EXPLORER'S GUIDES

Victoria
& Vancouver Island

EXPLORER'S GUIDES

FIRST EDITION

VICTORIA & VANCOUVER ISLAND

A GREAT DESTINATION

Eric Lucas

The Countryman Press
Woodstock, Vermont

LEFT: *Capital building in Victoria.*   iStockphoto/Ekins Designs

Explorers Guide Victoria & Vancouver Island: A Great Destination
978-1-58157-128-8

Interior photographs by the author unless otherwise specified
Maps by Erin Greb Cartography, © The Countryman Press
Book design by Bodenweber Design
Composition by Eugenie S. Delaney

Published by The Countryman Press, P.O. Box 748, Woodstock, VT 05091
Distributed by W. W. Norton & Company, Inc., 500 Fifth Avenue, New York, NY 10110
Printed in the United States of America

10 9 8 7 6 5 4 3 2 1

This book is dedicated to all the wonderful people of Canada,
from the First Nations bands who have worked hard
to preserve and protect their rich traditions;
to all the immigrants since who have built one of the planet's
most diverse and most welcoming countries.
Canada is truly a special place.

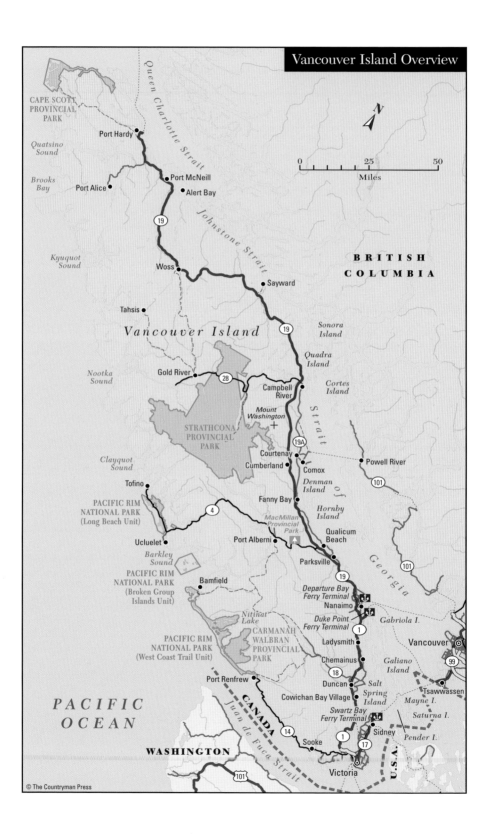

Vancouver Island Overview

CONTENTS

AN INTRODUCTION TO VANCOUVER ISLAND 9

1

VICTORIA AND THE CAPITAL REGION 27
   Sooke and West Coast 67
   Saanich Peninsula 71

2

GULF ISLANDS 81
   Salt Spring Island 84
   Pender Island 93
   Galiano Island 96
   Saturna Island 99
   Mayne Island 100
   Gabriola Island 100

3

MID-ISLAND FROM COWICHAN TO CAMPBELL RIVER 105
   Cowichan Valley 109
   Nanaimo 118
   Parksville/Qualicum 126
   Comox Valley 133
   Campbell River 143
   Discovery Islands 147
   Alberni Inlet and Valley 151

4

WEST COAST 157

5

NORTH ISLAND 181

INDEX 189

MAPS
   Vancouver Island Overview 6
   Capital Region 30
   Victoria 31
   Gulf Islands 82
   Mid-Island 106
   West Coast 158
   Tofino & Ucluelet 160
   North Island 182

An Introduction
to Vancouver Island

At one end of Vancouver Island, in Victoria, tall palm trees stand watch over a flower-bedecked harbor promenade with a distinctly Mediterranean air. In the background a world-famed Edwardian hotel offers high tea to international guests clinking bone china and sterling silver beneath crystal chandeliers.

At the other end of the island, 280 miles north-northwest, wilderness hikers stroll a 1-mile (1.6 km) crescent of ivory beach at Cape Scott, checking for wolf and bear tracks. Ancient cedar and spruce trees lean over storm-tossed dunes and drift logs, bald eagles call from nearby headlands, and seals and sea lions prowl the bay.

These two extremes typify Vancouver Island. Few places on earth offer as much cultural, climatic and geographic diversity as this 12,076-square-mile (19,434-square-km) bastion on the west coast of Canada. The southeast corner of the island is one apex of a triangle of civilization whose other points are Seattle and Vancouver; and in some regards Victoria, an erstwhile colonial capital of the British Empire, is the most civilized of the three. Few other places on earth still offer high tea as a daily tradition in elegant colonial surroundings.

Yet not far away, in a remote wilderness valley, stands one of earth's largest trees, a 312-foot (95 m) Sitka spruce that's emblematic of a maritime rainforest saved from logging by late 20th-century environmental activism. And a denizen of that rainforest, a cougar, once turned up in the Empress Hotel's parking garage in Victoria. (It was expeditiously trapped and returned to the forest, and all involved repaired upstairs for tea.)

Long inhabited by aboriginal peoples—at least as long as 10,000, and perhaps 30,000, years—the island's natural treasures have always been its draw. First Nations peoples thrived on salmon, shellfish, and berries. European settlers were drawn in the early 1800s by fish and timber, and fortunes were built on those two resources, plus coal. Trade and government became economic staples as gold rushes spurred booms in British Columbia's interior. Today, more than 1 million annual visitors come to experience the island's beauty and diversity.

Heading north from Victoria, in the Cowichan Valley, tidy vineyards supply a growing winery district in which visitors can enjoy a breathtaking wealth of locally grown sustainable foods. An hour onward, at Parksville, vacationing families gather on sun-warmed sand whose waters are as mild as milk.

LEFT: *Nordic skiing, Mount Washington*

Big Tree Trail, Meares Island

Another hour to the north is a family-friendly homegrown ski resort that often collects the greatest seasonal snow accumulation in North America. Yet late spring visitors to the Comox Valley below Mount Washington can golf in the afternoon following a half-day of skiing in the morning.

North of there, two hours and a ferry ride worth, is a tiny island with a world-class museum in which visitors can see stunning aboriginal art with a most memorable backstory—stolen from its First Nations owners a century ago, it has been returned to its home and lovingly displayed.

Just northeast of Victoria are a half-dozen delightfully scenic, friendly, and low-key smaller islands perfect for relaxed getaways. Meanwhile, out on the west coast of the island, Pacific swells roll into a long strand of beach at Tofino renowned as Canada's surfing mecca. Tour boats ply hundreds of miles of inlets and coves so visitors can watch whales and eagles, bears and otters, porpoises and spawning salmon.

All these attributes make Vancouver Island a fabulous visitor destination from almost any perspective. Adventurers, families, cosmopolitan global wanderers, bargain-hunting backpacker students, gourmands—there are innumerable attractions for each. Painting a picture of the island as a travel paradise is easy.

Yet "travel paradise" is a simplistic assessment of a place with far more breadth and depth. This is a complex natural and human community whose modern character reflects both its wealth and the ever-present potential for misuse.

Every modern achievement—the island is a world capital of the sustainability movement, particularly in agriculture and food preparation—rests astride a more troubling story. For all its sustainability, intense logging continues, and clear-cuts march to the very edge of world-class ecological preserves. Factory fish farms pollute remote bays at the same time island chefs mount a global campaign to conserve ocean fisheries. Wildlife abounds, and the ever-growing industry devoted to bringing tourists out to see wild creatures subjects them to disturbance and sometimes outright torment.

Visitors thus have a chance to enjoy and learn, taste and honor, touch and value one of the world's most precious places. This book is a guide to Vancouver Island's wonders with a discreet plea for its vulnerabilities; no one who loves it as I do can overlook either. When you respectfully savor its foods, swim its waters, scale its mountains, stroll its beaches, and admire its beauty, you are adding to this matchless wealth, and enriching your own life.

Vargas Island beach, Clayoquot Sound   Leslie Forsberg

Star of the tide pools   Leslie Forsberg

ABOUT THIS GUIDE

This book was born in my love for Vancouver Island, which I often name as the answer to the question every travel writer faces incessantly: What's your favorite place? I've been all over the world, and I find myself longing for places in and around Vancouver Island as much as or more than anywhere else. Luckily, I live quite close.

This is my fond portrait of and guide to traveling around the island and the many adjacent, smaller islands near it. As far as I know, this is the only guide devoted just to Vancouver Island (and its environs). A few explanatory remarks are in order:

Skunk cabbage

- This is a *selective* guide—not comprehensive. I've described the places, lodgings, attractions, restaurants, and other travel items I think are the best and most important. There are a fair number of well-known attractions on the island that you will not find here; I've left them out deliberately, usually because I believe they are unworthy of the visitor's time. There are more hotels, restaurants, stores, and so on—though I believe I have included all the best.

- This is not a budget travel guide, though I've included the economical lodgings, restaurants, and attractions I think are most worthwhile. I'm not a budget travel writer. There are many decent budget travel guides on the market . . . however, none (that I know of) covers only Vancouver Island.

- Canada is a metric country, like most of the others on earth. Remember that on the highway, my American friends: If you are going 60 mph, you are probably way over the speed limit, which is 60 *kilometers*, not miles, per hour. And, no, that excuse doesn't hold any water with the traffic enforcement Mounties any more. Many Canadians, who are user-friendly people indeed, will do their best to translate when they can.

HISTORY

Some of the chapters following contain a distinct history for the island's separate regions, but in each case the song is much the same: **First Nations** people for millennia enjoyed a relatively prosperous lifestyle based largely on salmon and cedar. Mostly members of three separate peoples, the Salish (south island), Kwakwaka'wakw (northeast island) and

Nuu-chah-nulth (Pacific Coast), they lived in large cedar longhouses, rode the seas in massive carved cedar canoes, and practiced periodic ceremonial feasts called potlatches.

Initial exploration in the 16th, 17th, and 18th centuries elicited little interest from British seafarers who sailed the island's coast and inland seas—Francis Drake, James Cook (he of Hawaiian tragedy fame)—and three major **Spanish expeditions'** only legacy is a plethora of place names such as Cortes and Juan de Fuca. All these were chartered to seek gold, other riches, and a northwest passage. All found only fish and forest.

The 19th century is when fish and forest became valuable commodities, and this is when the history of European settlement on Vancouver Island begins with establishment of a Hudson's Bay Company post at what is now Victoria on March 14, 1843. The island became a British crown colony in 1849; Victoria was declared the capital, and the chief honcho of the HBC post, James Douglas, became governor in 1851. Trade in beaver and otter pelts flourished for a short while, until interest in the area was boosted by discovery of gold in the BC interior in 1859. Victoria became a shipping and administrative center for the gold boom; when the island colony was consolidated with the mainland in 1866, it remained the capital, as it did when British Columbia joined the Canadian Confederation in 1871.

Timber and fisheries rapidly grew into the major industries as the interior gold rush faded; a brief boom returned with the late 19th-century Klondike gold rush in the Yukon. Meanwhile, federal authorities clamped down on indigenous First Nations culture in a campaign to "civilize" the island's native peoples. The ceremonial feast known as **potlatch was banned**; potlatch artifacts and regalia were stolen from their owners and sold overseas; children were seized from their families and sent to religious boarding schools where the effort continued to erase their cultural identity. I have personally met a First Nations artist who, as a boy, was forbidden to draw by the nuns at his school because it was considered a primitive, "Indian" pursuit.

Coal was discovered near Nanaimo in the late Victorian era and built fortunes in Victoria into the next century. Salmon canneries flourished along the Inside Passage from Campbell River north in the first half of the 20th century, while the island's **old-growth forests** were clear-cut in large parcels for the timber and pulp industries. Meanwhile, Victoria's fame as a travel destination grew for its real and supposed flavor as a former colonial outpost of the British Empire.

Forest sculpture—a cedar branch   Leslie Forsberg

In the second half of the 20th century the resource extraction industries began a long period of decline. The last coal was mined in 1968; the last cannery had closed before that. A fierce international environmental battle in the early 1990s forestalled a massive clear-cutting plan in Clayoquot Sound, near Tofino, and the timber industry entered a decline that continues in the 21st century. Today the entire island holds about 780,000 people—about half those in the greater Victoria region—a population growing mostly as immigrants, including Canadians, arrive to enjoy the lovely climate, relaxed lifestyle, amiable society, and infinite recreation opportunities.

FLORA

Forests are the ever-present mantle on the island, but they are more diverse than people think. The key trees in the evergreen woods are **Douglas fir, western hemlock**, and **western red cedar**, all of whose common names represent entertaining misnomers—Douglas fir is not a true fir, western hemlock has nothing to do with the famous poison that downed Socrates, and red cedar is not cedar at all. Each of these, as well as the strictly coastal **Sitka spruce** (yes, it's really a spruce), reaches gargantuan size or height or both in the uncut old-growth forests of the island. What's probably the world's biggest Sitka spruce stands 312 feet (95 m) tall in a hidden valley in Carmanah-Walbran Provincial Park; huge Douglas firs lie just off the road in MacMillan Provincial Park west of Parksville; the ancient gnarled cedar on Meares Island near Tofino, the Hanging Garden tree, is well over 1,000 years old.

Cathedral Grove, MacMillan Provincial Park   Boomer Jerritt/ Tourism Vancouver Island

Native forest denizen—a banana slug

Few of these giants are left, fewer still the places where visitors can see big trees reaching for the sky in undisturbed landscapes. Aside from the locales above, other good spots to see old growth include Strathcona Provincial Park, Cape Scott Park, Juan de Fuca Provincial Park, and Helliwell Provincial Park on Hornby Island. Other notable conifers include handsome **noble firs** and **grand firs**, both of whose names reflect their graceful shapes; **shore pine**, the coastal cousin of lodgepole pine, common on sandy ground in Pacific Rim National Park; and **Pacific yew**, the rare understory tree from which cancer-fighting tamoxifen was first derived. Yes, that's really a yew, and is closely related to the famed bow-wood trees of Europe.

Aside from the vast conifer forests of the island, several hardwoods are conspicuous. The southeast part of the island is the home of the **Garry oak** (essentially the same as the Oregon white oak), northernmost range for oaks in the Pacific Northwest. Tall **black cottonwoods** line rivers and streams, turning a beautiful butterscotch gold from late September to early December, depending on their location. Burly **bigleaf maples** are common on hills and drier locations, sometimes attaining great spread, also turning gold in autumn. **Red alder**, which grows in forest thickets along streams and rivers, is the favored wood for salmon-cooking fires, and was historically the subject of much disdain by anglers trying to crash through young thickets and by timber managers who once considered it a weed. But it has recently become an important timber species for its use in furniture and cabinet-making. The smooth, angular, ruddy amber trunks of **arbutus** trees (known as *madrona* in the States) lean out over rocky promontories and are much painted and photographed.

Native berry-bearing shrubs include **salal** and **salmonberry**, the latter's March and April blooms beloved of hummingbirds, the former's berries rarely used now but an important food for indigenous peoples historically.

Two introduced invasive plants are unfortunately widespread. The **Himalayan blackberry**, a relentlessly vigorous bramble, is the author of the vast berry thickets so common along roadsides, fencerows, and untended ground. Although there is a native blackberry species, it's small and uncommon; when you see blackberry jam, ice cream, wine, and pie, it is almost always made with Himalayan blackberries, which ripen in August.

But the most-reviled bane of farmers, landowners, and environmental advocates is

Scotch broom, a troublesome and incredibly prolific pioneer introduction meant to remind settlers of the heath back home. The gnarled, khaki-colored woody shrubs grow under almost all conditions, except absolute deep forest. Their early spring yellow blossoms mature to spew thousands of seeds every summer, are extremely difficult to eradicate, are highly flammable, and form dense thickets impossible to walk through, mow, or use as grazing ground. An island settler planted the first broom back in the late 19th century and bragged about it in a local newspaper. Millions have since cursed his folly.

FAUNA

Eagles and bears, wolves and whales—North America's most charismatic wild creatures ply the winds, lands, and waters of Vancouver Island. **Bald eagles** are numerous (BC as a whole has about 100,000) and usually within view every day, everywhere on the island. **Rufous hummingbirds** arrive from Mexico in late March. **Ravens**, the trickster birds of First Nations tradition, call from the woods at dawn. Innumerable ducks, geese, swans, and other **waterfowl** visit the island on their journeys north and south in spring and fall.

    Black bears prowl the woods and waterways of the island; there are no grizzlies on the island. **Cougars** (mountain lions) are believed by some scientists to be more numerous here than anywhere else on earth, with perhaps more than 5,000 ghosting their way through the deep woods in search of the favorite prey, deer. Moose haven't made it to the island, but **Roosevelt elk** are found in a few spots. Playful **river otters** are seen in both freshwater rivers and lakes, and saltwater bays; **sea otters** are spreading along the ocean coast after extinction in the late 19th century. **Harbour seals** poke along in near-shore

Resident Canada geese   Leslie Forsberg

Steller sea lion, Hornby Island   Boomer Jerritt/ Tourism Vancouver Island

waters. **California sea lions** bark from their haul-outs on buoys and rocks; the bigger and rarer **Steller sea lions** populate a few favored rookeries along the eastern shore of the island.

California **gray whales** cruise the ocean coast in spring and fall on their astounding annual 2,000-mile migration between Alaska and Mexico. Inland, pods of **orcas** (killer whales) inhabit the waters of the Salish Sea and are often seen from shore, especially in the Gulf Islands.

Please, for all these wonderful creatures, watch from a distance, quietly and respectfully.

And, high in the alpine fastnesses of the central range's wilderness, the **Vancouver Island marmot** is one of the most endangered animals on earth, with just a few hundred left. Few visitors ever see one (not to mention few residents) but, as much as anything, they symbolize both the unique character of the island and the damage human encroachment has caused. Habitat loss threatens the marmot. Let's hope that, however many people come to this beautiful place, we visitors do nothing to further damage the marmot's home.

CLIMATE & WHEN TO GO

Rain, rain, and more rain—the entire island is within a climate zone generally known as *temperate maritime*. That is, the key climatic influence is the Pacific Ocean, whose westerly winds bring in moisture and moderated temperatures. The counter to the ocean winds is the blocking power of the various mountains in the region—the Olympics to the south help keep Victoria relatively dry and sunny; the island's own central range keeps the mid-island coast from Nanaimo to Comox comparatively sunny and dry.

Out on the coast? Staggering amounts of precipitation soak the valleys and shores

Nature's horticulture Leslie Forsberg

struck by incoming weather. Henderson Lake, east of Ucluelet, is generally considered the wettest place in North America, with annual precipitation averaging 260 inches (655 cm). A Canadian weather station established there during the 1930s was soon abandoned because no ordinary human being could live there.

Generally speaking, island weather is nice from early May to early October, especially on the inland side of the island. April and October are shoulder months; July and August are the warmest, driest, sunniest, and not coincidentally, most crowded, months. I urge those who can plan trips with any flexibility to visit the island either May through mid-June, or in late September.

This is not to say winter is worthless. Storm watching on the coast is popular and invigorating. And I've enjoyed fine weather all over the island, including the coast, all months of the year. Fall, winter, and spring also bring the great virtue of fewer crowds, lower costs (substantially lower at many lodgings), no waiting in ferry lines, and so on. If you do visit the island at midwinter, bring wool, fleece, duck boots, sunglasses, and several good books.

At this northern latitude (almost 49 degrees north at Victoria) daylight ebbs and grows dramatically through the year, from barely 8 hours in dead of winter to almost 18 hours at midsummer. Even though the sun is down, light lingers at the end of June, when the glow from the sunset burnishes the northwest sky well past 11 PM in many locales, especially on the island's west coast. It's a great time for a late evening walk on the beach at Tofino.

GETTING THERE

The Trans-Canada Highway, Highway 1 in national numerical parlance, begins its 4,990-mile (8,030 km) transcontinental journey at the intersection of Dallas Road and Douglas Street, just up from the waterfront by Beacon Hill Park in Victoria. A plaque marks the spot; its Mile Zero designation indicates its age, predating Canada's adoption of the metric system in the 1970s. More interesting, though, is the question of how a continent-crossing highway can magically traverse 35½ miles (57 km) of inland sea, the Strait of Georgia. No bridges reach Vancouver Island. Do cars float?

Yep—on the BC Ferries Horseshoe Bay–Departure Bay route between West Vancouver and Nanaimo. Virtually all the artifacts of modern civilization, including travelers, reach the island by boat; a small number do by plane. BC Ferries carries the vast majority of people to and fro, between island terminals near Victoria, Nanaimo, and Comox; smaller terminals serve the adjacent islands. Islanders are much given to whining and moaning about the ferry system, but their animus is mistaken: BC ferries are safe, comfortable, clean, well run, and efficient, and on time much more often than are, say, commercial airlines.

Washington State's ferry system serves the island from Anacortes daily. The Victoria Clipper high-speed catamaran passenger ferries serve Victoria from Seattle; and a delightful, old-school family-owned company, Black Ball Transport, operates a car ferry between Port Angeles and Victoria. All these boats are often full to the brim, especially during summer months, holidays, and weekends. The wise traveler makes reservations well in advance. That bears repeating: *Make reservations, period.*

Victoria's compact, clean, user-friendly airport (YYJ) has flights to major American and Canadian cities, but Vancouver or Seattle are the nearest true international gateways from which it's just a short 40-minute flight into Victoria. Nanaimo and Comox have small airports with service to various Western Canada cities. Most international itineraries into Seattle or Vancouver can tack on a hop over to Victoria at reasonable extra cost.

There's only one controlled-access freeway on the island, Highway 19 between Nanaimo and Campbell River. Highway 1 between Nanaimo and Victoria has short controlled access, four-lane stretches, as does Highway 17 between Victoria and the airport and BC Ferries terminal at Swartz Bay. The entire rest of the island is served by two-lane paved roads on which patience is sometimes required as retired World War II light colonels *slowly* make their way in their RV—say, between Nanaimo and Tofino. This is an island. It's not a high-speed land.

Off the paved road system, gravel logging roads provide uncertain access to remote valleys, recreation sites, and beaches. Ask locally about conditions before traveling these back roads. Venture on them only with a sturdy vehicle, a good spare tire, and a full gas tank. These roads are the province of logging trucks whose drivers are not as belligerent as those in the States, but still: Keep your headlights on. Be alert. Keep far right on curves. And do give way—they are much, much bigger than you.

STAYING THERE

Three of the **best-known lodgings** in the world are on Vancouver Island: the Empress Hotel, the Wickaninnish Inn, and Sooke Harbour House—the first, an elegant Edwardian hotel; the second, a destination for winter storm watching; the latter, a pioneer of the slow food ethos. Victoria itself has a huge lodging industry whose venues range from the deluxe

Early spring forest delight, native trilliums Leslie Forsberg

elegance of the Empress to skungy hostels and boarding houses. Elsewhere on the island, lovely small inns are numerous, as are comfy B&Bs with gracious and knowledgeable hosts. In each city in this guide I have described the best-known, most appealing, and my own favorite lodgings. It is by no means a comprehensive inventory, though I believe I have included virtually all the island's best lodgings.

Victoria, Nanaimo, Campbell River, and Courtenay/Comox all have properties within various Canadian and international chains—Marriott has a huge convention hotel in Victoria, for instance. I have not listed these properties (excepting the Empress, which is part of the Fairmont chain), but they are easily found on the tourism Web sites for the bigger destinations. Coast Hotels is a particularly prominent Canadian company, akin to Marriott in the States; several Coast properties are on the island; visit www.coasthotels .com.

A word about **budget lodgings**: I've included the reputable hostels where appropriate, such as in Tofino, Victoria, and Nanaimo. Other hostels on the island, particularly in Victoria, are not in this guide because they are not remotely appropriate for thoughtful travelers. Also, economy hotels, mostly in Victoria, which pop up on search engines and as package lodgings; are not here because of poor quality, incessant noise, or other problems. Frankly, there is no great plethora of budget lodging on the island, except in the off-season, when a large portion of the island's lodging becomes economical. One of the biggest budget chains, which had about a dozen hotels around Victoria, went bankrupt a while back; so much for the budget travel industry.

For simplicity's sake I decided on simple **pricing categories**: Budget lodgings are priced below $100, for one room for two people; Moderate means $100–$200; Expensive is $200–$300; Very Expensive lies above $300. Those are high-season rates; off-season rates lessen remarkably, and I have noted so for some wonderful, deluxe properties that are outlandishly expensive in summer, yet fairly economical in winter and spring.

Now, the truth about lodging prices: The old concept of "rack rates," so dear to travel guide writers and editors and travel agents, is in reality a thing of the past. The advent of online room shopping has upended hotel pricing, and every hotel room is a time-sensitive commodity to be traded and bartered depending on supply and demand. "Internet specials" are not really special because they're online; they're priced lower because of excess room supply (and they circumvent commissions).

So, for most lodgings bigger than a half-dozen rooms, rates go up and down, and perhaps up and down again, according to booking levels—not according to whatever you might see as the "published" rate, in this book or elsewhere. Those are guidelines that distinguish bargain hostels, say, from deluxe resorts. The moral of the story—shop early, shop late, shop often.

ENOUGH TO EAT

Surrounded by the food riches of the sea, with many valleys enjoying balmy maritime climates, Vancouver Island is one of the most agriculturally productive and diverse places in North America. Here are prosperous family dairies, orchards, vineyards, vegetable farms, grain growers, and more. Mushrooms are common in the forests; seaweed and aquatic edibles, along the shore. Island residents have long relied on their own farmers for food, as shipping products in is expensive.

Quiet cove, Gulf Islands

Meanwhile, the island's cultural diversity and generally progressive bent have combined to create a distinctive modern cookery, known as **West Coast cuisine**, which melds all these local ingredients with European and Asian culinary techniques. Steamed jasmine rice, French pan-searing, traditional indigenous fish-smoking, curries, and cioppinos—all might appear on one menu. Fish-and-chips are a mainstay; grilled salmon and fried oysters are ubiquitous; wild mushrooms and island fruits and berries flavor almost every chef's fresh sheet. I make a point to enjoy West Coast foods all the time, every time, I am on the island. It is simply best. It's silly to have hamburgers (Canadian burgers aren't very good, frankly) or Midwest steaks while in the homeland of one of the world's greatest regional cuisines.

Seafood is the foundation of island cuisine, and a few explanations about fish and shellfish are in order:

- *Fresh is best.* Period. Oh, the frozen-food technology advocates fuss when I say this, but seafood connoisseurs all agree: Frozen fish simply doesn't bear up as well. Now, occasionally there are moments when there is no fresh salmon to be had, but that's the time to branch out and try halibut, lingcod, rockfish (red snapper), sablefish, and many other equally delightful species. Once in a rare blue moon, there is no fresh fish at all; then you might settle for flash-frozen salmon. It's not bad, just not as good as fresh.

- *Avoid farmed fish.* The island hosts innumerable salmon farms in remote inlets; they produce an inferior product laced with chemicals, and the industry causes incalculable damage to the environment. Please do not buy or consume farm-raised salmon. Few thoughtful chefs use it, anyway.

- *Lobsters don't live here.* Visitors are forever coming to the West Coast expecting to feast on lobster; and, yes, it is on the menu many places. However, it has flown farther than you—Canadian lobster is from the Atlantic coast, 3,107 miles (5,000 km) or so east. There is no local lobster on the Pacific coast of Canada. Snow crab and king crab are also shipped in from far away (Alaska) and are usually frozen. Dungeness crab is local, and better than snow and king crab, anyhow. Other local shellfish include oysters—fabulous oysters, as good as any on earth—clams, scallops, and exotic items such as barnacles and sea cucumbers.

I don't (much) mean to disparage seafood from elsewhere, but it's . . . there, not here. Aside from the fact that imported seafood generally doesn't taste as good (How do you feel after flying five hours?), it's not sustainable to travel thousands of miles to eat food that has also traveled thousands of miles.

More than almost anywhere else, the admonition to "eat local" is not only environmentally wise; on Vancouver Island, it's best in every way.

SAFETY

The island is, despite all the development along its shores, still largely a wilderness. It is the haunt of wolves, bears, and cougars—many of the latter, with perhaps the highest density of mountain lions on earth. Other wild animals, from beavers to squirrels to eagles to harbor seals, are commonly encountered, and all are wonderful aspects of life here and exceptional visitor amenities.

And, folks . . . They're wild animals. *They are not here for our amusement.* Please do not approach them, feed them, yell at them, swim with them, ride them, try to pose for pictures with them, or perform any of dozens of other Stupid Human Tricks that any veteran wildlife official will be happy to describe for you.

As an aside, my favorite story: A BC park manager happened on a tourist who was painting honey on his son's face so he could film a video of a roadside black bear licking the boy's nose. "Legally, I was supposed to shoot the bear," the park official tells me. "Really, I should have shot the parents. So I just drove away." True story. Evolution is failing us.

Aside from the immense damage done to wild populations from human interference, wild animals are not OSHA-trained. They may bite, claw, stomp, chase, and generally raise hell, which is what nature has designed them to do. Yep, even squirrels. Let them be and enjoy their beauty from a distance.

Luckily, there are no poisonous creatures on the island. Sea urchins have spines, but unless you are a scuba diver you'll not encounter them. There are a few mildly poisonous plants—don't eat red berries or mushrooms. Yes, there are many perfectly safe mushrooms and red berries, but they are for expert collectors, not for tourists. Even if you know mushrooms and wild berries elsewhere, these are likely different here.

The greatest dangers on the island are posed by the climate and the ocean. Hypothermia kills more people than any other natural hazard; please be sure to have adequate warm clothing whenever you are outdoors. Lightning is a hazard, especially in the mountains; seek safe (lower) ground when you hear thunder.

On all beaches facing the Pacific Ocean, please be alert for rogue waves, which can arise at any time. These rare but powerful swells carry a few incautious beachgoers out to sea each year along the Pacific Coast. They are very powerful, utterly unpredictable, and luckily quite rare.

CULTURAL & LEGAL DETAILS

Keep your hands off the car horn. Please.

Residents of big cities such as New York and Toronto are often puzzled by the sense of unease they experience in Victoria, Nanaimo—even Vancouver and other major Pacific Northwest cities. These places are *quiet*. A cultural bias toward civility, silence, and circumspection means you will rarely hear car horns honking, people yelling, or other obnoxious activities so common now in much of the rest of the world. Aggressive driving? Very rare—and if you witness it, most likely it's a Type A macho-boy from somewhere else speeding to catch a ferry back to the mainland.

As with the rest of Canada, courtesy and mild-mannered behavior are the norms here. If you are faced with a necessity of waiting in line (as with ferries): no cutting in, no rude jostling your fellow humans. No barking at waiters and waitresses, please. Hospitality and ferry workers are not servants. And, for my American friends, Canada is politically different from the United States—gay marriage has long been legal; firearms are shunned; global warming is a fact. Not that discussing these items is verboten, but Canadians are not in need of education by travelers from elsewhere. If you want to have an interesting discussion, inquire (amiably) of Canadians to explain how it works that they live in a completely independent country, but Queen Elizabeth is the head of state.

Yes, I have personally witnessed all the above types of discourteous behavior, many times. Let's all remember that we are guests here. Very welcome guests—tourism comprises a substantial portion of the island and provincial economies—but guests indeed.

Canada's famous symbol Leslie Forsberg

A few technical notes:

- Passports are mandatory for border crossings. There is an obscure little special enhanced ID available to U.S. residents that covers Canada travel, but it's a fairly pointless item that saves, at most, $100. Please get a passport. Vancouver Island is a special place; and so is the rest of the planet.

- Canadian border officials can and do stop incoming travelers who have ever been in legal trouble in the States, or elsewhere. If you were arrested for a fraternity bar fight 21 years ago, it may well show up when the customs and immigration agent runs your profile through the computer, and you may well be turned away. Yes, I've witnessed this, too.

- Be sure to have *notarized* parental permission letters for all children whenever married parents are not both present—e.g., when taking your kids' friends on a ski vacation, or a divorced dad bringing son Joey up for a fishing trip. Yes, border officials do ask— crossing the border is a common tactic in custodial disputes.

- Don't bring large amounts of cash—virtually all ATM cards work perfectly well in Canada. If you bring little or no cash (I sometimes have, say, only $2) be prepared to demonstrate financial viability, such as with a high-value credit card. Occasionally border officials will pull you aside and run a credit check. Smile nicely and say thanks. One cannot win disputes with border guards.

- The Canadian dollar is usually worth up to 10 percent more or less than the U.S. dollar. Many merchants, especially in areas frequented by American travelers, accept U.S. dollars more or less at face value, depending on the exchange rate. But there is no requirement that they do so—please don't complain if a merchant declines. And it's wise to convert Canadian currency back to U.S. before returning to the States, as the only American merchants that accept Canadian dollars are those quite near the border.

- Above all, have fun. Canada is a wonderful country, and Vancouver Island is a particularly wonderful part of it.

VICTORIA AND THE CAPITAL REGION

Nostalgia is a great thing until it grows musty and, well, old. That's the realization that came to Victoria early this century as its erstwhile English kitsch identity began to lose not only its appeal to travelers, but any semblance of an accurate reflection of the city. Yes, it was once an outpost of the British Empire—long, long ago (mid-19th century, to be exact). Yes, there are tearooms scattered about—mostly fusty haunts of blue-haired visitors from the prairies. Yes, there was a wax museum—which was a great place for low-brow visitors to waste $15 until declining patronage led to its closure in September 2010. That was a signature event in a profound transformation that has, alas, gone unnoticed in the travel industry. You'll have no trouble finding tour packages that still refer to "a little piece of Merrie Olde England." Poppycock, all of it.

Today's Victoria is a vibrant capital city humming with the workings of the BC government. It's a popular place for young couples to raise families who cannot afford to live anywhere in the sky-high real estate market of central Vancouver. It's the center of one of the world's most dynamic local-food movements, with some of the most adventurous chefs on the planet. It exhibits the same remarkable ethnic diversity as Vancouver, with a strong Asian tinge to its character. It is a leader in sustainability, with Canada's first carbon-neutral hotel (Inn at Laurel Point), its first carbon-neutral airline (Harbour Air), and one of the world's greenest buildings (Dockside Green). And it supports an arts and culture community second only to Vancouver in the province.

Does any of that sound like a cobwebbed bit of Victorian England? With 350,000 people in the metro area, known as the Capital Regional District, Victoria is a thriving modern city that enjoys all the advantages of urban heft, but suffers few of the disadvantages—little real traffic or air pollution, for instance.

It also remains one of the top visitor destinations in Canada. The Royal BC Museum, which stands between the iconic Empress Hotel and the often photographed Parliament Buildings, is among the most-visited museums in Canada. Countless surveys and polls award the city premier status among travel attractions—it's among the top five in North America, according to the annual Condé Nast reader survey.

Victoria is also the home of one of the finest collections of hotels and small inns in the

LEFT: *Great blue heron*

Parliament Buildings, Victoria Leslie Forsberg

world, a few of them kitschy, several of them ultra-deluxe over-the-top Victorian mansions aglow with brass and crystal, some glistening new-tech towers. It claims the second-highest per capita number of restaurants in North America (after San Francisco) and registers the highest vegetarian food sales per capita in North America. The metro area is home to what is surely North America's most famous gardens (Butchart). And the city's Inner Harbour thrums with almost constant seaplane traffic, the pontoon-clad Beavers and Otters carrying visitors, government officials, and business people in and out. In effect, it's an international airport.

In other words, even though they are still here, lace doilies, tea and crumpets, stately carriages and lavender sachets are old news. The new Victoria is better represented by the New Age body lotions at Silk Road; the divine sustainably harvested fish-and-chips at Red Fish Blue Fish (best anywhere, in my opinion); the splendid Galloping Goose recreation path, an old railroad grade that runs from the city center to the mountains; and the sensational Pacific Rim indigenous art at Alcheringa Gallery.

This is not to say the classic Victoria has disappeared—far from it. You can still find finger sandwiches and Scottish tartans here. Perhaps the best amalgam of the city's old and new characters is the annual **Victoria Tea Festival**, begun in 2006, which celebrates tea in all its aspects around the globe, from English high tea to the Japanese tea ceremony, in mid-February (www.victoriateafestival.com). A raft of other intriguing festivals abound. **Victoria Dragon Boat Festival** brings these colorful craft to the waters of the city's harbor each August (www.victoriadragonboat.com). The **Victoria Film Festival** is more intimate than its big-city counterparts, but still brings more than 100 films from around the world to the city each February (victoriafilmfestival.com). Other notable annual events include **JazzFest International** (www.jazzvictoria.ca), which spans June through early July and reflects the love of jazz on an island that nurtured Nanaimo native Diana Krall; **Symphony Splash**, in August, which finds Victoria's excellent symphony on a barge in the Inner Harbour for a performance that concludes with Tchaikovsky's 1812 Overture, complete with fireworks and cannon (www.victoriasymphony.ca); and **Feast of Fields**, the annual mid-September outdoor dining celebration of local foods, farmers, fishers, chefs, and gourmands (www.feastoffields.com).

The best source for general information on visiting Victoria is **Tourism Victoria** (250-953-2033, 1-800-663-3883, www.tourismvictoria.com). The main tourism **Visitor Centre** is at 812 Wharf Street, V8W 1T3, just above the Inner Harbour, on the corner northwest of the Empress Hotel; open daily 9–5.

I've been visiting Victoria regularly for almost 20 years now, and I've watched the city's transformation from kitschy to cutting-edge with fond appreciation. Statistics Canada rates it the country's fittest city and Canada's cycling capital. The city's tourism folks a few years back pitched all nostalgic references to colonial history and adopted a new slogan: "Full of Life." Exactly, wonderfully so.

HISTORY

Indigenous Salish people have lived on the Saanich Peninsula for thousands of years, thriving on the plentiful natural resources—seafood, shellfish, and berries, chiefly—and creating an artistically and culturally rich civilization. Huge cedar canoes carried people to and fro among the islands; cedar logs were carved into the planks, poles, and beams needed to make massive longhouses that afforded shelter to extended families and clan groups. Songs, dances, chants, and stories relayed the history and legends of the bands down through generations. Many of these aspects of First Nations life thrive today as the various bands throughout Vancouver Island reclaim their traditions and identity.

Although Sir Francis Drake, Captain James Cook, and several Spanish explorers sailed by the island in the 16th and 17th centuries, it was not until 1795 that a European power took interest in the territory. That's when George Vancouver explored the region and negotiated title to the island from the Spanish, who considered it low-value wilderness.

Real settlement did not take place until 1843, when Hudson's Bay Company representative James Douglas established a fort on the obviously prime anchorage of the Inner Harbour, at the present-day site of Bastion Square. Douglas named the outpost after Britain's queen, and as logging, fishing, fur trapping, coal mining, and other resource-extraction industries brought people and industry to the island, Victoria assumed its role as the island's capital. Although the fervor of settlement shifted to the mainland after gold was discovered in the interior Cariboo region in 1858, the city was declared the capital of the colony of British Columbia in 1868, and maintained that role when British Columbia joined the Canadian federation in 1871.

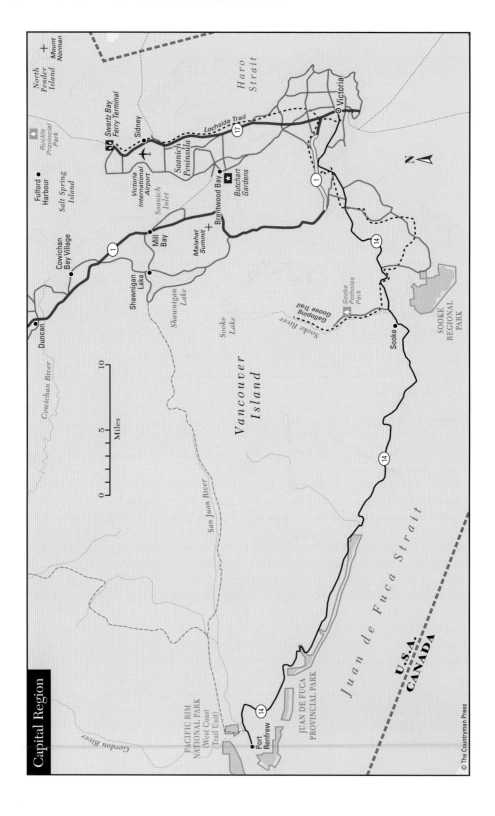

Capital Region

© The Countryman Press

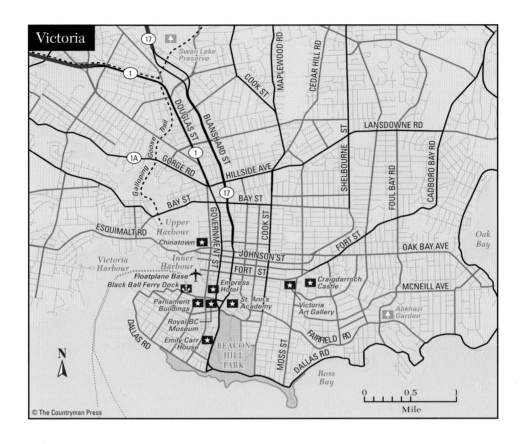

While population growth and development boomed on the mainland, the island slowly fashioned an identity as a source of timber, fish, and coal. The Victoria-based Dunsmuir family became the province's richest, on par with the rail barons of California, by mining coal mid-island and building rail lines to ship it and the island's timber to port; the Dunsmuir legacy can be seen at Craigdarroch Castle and Hatley Castle, two huge estate manors that testify to the heft of turn-of-the-century industrial wealth. Victoria settled into a role as a relatively sedate government and retirement center, and the colonial capital aura that adheres to the city still was cemented in the late 19th and early 20th centuries—despite the fact that, in reality, Victoria was an outpost of the British empire for just 28 years.

Although its colonial heritage is far in the past, its status as a government center is as strong as ever. About 20 percent of the capital region's residents have government jobs; tourism is also a major employer. Those seeking flavors of Victoria's empire past will find them at the city's famous Murchie's tea merchants on Government Street. Just a few blocks down, also on Government, visitors seeking the flavors of Victoria's more cosmopolitan modern identity will find them at the much different Silk Road tea shop. When I'm in the city, I almost always stop in at both.

By the way, the waters east of Victoria, Cadboro Bay, are the home of a legendary sea creature, *Cadborosaurus*. Although sightings have been numerous over the years, as with the Loch Ness monster and Ogopogo in BC's Okanagan Lake, no one has ever provided irrefutable documentation of the creature's existence. If you happen to be beachcombing along the bay, or driving the scenic Marine Drive, and can capture Caddy on camera or video, you will become very, very famous.

TRANSPORTATION

Ships, planes, buses, and trains—all head to Victoria which, as the capital of an island, requires almost all visitors to utilize some form of mass transportation to get there.

Victoria International Airport (YYJ) is about 25 minutes north of downtown along Highway 17 on the Saanich Peninsula—a very scenic setting for an airport, with the Gulf Islands and Strait of Georgia just northeast, and Malahat Mountain west. Inbound and outbound passengers usually get quite a panorama of the region. YYJ has daily service to Vancouver, Seattle, San Francisco, Edmonton, Toronto, and Calgary, with connecting service anywhere in the world through Vancouver International Airport; visit www.victoria airport.com. Nonstop flights also reach the BC cities of Nanaimo, Abbotsford, and Kelowna. Major carriers are Air Canada, WestJet, Horizon Air, and United; plus local carriers Island Express, Orca, and Pacific Coastal.

By far the most common way to reach the island, though, is on one of the many ferries that cross the Strait of Georgia or Strait of Juan de Fuca. The prime service provider is **BC Ferries**, the autonomous provincial corporation that is one of the largest such services in the world (250-386-3431, 1-888-223-3779, www.bcferries.com). The key access route to Victoria is from the major terminal 40 minutes south of downtown Vancouver at Tsawassen, from which boats take about 95 minutes to cross to Swartz Bay, a half-hour

Fueling up in the ferry line Leslie Forsberg

Victoria Harbour Ferry Leslie Forsberg

north of downtown Victoria at the end of Highway 17. Boats depart almost hourly from 7 AM to 9 or 10 PM, with extra sailings on holidays and weekends. These ferries are among the largest in the world, 558-foot (170 m), sparkling white five-deck behemoths capable of holding 470 vehicles and more than 2,000 passengers. Sundecks, restaurants and coffee shops, playrooms, and shops entertain passengers not sufficiently enthralled by the scenic journey. I've been across hundreds of times, and I never tire of simply watching the passing seascape, framed by distant snowy mountains. BC ferries also sail between Swartz Bay and the various Gulf islands; and into Nanaimo, two hours north of Victoria.

Reservations are available on the Tsawassen–Swartz Bay route for a surcharge of $17.50, pushing the ordinary $73 cost for a car with two adults up to $90. Believe me, this extra fee is worth it, and *reservations are essential for travel on weekends and holidays* unless travelers are willing and able to deal with the potential for hours-long waits. BC residents are wont to grouse about their ferries, but like Londoners whingeing about the Tube, they know not whereof they speak: service is largely on time, friendly, and efficient.

Washington State Ferries operates daily sailings from the U.S. mainland, through the San Juan Islands, and into Sidney, adjacent to the Victoria airport (www.wsdot.wa.gov/ferries). Two boats a day travel this route in summer; one daily the rest of the year, and *reservations are highly advisable.*

Two ferry services sail into Victoria's Inner Harbour, both from the United States. The **MV** *Coho* (Black Ball Ferry) departs from Port Angeles, on Washington State's Olympic Peninsula, and takes 90 minutes to reach its dock about ⅛ mile (a few hundred meters) from the Empress. (It's amazing how the captains maneuver the huge ship in the relatively tiny harbor.) The Coho carries both cars and passengers, and Black Ball is a reliable, family-owned company that has been sailing this route more than half a century. There are four sailings a day in summer, two the rest of the year. And as with all Victoria-bound ferries, *reservations are highly advisable* (250-386-2202, cohoferry.com). Please note that U.S.-bound travelers go through customs in Victoria, and should arrive at least two hours early.

The famed **Victoria Clipper** is a high-speed catamaran that sails from downtown Seattle to the Inner Harbour. The crossing takes about three hours; there are three sailings daily in summer and one or two a day the rest of the year (206-443-2560, 1-800-888-2535, www.clippervacations.com). It's a scenic passage, but the boats are somewhat cramped for such a long journey—though certainly no more so than the average commercial jet these days. The company offers travelers many all-inclusive packages for trips to Victoria.

Nifty helicopter service between downtown Vancouver and Victoria Harbour is offered by **Helijet**; the flight is just 35 minutes and offers very scenic views. The fare is less than you'd expect—$149 off-peak on weekends (604-273-4688, 1-800-665-4354, www .helijet.com).

Floatplane outbound

With a harbor at its center, Victoria has one of the busiest **floatplane** ports in the world, just north of the Empress where the Gorge Waterway meets the Inner Harbour. More than 100 flights a day arrive or depart here during the busy summer months, and the sight of a floatplane banking eastward above a ferry in the harbor is an iconic Victoria image. **Harbour Air** is the prime carrier here, with numerous daily flights to and from both downtown Vancouver and Vancouver International Airport, using sturdy DeHavilland Beavers, and Otters. Harbour Air is one of the world's biggest floatplane operators (250-384-2215, 1-800-665-0212, www.harbour-air.com). **West Coast Air** (now a subsidiary of Harbour Air) serves the same Victoria-downtown Vancouver route (604-278-3478, 1-800-665-0212, www.westcoastair.com). Seattle-based **Kenmore Air**, one of the biggest and most experienced floatplane operators in the world, offers service from that city's downtown Lake Union (425-486-1257, 1-866-435-9524, www .kenmoreair.com).

Pacific Coach Line offers comfy bus service to and from Victoria and Vancouver's downtown, cruise ship terminal, and airport; travel includes ferry tickets. Reservations are best during peak travel periods (250-385-4411, 1-800-661-1725, www.pacificcoach.com). The company's new 3-**City Circle** package is an excellent choice for the many travelers who engineer a journey between all three of the region's major cities, Victoria, Vancouver, and Seattle. A 3-City-Circle ticket costs $150 and provides conveyance among all three cities, with passage on the Victoria Clipper and BC Ferries included. Travel can start in any of the three cities, and travelers have up to a year to complete the circuit one way.

Tofino Bus offers daily service to and from Vancouver Island's West Coast (see chapter 5) (250-725-2871, 1-866-986-3466, www.tofinobus.com). **Greyhound Canada** offers bus service into and out of Victoria, but their Web site and customer service are dicey at best (1-800-661-8747, www.greyhound.ca). **Gray Line** offers regularly scheduled bus tours of Victoria and local sights (250-744-3566, 1-800-663-8390, www.graylinewest.com).

Bus service in and around the city, **Victoria Regional Transit**, is operated by BC Transit; there are two fare zones, Victoria proper, and the rest of the metro area. Normal adult fare is $2.50, and a 10-ticket book is $22.50 (250-382-6161, www.bctransit.com).

Via Rail is the Canadian national passenger rail system, with frequent service across Canada—yes, including Victoria (passengers cross the water on a ferry). The company also operates daily service between Victoria and Nanaimo and Courtenay (1-888-842-7245, www.viarail.ca).

A most handy way to get around the downtown area is on the **tub ferries** that ply the Inner Harbour and Gorge Waterway. Chugging back and forth like gaily colored little cabooses, these boats hold about a dozen passengers and trundle among 19 docks, from the Empress to Fisherman's Wharf, from far up the Gorge Waterway out to the Outer Harbour. A ferry happens by every 15 minutes in summer, every 20 minutes the rest of the year. Prices range from $5 up; full tours are available at $26; and it's a dandy way to get around. Visit www.victoriaharbourferry.com for maps and exact fares.

Central Victoria is an eminently **walkable** city—in fact, walking is by far the best way to get around and see the sights. If you are planning to stay at a central hotel or inn and spend your time in the city, there is no need for a rental car. Most major car-rental companies do have outlets at or near Victoria airport, and downtown as well; if you are driving in the region, it's a half-hour to the airport from downtown, and 10 minutes more to the Swartz Bay ferry terminal. Sooke is about 35 minutes west, Cowichan Valley an hour or more north, Nanaimo at least two hours, and Tofino at least four.

WEATHER

Victoria happily advertises itself as the home of Canada's mildest climate. Indeed, poised on the inland foot of Vancouver Island, washed by mild sea breezes and sheltered from weather systems by three mountain ranges, mild is the order of the day . . . most days. The island's own central range blunts North Pacific weather systems; the Olympic Mountains to the south, in the United States, dry the mid-Pacific moisture streams that soak the Washington coast; and the Coast Range on the BC mainland largely blocks the Arctic air from Yukon and Northwest territories that occasionally brings snow to the region. The same seas that moderate winter temperatures do the same for summer heat—very rarely does the temperature rise above 30°C (86°F).

Winters are generally so mild that the city holds an annual "Flower Count" in late February during which residents count the flowers in their yards—daffodils, crocus, rhododendrons, magnolias, and such—and call the total in to a local radio station. The result is invariably in the millions (yes, millions—21 million blossoms in 2010), and the total is gleefully reported across Canada to Albertans, Manitobans, and Ontarians shivering in subzero temperatures. Might Victoria residents exaggerate their counts? Possibly. Fact remains, there are zero flowers blooming anywhere else in Canada (except for the Vancouver area) then. Learn more about this dazzlingly inventive promotion at www.flower count.com.

The summertime average high is 22°C (71°F), with overnight lows near 11°C (51°F), so you'll need a jacket for evenings. Wintertime highs are around 46°F (8°C), with lows near freezing. Snow is rare, and May through September are largely dry months.

Houseboats at Fisherman's Wharf Leslie Forsberg

But . . . it can rain almost any day of the year. The occasional 20-inch (50 cm) snow ties the metro area in knots for a few days, about once a decade. Thunderstorms are rare. Winds are more common, as the Strait of Juan de Fuca funnels incoming Pacific air past the city. Annual precipitation is 24 inches (61 cm), almost all rain—considerably less than in Seattle and Vancouver. To understand the difference made by the various mountains sheltering Victoria, Port Renfrew, on the open ocean coast just 80 kilometers west, receives 144 inches (367 cm) of rain a year.

Overall, you'll never be either hot or really cold in Victoria. You're more likely to get misted than drenched. You'll need sunglasses more than rainhats, most of the year. And there are only a few days a year you won't need some sort of jacket at some point. It's a city for layered clothing, in other words—and Government Street has a plethora of shops to supply you if you neglected to bring enough.

LODGING

It's no surprise that Victoria has one of the biggest and most diverse lodging communities in western North America—almost 10,000 rooms in more than 200 hotels, inns, and B&Bs. This is, after all, one of the top tourist destinations on the continent, and tourism is an economic mainstay. Here are massive world-famed historic hotels, spiffy modern resorts, ultra-deluxe small inns housed in Victorian mansions, and cozy neighborhood B&Bs. Mainstream hotels and motels run the gamut from a huge, new, meetings-oriented Marriott to the usual Holiday Inns, Ramadas, and such. The downtown Travellers Inn offers clean, economical motel-style lodging along the main route in and out of town. Rooms are not fancy, but they are serviceable enough for car-borne travelers who simply want a bed for the night in the area (www.travellersinn.com).

Visitors interested in a real Victoria experience will be best served to ignore the name-brand chains and explore one of the city's many independent hotels, most of which are within a few blocks of the Inner Harbour. Or, equally appealing, the city's well-preserved neighborhoods hold a wide selection of Victorian and Edwardian homes and manor houses that have been transformed into small inns. Many of my favorites follow, but there are numerous others as well; consult www.tourism victoria.com.

ABIGAIL'S HOTEL
250-386-8721 or 1-800-663-7667
www.abigailshotel.com
innkeeper@abigailshotel.com
906 McClure St., Victoria, BC V8V 3E7
Three blocks east of the Inner Harbour
Price: Moderate to Expensive
Credit cards: Yes
Handicapped Access: Full
Special Features: Pets welcome, free WiFi, free local calls

Fervent customer loyalty has kept Abigail's one of Victoria's top small hotels for years—peruse the guest book and you'll see innumerable comments from visitors there for their umpteenth return to the hotel. Poised on a quiet back street between downtown and Rockland Hill, the main building sports the sort of neo-Tudor design that typified the image of the city for so long in Victoria. Never mind that, though: Abigail's is a spiffy small inn with comfy, deluxe rooms, lots of crimson and brocade, four-poster canopy beds—the full-meal deal when it comes to a historic inn filled with antiques. (It was actually built in the 1930s as a Tudor revival apartment house.) The inn is justifiably famed for its three-course

Abigail's Hotel, Victoria   Leslie Forsberg

breakfasts, which always include baked-in-house pastries, fresh fruit, and a hot entrée such as a frittata with baked yams. Afternoon tea also includes savory appetizers. At 23 rooms, it's small enough to be intimate but big enough to support its own in-house spa.

AMETHYST INN
250-595-2053 or 1-888-265-6499
www.amethyst-inn.com
innkeeper@amethyst-inn.com
1501 Fort St., Victoria, BC V8S 1Z6
Near Regents Park, on the north side of Rockland Hill
Price: Moderate to Expensive
Credit cards: Yes
Handicapped Access: Limited
Special Features: Free WiFi

Built in 1888 as one of Victoria's finest inns, this large property (15 rooms) is located up Fort Street, convenient to that street's famous antiques stores, and close to the Victoria Art Gallery and Craigdarroch Castle. The Inner Harbour and downtown are about a 20-minute walk. Rooms and suites in the large, columned clapboard building range from cozy (and fairly economical) to the sumptuous Royal Suite, whose name is not too hyperbolic. Décor is Edwardian or Victorian throughout, with each room different and offering amenities such as fireplaces, soaking tubs, and canopy beds. Breakfasts span the range from pancakes and scrambled eggs to handmade omelets. The location distinguishes this inn from most others in the city.

ASHCROFT HOUSE
250-386-8721 or 1-800-663-7667
www.ashcrofthousebandb.com
paulanne@ashcrofthousebandb.com
670 Battery St., Victoria, BC V8V 1E5
East of downtown, near Beacon Hill Park

Price: Moderate
Credit cards: Yes
Handicapped Access: Partial
Special Features: Free WiFi, free local calls, laundry facilities

This cheery Victorian near Beacon Hill Park is in a quiet neighborhood away from the downtown bustle, yet the city's sights are within 10 minutes walk. Built in 1898 by English aristocrat E. H. H. Taylor, the house's big windows bring in light, and its 4,200 square feet amply accommodate the five rooms and public spaces. Although appropriate to the period, the décor is less gaudy than at some Victorian inns, and the Mediterranean colors are sunny. Nearby Beacon Hill Park is a wonderful place for a flower-garden stroll.

BEACONSFIELD INN
250-384-4044 or 1-888-884-4044
www.beaconsfieldinn.com
info@beaconsfieldinn.com
998 Humboldt St., Victoria, BC V8V 2Z8
Between downtown and Rockland Hill
Price: Moderate to Expensive
Credit cards: Yes
Handicapped Access: Partial
Special Features: Free WiFi, free local and North American calls

Although it fashions itself a boutique hotel, Beaconsfield has just nine rooms. Room rates include not only lodging and breakfast, but evening sherry and late-night coffee and cookies. Designed by well-known Victoria architect Samuel Maclure, the colorful paint scheme on the 1905 Edwardian property's covered veranda reflects the lavish décor within, with canopy beds, overstuffed vermilion armchairs, plum carpets, carnelian walls, tile baths, soaking tubs, and fireplaces. The book-lined library is the site for the afternoon tea and evening sherry, and it's all much like a clubby London hotel.

THE EMPRESS HOTEL
250-384-8111 or 1-866-540-4429
www.fairmont.com/empress
theempress@fairmont.com
721 Government St., Victoria, BC V8W 1W5
On the Inner Harbour, just above the yacht basin
Price: Expensive
Credit cards: Yes
Handicapped Access: Full
Special Features: Pets welcome

Hardly anyone uses the word *hotel* when speaking of this Victoria institution, which is one of the best-known lodgings on earth. It's just "the Empress," a name deliberately chosen for its evocative character, but one that fits its subject admirably a century after its opening in 1908 as one of the Canadian Pacific Railroad's signature destinations. Its regal stone-and-copper-turret presence looming over the Inner Harbour like a castle, this is indisputably the grande dame of Pacific Coast hotels. Canadian Pacific hired Francis X. Rattenbury, architect of the Parliament Buildings across the way, to create an imposing postcolonial landmark, and he succeeded admirably. Although it does not in fact date to colonial times, the hotel calls to mind the Victorian pinnacle of empire during which the city named for the queen came of age.

Much of the hotel's nostalgic quality derives from the studied elegance of its interiors, which feature polished brass, glistening crystal, hushed wood trim, wainscoting, and an empire of ivory paint. The lobby is the setting for the Empress's famous afternoon High Tea service, which is elegant if not sumptuous (no danger of overeating) and very, very popular. Eight hundred guests a day in summer months take tea; reserve far ahead if it's something you feel you must do. Far more interesting is the downstairs Bengal Lounge, a comfy café decorated with tiger skins given the hotel in 1940 by an Indian maharajah, and

Empress Hotel, Inner Harbour Leslie Forsberg

featuring a splendid curry bar that has been one of the city's best lunch spots for more than a half-century.

The massive stone landmark holds 477 rooms with Edwardian-style furnishings—lots of dark oak and walnut, prim upholstery, and wainscoted walls. Although most visitors want a harbor-view room, the rear rooms are quieter and often cheaper. It's best to view the harbor while you're out and about in the city.

The Willow Stream Spa not only offers the first-class treatments and service you'd expect in one of Fairmont's lead properties, it includes several treatments featuring regionally appropriate ingredients derived from forest and seashore.

Most of the hotel's rooms go for more than $300 in summer. Is it worth it? I'd say everyone should stay at the Empress at least once. It's a quintessential part of the city's culture and truly one of a kind in North America.

FAIRHOLME MANOR

250-598-3240 or 1-877-511-3322
www.fairholmemanor.com
info@fairholmemanor.com
638 Rockland Place, Victoria, BC V8S 3R2
In Rockland, 10 minutes east of downtown
Price: Expensive
Credit cards: Yes
Handicapped Access: Partial
Special Features: Pets welcome, free WiFi, free local calls

This divinely romantic manor house atop Rockland Hill is more Mediterranean than British in atmosphere—even though it's practically next door to the lovely English-style gardens at Government House, the estate where British royal representatives stay when they are in the vicinity. Fairholme is an Italianate mansion built in 1885 by a Victoria doctor and operated as a deluxe B&B since 1996 by Austrian expat Sylvia Main, who brings a distinct European sensibility to her inn in many ways. The six rooms are actually vast suites with 14-foot ceilings, sitting areas, massive bay windows, fireplaces, hardwood floors, window benches, and more. The 1-acre grounds, though no match for the 36-acre gardens next door, are lovely and serene. And the proprietress's breakfasts, molded by her Austrian upbringing, feature fresh baked goods and entrées such as lemon ricotta pancakes or eggs Florentine. Often listed in guides for romance, Fairholme is truly a place that deserves such fame.

HATERLEIGH HERITAGE INN

250-384-9995 or 1-866-234-2244
www.haterleigh.com
guestservices@laurelpoint.com
243 Kingston St., Victoria, BC V8V 1V5
Price: Moderate to Expensive
Credit cards: Yes
Handicapped Access: Partial
Special Features: No pets, free WiFi, free local calls, off-street parking

An abundance of stained-glass windows, shimmering dark woodwork, glistening cut crystal, and polished brass make this opulent 1901 Victorian the epitome of a luxurious Victoria B&B. It's just a block from the Inner Harbour, near the Parliament Buildings, and convenient for walking to virtually all the city's sights. The seven rooms feature Victorian antique furnishings, with soaking tubs in most, and the usual afternoon tea is complemented by a service not often found at small inns: concierge assistance with local tours and bookings.

HI VICTORIA HOSTEL

250-385-4511 or 1-888-883-0099
www.hihostels.ca
516 Yates St., Victoria, BC V8W 1K8
Northwest end of downtown, near the Gorge Waterway
Price: Budget
Credit cards: Yes
Handicapped Access: Partial
Special Features: Free WiFi, free local calls

Best to beware the other hostels in Victoria, some of which stretch the term *backpacker* as far as it can go. This Hostelling International facility near Chinatown is a clean, quiet, well-furnished facility in a heritage building, and draws the type of circumspect guests one expects from HI travelers. Rooms range from the traditional bunk halls to small, private family accommodations, some of them with private baths. Shared-room bunks max out at $28 in summer peak season, so this is the ultra-budget choice for Victoria visitors.

HOTEL GRAND PACIFIC

250-386-0450 or 1-800-663-7550
www.hotelgrandpacific.com
greserve@hotelgrandpacific.com
463 Belleville St., Victoria, BC V8V 1X3
On Inner Harbour, just south of the Parliament Buildings

Price: Expensive
Credit cards: Yes
Handicapped Access: Full
Special Features: Pets welcome (extra fee), free WiFi

Only the Empress enjoys a location as handy as the Grand Pacific among Victoria hotels—the Parliament Buildings are next door, the Royal BC Museum a block away, the Inner Harbour at its doorstep. The Black Ball ferry from Port Angeles docks across the street, practically, so it is eminently possible for visitors from the States to leave their car in the United States and travel to Victoria on foot. The hotel itself is a modern contrast to the empire of historic lodging in the city, a turreted 10-story high-rise whose rooms feature modern, vaguely Edwardian furnishings—dark walnut, teal armchairs, ivory walls. The service ethic brought the hotel an award as Canada's best in 2008 from *Condé Nast Traveler* magazine.

HOTEL OSWEGO

250-386-8721 or 1-800-663-7667
www.laurelpoint.com
guestservices@laurelpoint.com
680 Montreal St., Victoria, BC V8V 1Z8
On Laurel Point, just south of the Inner Harbour
Price: Expensive
Credit cards: Yes
Handicapped Access: Full
Special Features: Pets welcome, free WiFi, free local calls

Throw a pebble almost anywhere and you'll hit a boutique hotel claiming to offer unique, customer-oriented luxury. But how many put, for example, French press coffeemakers in the rooms, with a daily supply of fresh-roasted coffee to ensure real quality? The Oswego is tucked into a quiet corner of the James Bay neighborhood, barely a five minutes' walk from the Inner Harbour, and counters the classic Victoria hotel experience with a sleek sophistication more like that on offer at Vancouver hotels. Black wood furniture, metal trim, and earth tone carpets and fabrics all meld into a contemporary décor that matches the high-rise building. Large windows look out over the city, and full kitchens obviate the usual morning trudge down to a café.

HOTEL RIALTO
250-383-4157 or 1-800-332-9981
www.hotelrialto.ca
stay@hotelrialto.ca
653 Pandora St., Victoria, BC V8W 1N8
Downtown, near Chinatown
Price: Moderate
Credit cards: Yes
Handicapped Access: Full
Free WiFi, free local calls, on-street parking
Handicapped Access: Full

With a zillion restored heritage homes in Victoria offering B&B accommodations, the Rialto offers an intriguing counterpoint—a restored commercial building that has been beautifully transformed into a boutique hotel. Italian marble, wall frescoes, hardwood floors, and other glamorous touches mark the four-story, 1912 stone-and-brick Italianate facility (though it was actually built by a Chinese merchant). Despite the history, the room furnishings are crisp: modern beds, linens, and woodwork, flat-panel TVs, and such. Best to ask for a room off the street—it's not a quiet neighborhood. Prices are engaging, with even a king-size-bed suite less than $200.

HUMBOLDT HOUSE
250-383-0152 or 1-888-383-0327
www.humboldthouse.com
rooms@humboldthouse.com
867 Humboldt St., Victoria, BC V8V 2Z6
On Laurel Point, just south of the Inner Harbour
Price: Expensive

Credit cards: Yes
Handicapped Access: Partial
Special Features: Free WiFi, free parking

Comfort equals 9th-century opulence here at this stately clapboard 1893 Victorian quite near downtown and the Inner Harbour. The six spacious suites all vary in décor, which features rich Victorian colors such as vermilion, fuchsia, and teal, as well as Oriental throw rugs, wood-burning fireplaces, and soaking tubs. Breakfast is served privately to each room using a pass-through cupboard. Despite the proximity to downtown (just two blocks to the Inner Harbour), the area abutting St. Ann's Academy is quiet.

INN AT LAUREL POINT
250-386-8721 or 1-800-663-7667
www.laurelpoint.com
guestservices@laurelpoint.com
680 Montreal St., Victoria, BC V8V 1Z8
On Laurel Point, just south of the Inner Harbour
Price: Expensive
Credit cards: Yes
Handicapped Access: Full
Special Features: Pets welcome, free WiFi, free local calls

Poised at the entrance to Victoria's Inner Harbour like a huge ivory flagship, this chic hotel's newest and most conspicuous wing was designed by famed Canadian architect Arthur Erickson (best known for the Law Courts in Vancouver). The graceful exterior design is matched within the 65 Erickson Wing guest suites, which are spacious and understated, feature lots of light-colored wood trim, and offer smashing views of the harbor, mountains, and Strait of Juan de Fuca. Priceless First Nations and Pacific Rim art is scattered about the open, airy public spaces; the smaller but very fine rooms in the Laurel Wing are more economical; earth tones such as sand and maple throughout lend an air of calm solidity; and the location, right next to the Harbour Promenade, is ideal. The hotel is carbon-neutral, first lodging in BC to achieve that distinction.

JAMES BAY INN
250-384-7151 or 1-800-836-2649
www.jamesbayinn.com
info@jamesbayinn.com
270 Government St., Victoria, BC V8V 2L2
James Bay neighborhood, south of downtown
Price: Budget to Moderate
Credit cards: Yes
Handicapped Access: Full
Special Features: Pets welcome, free parking

Its 45 rooms make James Bay a bit larger than most of Victoria's heritage inns—it opened in 1911—and that helps maintain its economy: Standard hotel rooms can usually be found here under $100. Although small-ish, rooms are comfortable and feature early 20th-century décor, and the adjoining heritage house offers more deluxe suites. The surrounding residential neighborhood is quiet. Wintertime rates for longer stays are remarkable—pay for 15 days and you get 15 more free.

MAGNOLIA HOTEL
250-381-0999 or 1-877-624-6654
www.magnoliahotel.com
sales@magnoliahotel.com
6123 Courtney St., Victoria, BC V8W 1B8
On Laurel Point, just south of the Inner Harbour
Price: Moderate to Expensive
Credit cards: Yes
Handicapped Access: Full
Special Features: Pets welcome (extra fee), free WiFi, free local calls, continental breakfast included

Ideally located just a block from Government Street, a block from the Inner Harbour, close to Chinatown and the Yale Street shopping district, the Magnolia is a true boutique hotel—only 64 rooms—whose classic elegance is neo-Edwardian in appearance but very modern in prove-nance. Deep-colored fabrics (royal purple, forest green), Oriental rugs, walnut panel-ing, brass fixtures, and other classic ele-ments contrast with the airy feel lent by floor-to-ceiling windows. The thumping ground-floor nightclub that used to create a noise problem on the lower floors has been, thankfully, replaced by a most excel-lent steakhouse, Prime (see Dining).

SELKIRK GUEST HOUSE
250-389-1213 or 1-800-974-6638
www.selkirkguesthouse.com
info@selkirkguesthouse.com
934 Selkirk Ave., Victoria, BC V9A 2V1
Along the Gorge Waterway, north of downtown
Price: Moderate
Credit cards: Yes
Handicapped Access: Partial
Special Features: Pets welcome, free WiFi, free local calls, laundry facilities, shared kitchen

This 1909 waterfront home bears hints of the then-extant Tudor revival style with its gables and green trim. Rooms range from standard queen-size-bed rooms to suites with wood-burning fireplace, clawfoot tub, private entrance, and a bunk bed. Breakfast costs an extra $8. The wonderful Galloping Goose Regional Trail is nearby, and though it is far from downtown in terms of quiet, Old Town Victoria is only a 20-minute walk on quiet streets and then over the famed Blue Bridge. The waterfront hot tub is a divine extra amenity.

SPINNAKERS GUESTHOUSE
250-386-8721 or 1-800-663-7667
www.laurelpoint.com
guestservices@laurelpoint.com
680 Montreal St., Victoria, BC V8V 1Z8

On Laurel Point, just south of the
Inner Harbour
Price: Moderate
Credit cards: Yes
Handicapped Access: Full
Special Features: Free WiFi, free local calls,
breakfast included

Actually a small aggregation of residential
buildings around Spinnakers Brewpub,
this dandy small inn overlooks the outer
entrance to the Inner Harbour. Five rooms
are in a heritage 1884 Victorian home, with
period amenities ranging from clawfoot
tubs to wood-burning fireplaces. Old-
growth Douglas fir floors lend a warm tone
throughout. The four newer Garden Suites
all feature soaking tubs and kitchen facilities. The separate bungalow has a soaking
tub, kitchen, rain shower, and living room.

VILLA MARCO POLO
250-370-1524 or 1-800-663-7667
www.villamarcopolo.com
enquire@villamarcopolo.com
1524 Shasta Pl., Victoria, BC V8S 1X9
On Laurel Point, just south of the Inner
Harbour
Price: Moderate to Expensive
Credit cards: Yes
Handicapped Access: Full
Special Features: Free WiFi, free local calls,
breakfast included

The sunny Mediterranean atmosphere
here is a pleasant contrast to the stuffier
Edwardian or Victorian themes so prevalent among the city's historic inns. The
mansion was built in 1923 in the quiet
Rockland neighborhood about 10 minutes
from downtown. Marco Polo's four spacious
suites reflect stops along the famous
explorer's journeys—the dandy Silk Road
suite, for instance, has a Maxfield
Parrish—style mural on the barrel vault
ceiling, Persian carpet, a wood-burning
fireplace, and leaded glass windows.
Breakfasts feature breads and pastries from

the inn's own kitchens, and locally sourced
fruits and meats; and are served in the sun-
room, on the patio, or in the guests' own
suite. A large parlor, hallway, and upstairs
library with a huge games selection offer
more public space than does the usual
small inn. Despite all the splashy luxury,
two of the suites go for less than $200, a
good deal for what you get.

DINING

Victoria is not only the capital of British
Columbia, it's the capital of a region,
southern Vancouver Island, that is itself a
capital of the global slow food phenomenon. Slow food celebrates carefully prepared meals relying largely on local
ingredients produced in as natural a fashion as possible, and both the Saanich
Peninsula and Cowichan Valley north of
Victoria hold dozens of farms and food producers practicing this philosophy. Add the
Gulf Islands (Salt Spring is the home of two
of the best artisan cheese makers in North
America) and the waters of the Salish Sea
and Pacific Ocean, and there is very little a
chef might ever want or need that cannot be
found within 60 miles (100 km) or so.

The overarching term for the modern
regional cuisine of British Columbia,
including the island, is "West Coast," and
dozens of restaurants describe their menus
thus. Victoria claims to have the second-
highest number of restaurants per capita in
North America, after San Francisco, and
while visitor attention naturally focuses on
all the excellent options around the Inner
Harbour, there are numerous residential
areas with small commercial districts holding great restaurants, cafés, and pubs.

Cook Street Village is an ideal example
of the Canadian paradigm in urban neighborhoods. Here, within a few blocks along
Cook Street, are a good pizza joint (Pizzeria
Prima Strada, www.pizzeriaprimastrada
.com); a superb liquor store, BC Liquor

A popular tavern in Victoria's Fernwood neighborhood   Leslie Forsberg

Guys, specializing in rare craft beers and BC wines, such as the very hard-to-get Blue Mountain vintages (bcliquorguys@blogspot .com); a great local bakery, **Bubby Rose's**, famed for its cinnamon rolls (www.bubby rosesbakery.com); a local coffee roaster, **Caffe Fantastico** (www.caffefantastico .com) competing amiably with a Starbucks and a Serious Coffee outlet; numerous small shops and cafés; and the excellent Beagle Pub (see listings). The **food-cart court** at 325 Cook Street, in a once-vacant lot, illustrates a phenomenon growing in popularity up and down the West Coast from here to Portland, with fish-and-chips, tacos, pastries, and more, depending on the day.

Other examples of urban neighborhood villages in Victoria, all worth a dinnertime stroll, are **Oak Bay Village** (www.oakbay tourism.com), **Cadboro Bay Village** (www .cadbororbayvillage.com); **Estevan Village**, in Oak Bay.

The most conspicuous local coffee-roasting chain is **Serious Coffee**, which started up-island at Mill Bay and now has outlets throughout Southern Vancouver Island. Yes, *serious* suits its name—the chain's roasts are robust and served up strong.

BARB'S
250-386-2010
www.barbsplace.ca
310 St. Lawrence St., Victoria, BC V8V 1Y4, at Fisherman's Wharf
Open: Daily 11 AM—sundown, March—October

Price: Budget to Moderate
Credit cards: Yes
Cuisine: Seafood
Serving: L, D
Handicapped Access: Yes
Special Features: Nightly prix fixe menu,
brunch till 4 PM

Long the standout purveyor of fish-and-chips in Victoria, this ever-busy stand at Fisherman's Wharf still draws crowds for its more-traditional (compared to RFBF) approach to its food. The setting is splendid, on floating docks at the entrance to the Inner Harbour—a stroll among the neighboring houseboats (there are few actual fishing boats here) is a pleasant way to pass the time while you await your order. Aside from the classic cod or haddock, salmon, and halibut fish-and-chips, which are good but not great, there are quite good clam strips, a fried oyster dinner that's dandy, and great oyster burgers. The coleslaw is excellent, and the tables set hither and yon along the dock provide a most atmospheric dining venue. Barb's is easily reached by walking the harbor shoreline path, about 15 minutes from the Empress.

BEACON DRIVE-IN

250-385-7521
126 Douglas St., Victoria, BC V8V 2N9
Right across from Beacon Hill Park
Open: Daily 9 AM–10 PM
Price: Budget
Credit cards: No
Cuisine: Fast food
Serving: B, L, D
Handicapped Access: Yes

How rare is a true, old-fashioned drive-in joint? Rare indeed—this Victoria institution isn't really a drive-in any more, though there is no table service and tables are limited, especially inside. But it is fondly remembered by thousands of residents and visitors who came here as kids, and the food is a throwback to times past: soft-serve ice cream and shakes that are either delightfully light and smooth or flavorless and mushy, depending on your perspective. The burgers, fries, and fish-and-chips are either just like you remember from the '60s—or leathery, greasy, and stale, again depending on your perspective. What's indisputable is that this is a longtime Victoria favorite, a local mainstay with many nostalgic fans.

THE BEAGLE PUB

250-382-3301
www.beaglepub.com
301 Cook St., Victoria, BC V8V 3X5
Open: Daily 11 AM–11 PM
Price: Moderate
Credit cards: Yes
Cuisine: Pub food
Serving: L, D
Handicapped Access: Yes
Special Features: Nightly prix fixe menu,
brunch till 4 PM

As in England, a neighborhood tavern can be a fine place for dinner in Canada, and this bustling place at the end of Cook Street exemplifies the phenomenon. Invariably filled with a crowd of people variously watching sports (the TVs are kept at a discreetly low volume), families and friends having dinner, and Victoria office workers having a drink at the end of the day, it's wonderfully convivial. Despite the crowds, the staff does an excellent job of seating diners, taking orders and making sure customers are satisfied. (I once succeeded in sending back an overcooked burger, which was replaced by a medium-rare one, a near impossibility in Canada.) Stained glass, warm woods, and colorful furniture set the tone; a small sidewalk patio is shielded from cool breezes by glass panels. The menu includes *poutine*, the classic French Canadian fries–and–cheese curds dish; yam fries; and an exotic pub favorite, fried risotto cakes. The BLAT sandwich (bacon, lettuce, avocado, and tomato) is lovely; the bison and halibut burgers are admirable examples of alternatives to the classic beef patty.

BLUE FOX

250-380-1683
www.bonrouge.ca
919 Fort St., Victoria, BC V8V 3K2
Open: weekdays 7:30 AM–4 PM, weekends 8 AM–3 PM
Price: Budget to Moderate
Credit cards: Yes
Cuisine: Café
Serving: B, L,
Handicapped Access: Yes

Oh, how the line grows outside Blue Fox on weekend mornings as would-be break-fasters gather. Sometimes the queue stretches down the block and around the corner, all for a chance at the relatively small café's no-holds-barred platters of eggs, French toast, pancakes, huevos rancheros, eggs Benedict, and more. There's nothing exotic here, just heaps of good food cooked up comfort style, suffi-cient to feed soldiers marching across continents (which some critics dismiss as greasy-spoon junk). There have been com-plaints lately about slipping quality and shoddy service, a shame for this 20-year mainstay of Victoria café culture. An alter-native to the breakfast frenzy is lunch, which offers up burgers and sandwiches, also in Bunyan-esque proportions.

BON ROUGE

250-220-8008
www.bonrouge.ca
611 Courtney St., Victoria, BC V8W 1B7
Open: Daily 11 AM–10 PM, till 11 PM Friday and Saturday
Price: Moderate to Expensive
Credit cards: Yes
Cuisine: French
Serving: L, D

Handicapped Access: Yes
Special Features: Nightly prix fixe menu, brunch till 4 PM

Both the food and the décor are an able representation of the French café this downtown standout aspires to be. Crimson walls, black-and-white tile floors, white linen-covered tables, and windowside banquets—the interior is Parisian bistro style. The menu features bistro standbys, including an excellent steak frites (yes, served in a cast-iron skillet) and beef tartare, as well as bouillabaisse, duck con-fit, and regional dishes such as smoked black cod. The atmosphere reaches high-buzz level most nights at 8 PM, and the serv-ice is generally exceptional. The nightly $29 prix fixe menu is an excellent bargain for a fine-dining, romantic dinner shrine.

CAFÉ BRIO

250-383-0009
www.café-brio.com
944 Fort St., Victoria, BC V8V 3K2
Open: Daily 5:30 PM–9:30 PM
Price: Expensive
Credit cards: Yes
Cuisine: West Coast/Italian
Serving: D
Handicapped Access: Yes
Special Features: Nightly prix fixe menu, brunch till 4 PM

Opened in 1997 by pioneers of West Coast/New Age cuisine in Victoria, Silvia Marcolini and Greg Hays, Café Brio has long since become one of the pillars of the gourmet establishment on Vancouver Island, housed in a heritage brick building with sunny mustard stucco walls at the upper end of the city's antiques row. The décor is spare but enlivened by fine art on the walls, warmed by liberal use of recycled Douglas fir. The menu is highly committed to the regional slow-food philosophy (*cucina domestica,* in Italian) prevalent on the island. Thus, while the recipes are

Italian, the foods are local—island-raised pork, venison, lamb, and shellfish, with island-grown fruits and vegetables. The result is dishes such as pork belly braised in tomatoes and molasses, venison with celery root, pear and nettle risotto, and marinated squid with squid-ink risotto, a delightful exotic signature dish. There's a separate menu for *salumi* (hand-cured meats) and desserts range from dark chocolate to a cheese plate. One shouldn't overlook the stuffed olives made by the proprietress's mother back in Italy— probably the one item on the menu that has traveled farthest.

CAMILLE'S

250-381-3433
www.camillesrestaurant.com
45 Bastion Square, Victoria, BC V8W 1J1
Open: 5:30 PM–9 PM Tuesday–Saturday
Price: Expensive
Credit cards: Yes
Cuisine: West Coast
Serving: D
Handicapped Access: Yes
Special Features: Nightly chef's tasting menu, $60

One of the paragons of West Coast cuisine in Victoria, this is also a deliciously atmospheric European-style bistro set in the daylight basement of a heritage building one the south side of Bastion Square. Candlelight and a soft blues/jazz soundtrack establish a cosmopolitan atmosphere amid the brick-walled dining rooms. The menu changes daily, but always features mostly island ingredients in a wide-ranging cuisine that melds Asian, French, and Mediterranean influences. The signature soup is a bisque made with lemon, ginger, and North Pacific spot prawns. Bouillabaisse, scallops, salmon, halibut, curry, lamb, duck, and beef tenderloin flesh out the menu. This is one of the most romantic celebration dining spots in BC.

DON MEE

250-383-1032
www.donmee.com
538 Fisgard St., Victoria, BC V8W 1R4, upstairs midblock
Open: Daily 11 AM–9:30 PM, best to arrive before 1 PM for dim sum
Price: Moderate
Credit cards: Yes
Cuisine: Mandarin, dim sum
Serving: L, D
Handicapped Access: Yes
Special Features: Dim sum lunch

Dim sum is one of those exotic, arcane culinary pursuits that turns some people, such as your correspondent, into quasi-zealots. I've researched the topic in both North America and Asia, and the dim sum here in Victoria Chinatown is as good as any in Hong Kong, Beijing, San Francisco, or Los Angeles. Early each morning, the dim sum chefs start preparing the dumplings, rolls, and other delights; each day around 11:30 AM, the dim sum ladies start trundling through the restaurant with baskets and platters of these savory treats. There are literally hundreds of types of dim sum, but you can expect shrimp dumplings, crab rolls, bean curd creations, taro dumplings, and of course the famous chicken feet, which you should try at least once to say you did it. (They're not actually very interesting.) After several shared baskets or platters of savory dim sum, diners traditionally finish with a couple sweet treats, such as egg custard balls, mango puddings, steamed sponge cake, and more. Be sure to arrive before 1 PM, as the dim sum carts start to empty out soon after that.

When the dim sum carts run out, the menu shifts to Mandarin and Szechuan cuisine, such as barbecued duck, prawns in black bean sauce, and kung pao chicken. All are executed well, and the atmosphere is abuzz with Mandarin and Cantonese conversation. I rate this the top Chinese restaurant in Victoria.

FERRIS' OYSTER BAR

250-360-1824
www.ferrisoysterbar.com
536 Yates St., Victoria, BC V8W 1K8
Open: downstairs, 11:30 AM–11 PM daily;
upstairs 5 PM–11 PM Sunday–Thursday,
4 PM–midnight Friday and Saturday
Price: Moderate to Expensive
Credit cards: Yes
Cuisine: French
Serving: L, D
Handicapped Access: Yes
Special Features: Reservations are limited,
phone only

Few shellfish restaurants could equal the boast at Ferris—the menu features only oysters grown in British Columbia waters. Since the province's shellfish industry is large and diverse, that is not a limiting factor, and oysters here come fresh shucked in several varieties, pan fried or panko coated, and in eight baked versions that range from creamy pesto to chipotle and lime butter. The rest of the menu features clams and mussels, prawns, pitas, burgers, and such, all very good, but it's silly to come here and not focus on the signature food. The décor in both the downstairs Grill and upstairs Oyster Bar reflects the heritage building in which they are located, with lots of recycled wood, brickwork, and warm light.

FOL EPI BAKERY

250-477-8882
398 Harbour Rd., Victoria, BC V9A 0B7
Open: 7:30 AM–5 PM Monday–Saturday
Price: Budget
Credit cards: No
Cuisine: Baked goods
Serving: B, L
Handicapped Access: Yes

Housed in a spiffy new residential condo development, Dockside Green, along the Gorge Waterway northwest of downtown,

Fol Epi is fervently committed to using organic, sustainable, regional ingredients. Most notable is the bread made with Red Fife wheat, a Canadian heritage variety grown on the island and in the prairies, notable for its robust flavor and high nutritional profile. Rye and other whole-grain breads are the main items on offer, though there are also croissants, pastries, small pizzas, muffins, and espresso drinks. The wood-fired oven lends depth to the flavor of everything. It's right by the start of the Galloping Goose Trail, and I can't think of a better way to do the trail than to start with pastry and coffee here, grab a loaf of bread to supplement a chunk of island cheese, and head out on the trail for a picnic in a field somewhere toward Sooke.

FOO ASIAN

250-383-3111
www.foofood.ca
769 Yates St., Victoria, BC V8W 1L4
Open: 11:30 AM–10 PM weekdays, 5 PM–10 PM weekends
Price: Budget
Credit cards: Yes
Cuisine: Asian fusion
Serving: L, D
Handicapped Access: Yes
Special Features: Nightly prix fixe menu, brunch till 4 PM

This restaurant's inspired meld of Asian cuisines and Vancouver Island ingredients is broad-ranging, from Chinese-style pot stickers to Thai curries. Housed in a former service station, the ambience blends urban buzz with fast-food sleekness. Everything's good, but the standouts are glazed octopus salad in chile-lime dressing, *laksa* (Malaysian bouillabaisse) with local fresh fish, and the beef short rib chow mein. A splendid dinner for two runs about $20.

JOHN'S PLACE
250-389-0711
www.jonsplace.ca
723 Pandora Ave., Victoria, BC V8W 1N9
Open: 7 AM–9 PM weekdays, 8 AM–9 PM
Saturday and Sunday
Price: Budget to Moderate
Credit cards: Yes
Cuisine: Diner
Serving: B, L, D
Handicapped Access: Yes

Although this iconic comfort food joint
advertises itself as a diner, its menu ranges
much further afield—banana kiwi waffles,
Grand Marnier lattes, wild salmon grilled
with maple syrup and pecans, and sour
cream apple pie. *Eclectic* is the real description of the food here; platters are more
than filling. The décor is heavy on auto-
graphed celebrity pictures.

MING'S
250-385-4405
www.mings.ca
611 Courtney St., Victoria, BC V8W 2K9
Open: Daily 5 PM–10 PM, till 11 PM Friday
and Saturday
Price: Moderate to Expensive
Credit cards: Yes
Cuisine: Mandarin
Serving: D
Handicapped Access: Yes
Special Features: Nightly prix fixe menu,
brunch till 4 PM

Ming's is the mainstream classic Mandarin
restaurant in Victoria, downtown a few
blocks from Chinatown proper in a modern
white edifice that seems more abstract than
Chinese in inspiration. Inside, though,
there are moon gates, fish tanks, and the
usual trappings of a Chinese restaurant.
Aside from the usual suspects such as won-
ton soup and Peking duck, there are more
interesting dishes such as winter melon
soup, plum duck, lobster Cantonese (in
black bean sauce), and sweet-and-sour

mushrooms. The menu is more manageable
than the usual encyclopedic compendium at
Chinese restaurants, and the food preparation and service are excellent.

PAPRIKA BISTRO
250-592-7424
www.paprika-bistro.com
2524 Estevan Ave., Victoria, BC V8R 2S7
Open: Daily 5 PM–9 PM, till 10 PM Friday
and Saturday
Price: Moderate
Credit cards: Yes
Cuisine: West Coast
Serving: D
Handicapped Access: Yes
Special Features: Nightly three-course fixed
menu available till 6 PM

This is one of the finest examples of a
Victoria phenomenon, the neighborhood
fine dining bistro far from tourist areas.
You have to take a car to get here from
downtown, but it's worth the cab ride if you
have sensibly not brought a vehicle to
Victoria. Geoff Parker and Anna Hunt,
both longtime veterans in the hospitality
industry, operate Paprika as a family destination, with a low-key atmosphere, seats
for just 60 diners, and impeccably friendly
service. The European-inspired menu
ranges from beef tartare to Qualicum scallops to Cowichan Bay duck, and apricot
risotto cake. A dinner visit here should
include an hour of presupper strolling the
surrounding village commercial district.

PRIME STEAKHOUSE
250-386-2010
www.primesteak.ca
621 Courtney St., Victoria, BC V8W 1C1,
in the Magnolia Hotel
Open: Daily 11:30 AM–11 PM
Price: Expensive
Credit cards: Yes
Cuisine: Chophouse
Serving: L, D

Handicapped Access: Yes
Special Features: Nightly prix fixe menu, brunch till 4 PM

Although beef has been a mainstay of British cuisine for centuries, it wasn't until this glitzy new emporium opened in 2009 that downtown Victoria boasted a sterling example of what's best known as a chop-house. Dark wood paneling; even darker leather seating; burgundy carpeting; and crystal, ebony, and crimson accents set the sleek tone. The menu hews to mainstream dishes, from halibut to stroganoff and rack of lamb, but of course it is the steaks that stand out. Prime's six different steaks depart a bit from the norm—the New York cut is cooked and served bone in, there is both rib eye and filet mignon—but what distinguishes the food most is the sheer excellence of the food and its execution: If you tell them medium with just a touch of pink in the center on a 2-inch-thick base-ball sirloin, that is exactly what you'll get. Notable sides include sensational onion rings in a panko crust.

RED FISH BLUE FISH
250-298-6877
www.redfish-bluefish.com
1006 Wharf St., Victoria, BC V8W 1T4
(near the floatplane base)
Open: Daily 11 AM–10 PM, closed December and January
Price: Budget to Moderate
Credit cards: Yes
Cuisine: Seafood
Serving: L, D
Handicapped Access: Yes
Special Features: The entire menu is based on sustainable ingredients.

Is this wonderful little waterfront stand the best fish-and-chips in the world? I have often argued that, though of course neither I nor anyone else has ever tried all the world's fish-and-chips, and there are even local connoisseurs who prefer other island

purveyors (see the Nanaimo section). The signature dish consists of moist, tempura-battered halibut, cod, or salmon (the best), and the chips are made of hand-cut Kennebec potatoes—though the coleslaw is actually even better. The *tacones* are hand-rolled tortillas filled with everything from barbecued salmon to chipotle shrimp; the Fanny Bay oyster sandwich has shallot aioli; and the Pacific Rim chowder puts to shame the usual dreary pale soup, here including chipotle, coconut, corn, and garlic. Honestly, everything on the menu is great. The harbor-side wharf setting is atmospheric (though the seating is a bit scant); the prices are great (a fabulous dinner for two runs about $35); and the restaurant's commitment to sustainability stretches as far as the recyclable serving utensils and takeout containers.

SPINNAKER'S GASTRO BREWPUB
250-386-2739 or 1-877-838-2739
www.spinnakers.com
308 Catherine St., Victoria, BC V9A 3S8
Open: Daily 11 AM–10:30 PM
Price: Moderate to Expensive
Credit cards: Yes
Cuisine: Pub food
Serving: L, D
Handicapped Access: Yes
Special Features: Aside from the brews, you can buy the malt vinegar to take home.

Spinnaker's advertises itself as Canada's oldest brewpub (not everyone agrees), and sure enough, there are fine ales and beers made here, with many seasonal offerings. It is also a superlative place to sample a pub-food dinner, one of the mainstays of life in Canada. The menu ranges from traditional (bangers and mashed potatoes) to distinctly New Age items such as a locally made vege-tarian burger made from beets and pota-toes. Thin-crust pizzas are baked in a brick oven, and salad dressings are notable for the Spinnaker-made vinegar that's used in them. In the same complex, Sips Artisan Bistro pairs BC beer and wine with BC-made cheese and charcuterie, ranging from Salt Spring chèvre to North Vancouver venison chorizo. The attractive setting overlooks the entrance to the Inner Harbour and offers a great place to spend a summer evening.

STAGE
250-388-4222
www.stagewinebar.com
1307 Gladstone Ave., Victoria, BC V8R 1R9
Open: Daily 5–midnight, till 10 PM Sunday and Monday
Price: Moderate
Credit cards: Yes
Cuisine: Tapas
Serving: D
Handicapped Access: Yes
Special Features: Reservations by phone only

Housed in a heritage building near Fernwood Square, Stage is ultra-atmospheric—old brick walls frame high ceilings, muted light glistens on crystal, theater-goers buzz before and after shows at the nearby Belfry. Operated by the couple behind the superb Paprika (see listing), George and Linda Szasz, Stage fashions itself a "small plates wine bar," and offers the chance for a light dinner or full repast. Artisan cheese, scrumptious olives, pork belly over stewed beans, and handmade sausage are mainstays. Particularly popular are the *langos*, Hungarian fried bread sprinkled with salt and garlic, reflecting George's heritage. Although the extensive wine list includes fine BC vintages, it ranges the world, and there are more than a dozen available by the glass.

WILD FIRE BAKERY
250-381-3473
www.wildfirebakery.ca
1517 Quadra St., Victoria, BC V8W 2L3
Open: 7:30 AM–6 PM weekdays, 8 AM–5 PM Saturday
Price: Budget
Credit cards: Yes
Cuisine: Baked goods
Serving: B, L
Handicapped Access: Yes
Special Features: Breads can be ordered ahead online.

One of the earliest practitioners of healthful baking using sustainable ingredients in Victoria is this now-famous spot downtown. A wide range of European-style breads is supplemented by muffins, *levains* (sourdough bread), tarts, cookies, shortbreads, and flourless hazelnut cake. Lunch is hearty soups, sandwiches, and salads, plus vegetarian pizzas baked in wood-fired ovens.

WILLIE'S BAKERY
250-381-8414
www.williesbakery.com
537 Johnson St., Victoria, BC V8W 1M2
Open: Daily 6 AM–5 PM, weekends 8 AM–5 PM
Price: Moderate to Expensive
Credit cards: Yes
Cuisine: Baked goods, café lunch
Serving: B, L
Handicapped Access: Yes
Special Features: Although it's a bakery, Willie's offers beer and wine.

Although it's nominally in Chinatown, there's nothing Chinese about this quintessential bakery housed in a heritage building. Savory and sweet muffins, breads, and pastries line the shelves in the glass cabinets; the seating area ambience benefits from eclectic furniture and the brick walls, high ceilings, and wooden beams of the heritage building. The breakfast menu ranges from pancakes (house-made buttermilk batter) to eggs Benedict, banana-pecan French toast, and panini. It all sounds very contemporary, but Willie's was founded in 1887 in this very spot and is BC's oldest bakery, though it closed for a time in the late 20th century and was reopened in 1999 under new ownership. There's a nice outdoor patio at the Johnson street store for summer use, and Willie's operates a café next to the gift shop at the Royal BC Museum. Two historic suites above the bakery are **B&B lodgings** (Isabella suites, available through Willie's), with the breakfast part of that equation consisting of bakery delights, of course.

CULTURE

As the erstwhile colonial capital of the British empire in the eastern Pacific, the current capital of British Columbia, and one of the top tourist destinations in the Pacific Northwest, Victoria is splendidly arrayed with cultural attractions far beyond the usual for a city its size. Here is one of the best museums in North America, a small but grand totem collection, a dandy small art museum, a Chinatown that is simultaneously the oldest and smallest in Canada, an active theatre community, a symphony orchestra, and plenty of nightclubs and performance venues, though nothing like in Vancouver or Whistler. Visitors do not usually come to Victoria for the cultural offerings, aside from those at the Royal BC Museum; but there is plenty here for visitors to enjoy.

Piping in the sunset, Inner Harbour Leslie Forsberg

Several tour companies offer carriage rides around the Inner Harbour, through Old Town and Chinatown and such. On a cool evening, with the Parliament Buildings all alight, buskers along the promenade and the city's many hanging flower baskets overhead, it's a most romantic journey.

The superb **Victoria Symphony** (www .victoriasymphony.ca) is led by Tania Miller, one of the few female symphony maestros in North America, and is the equal in live performance of much bigger orchestras in much larger cities. The annual subscription program offers a full slate of concerts in the classical and pop pantheon, including especially lively concerts devoted to movie themes and music associated with Shakespeare; the symphony does not shrink from pieces as substantial as the Verdi Requiem. The main performance venue is the opulent 1913 Royal Theatre, a restored Beaux Arts–style venue that has hosted stars from Sarah Bernhardt to Luciano Pavarotti. The symphony also offers numerous summer concerts at Butchart Gardens, and a hugely popular event, **Symphony Splash**, which consists of an August concert from a barge moored in the Inner Harbour, complete with fireworks and a cannon.

Several theater companies offer yea-round slates of plays that range from classics to modern, path-breaking works. **Belfry Theatre**, which utilizes a historic Baptist church near Fernwood Square, offers a year-round series specializing in new productions of modern works that challenge social and cultural norms (www.belfry.bc.ca, 250-385-6815), with an emphasis on Canadian playwrights. **Blue Bridge Repertory Theatre** is Victoria's mainline company, offering classics from Shakespeare to Albee (bluebridgetheatre.ca). **Pacific Opera Victoria** presents four productions a year from the classic opera repertoire (pov.bc.ca).

Monday Magazine is Victoria's excellent free-distribution weekly arts and entertainment publication, with a healthy dose of political and cultural commentary thrown in. Look for it in coffee shops, cafés, hotel lobbies, and such.

Fair warning: **Caution**, alas, must be exercised when passing through the area along Pandora Street near Harris Green Park, east of Vancouver Street. Like a few blocks in the east end of downtown Vancouver, this area has been taken over by transients and drug users and is not safe, especially at night. Luckily, it's not very near any of the attractions downtown, but visitors should be aware and avoid it.

ABKHAZI GARDEN
250-598-8096
blog.conservancy.bc.ca
1964 Fairfield Rd., Victoria, BC V8S 1H2
Open: Daily 11 AM–5 PM, closes 4 PM in winter
Admission: Adults $10, students and seniors $7.50

A true labor of love, this naturalistic garden space on a rocky slope on the east side of Rockland blends casual plantings—rhododendrons, azaleas, bamboo, and other exotics—into the native habitat of Garry oak. It's tempting to describe it as the antithesis of Butchart Gardens, but that's not fair to either. Nicholas and Peggy Abkhazi, both World War II refugees of sorts, settled on this 1-acre parcel in 1946 and set about transforming it into what she compared to a Chinese scroll painting. As you wander along the garden paths, it is like discovering new scenes and vistas at each turn—a swale of lawn bordered by heather resembles the Yangtze River; the garden design elegantly leads the eye to the rocky outcrop that held the Abkhazis' modest home. The property is now owned by the Land Conservancy and operated as a nonprofit.

ART GALLERY OF VICTORIA
250-384-4171
aggva.org
1040 Moss St., Victoria, BC V8V 4P1
Open: Daily 9 AM–5 PM, extended hours Thursday, closed Monday
Admission: Adults $13, students and seniors $11

Although it's a relatively small facility, this hillside museum makes up in quality what it may lack in size. The gallery itself is adjacent to an 1889 hillside mansion on Rockland Hill, and includes a lovely outdoor Asian garden. The collection of 17,000 works is the largest such in British Columbia, though only a small portion is on view at any given time.

In particular, the museum's new gallery devoted to Victoria native daughter **Emily Carr** is the most notable public display of this iconic artist's work, and it fills a need long unmet by the largest holder of Carr pieces, the Vancouver Art Gallery (some of whose holdings have been lent to Victoria for this gallery). Not only are more Carr works on display here than anywhere else, their juxtaposition with other artists who were her peers lends depth to the display. Inclusion of numerous lighter-hued pieces dispels the popular conception of Carr's work as relentlessly dark, and her adaptation of impressionist and expressionist techniques is explored.

The gallery also has an exquisite collection of **Asian artworks** (one of the best such collections in North America), and regularly mounts exhibits of work by other island and Western Canada artists.

BASTION SQUARE

The small public plaza between Government and Wharf streets, north of Courtney, is the site of the original fort (bastion) the Hudson's Bay Company established in 1863. Cafés and shops surround the cobblestone square, which slopes toward the harbor, just across Wharf Street. The smallish **Maritime Museum of British Columbia** is on one side of the plaza (28 Bastion Square, 250-385-4222, www .mmbc.bc.ca). Among the artifacts here is *Tillikum,* a hand-carved canoe that sailed from Victoria to England from 1901 to 1904 in a colorful career as a sail-driven dugout. A modest food and crafts market occupies the square weekends in summer.

Chinatown storefront   Leslie Forsberg

CHINATOWN

Between Government and Wharf streets and Fisgard and Herald streets

North American cities are wont to claim the largest, or oldest, or most-visited, or whatever, Chinatown. Victoria lays claim to the oldest in Canada and, if anything, smallest—it's just a couple blocks at the north end of downtown, between Government and Store streets. One of the main attractions here is **Fan Tan Alley**, the sort of odd item that used to show up in Ripley's Believe It or Not: "Too narrow for two men to pass abreast!" And so it is, along a short stretch, inducing claustrophobia as you pass through a section only 3 feet (90 cm) wide, with towering brick walls on each side. It is the narrowest "street" in Canada, and the odd little stores tucked in along its 240-foot (73 m) length (a record shop, a Chinese café) look only slightly upgraded since its historic days as the home of opium and gambling dens.

The rest of Chinatown consists of Herald and Fisgard streets, between Government and Wharf streets. A gaily decorated 1981 archway, the **Gate of Harmonious Interest**, marks the district in its spot on Fisgard near Government Street and is its symbolic entrance. The rest of the district offers up Chinese restaurants and cafés, Asian grocery stores, and novelty shops. A local tour company, Hidden Dragon, offers guided tours of the district (www.oldchinatown.com).

Most stores open at 10 AM, restaurants at 11. Dim sum seekers are best advised to arrive at their chosen restaurant no later than 1 PM, as the best delicacies sell out in short order after service starts just before noon.

CRAIGDARROCH CASTLE
250-592-5323
www.craigdarrochcastle.com
1050 Joan Crescent, Victoria, BC V8S 3L5
Open: Daily 10 AM–4:30 PM, 9 AM–7 PM summer
Admission: Adults $13.75, students $8.75

Most buildings in North America called "castles" are puny attempts at such, but this towering mansion on Rockland Hill comes close. Built by Scottish coal baron Robert Dunsmuir in the 19th century as his manse, it is a four-story, 39-room, 20,000-square-foot edifice that, despite its bulk, exhibits an elegance and refinement unusual in what are known as "bonanza castles." Built by 19th-century tycoons whose fortunes usually derived from mining or railroads (in Dunsmuir's case, both), such homes were meant to convey the wealth and significance of the builder. Here, no effort was spared to satisfy that goal. The exterior design, a sort of Romanesque revival popular at the time, features massive stone cut blocks with turrets, garrets, and towers on every side. The interior is a jaw-dropping treasure chest of finely carved oak, mahogany, cedar, cherry, and exotic tropical woods. Stained glass sprays a rainbow of light, and vast parlors and halls offer dancing and dining spaces equal to the average home.

Its history is an excellent example of the term *overweening*—the building was finished in 1890, but Dunsmuir never lived in it, as he had died the year before. His widow remained in the castle until 1908, and one can only wonder what it was like for her in this immense home without its creator. Visiting today not only affords a look at an architectural wonder, it spurs reflection on what really matters in life.

EMILY CARR HOUSE
250-383-5843
www.emilycarr.com
207 Government St., Victoria, BC V8V 2K8
Open: Daily 11 AM–4 PM, closed in winter
Admission: Adults $5

Canada's most famous female artist was born in Victoria in this 1864 house in 1871, just after British Columbia shifted from British colony to Canadian province. Although she didn't live here after her leaving to study art in San Francisco as a young woman, the house remained in the Carr family's hands until the early 20th century, and she built her own house next door in 1913. The provincial government bought the original Carr home in 1976, and it has been restored to its Victorian appearance. Aside from the connection the famous artist, it is a superb example of a 19th-century Italianate home, and the surrounding gardens reflect the tidy Victorian style. Exhibits describe Carr's life and place in 20th-century art, and a small gift shop/gallery offers the work of regional artists of today.

GOVERNMENT HOUSE
250-387-2080
www.ltgov.bc.ca
1401 Rockland Ave., Victoria, BC V8S 1V9
Gardens open: Daily dawn–dusk
Admission: Free

This manor atop Rockland Hill is the residence for members of the royal family when they visit Victoria, and the official residence of the province's lieutenant governor, who is also the queen's representative in BC. (If you want to have a colorful conversation, ask Canadians to explain the complicated system under which Canada is completely independent of Great Britain, but the queen is still the head of state.) The house's extensive gardens are open to the public during daylight hours. The formal English-style cottage gardens feature many roses, a lily pond, and small waterfall. It's a pleasant (and free) contrast to the usual crowded frenzy at Butchart Gardens. There is also a large Garry oak prairie preserve on the property.

HATLEY CASTLE
250-391-2666
www.hatleypark.ca
2005 Sooke Rd., Victoria, BC V9B 5Y2
Open: Daily 10 AM–4 PM,
Admission: Adults $18, students $10.50; gardens, $4.75
Entrance into castle by guided tour only; by appointment only in winter

As with Craigdarroch, this "castle" is actually an extravagant manor house, built in 1908 by island coal and railroad baron James Dunsmuir. Yes, he was the son of Robert Dunsmuir, who built Craigdarroch; James spared no expense on this project after winning a bitter inheritance battle with his mother that went all the way to the Privy Council in London. The vast 40-room building exemplifies the very best an Edwardian tycoon could buy, and in turn mimics a 15th-century Scottish castle. The ivy-covered stone walls harbor vast rooms with oak beams and paneling, crystal chandeliers, teak floors, marble fireplaces, and fine detail such as sculpted ceilings, though the furnishings are not original. The gardens immediately around the home are carefully tended, but the surrounding 565-acre estate preserves old-growth forest of Douglas fir, arbutus, and Garry oak. The entire complex also holds Royal Roads University. The castle itself has often been used as a film set. "Money doesn't matter, just build what I want," James Dunsmuir famously told architect Samuel Maclure. Like his father and his industrialist brethren in the United States, Dunsmuir was famous for his heavy-handed suppression of labor organization for his workers in order to maximize business receipts. Here and at Craigdarroch one can admire the craftsmanship that money buys, and ponder the cultural cost of such great wealth.

INNER HARBOUR
Along Government Street between Wharf Street and Belleville Street

The Inner Harbour is the focal point of downtown Victoria. The Empress Hotel bestrides the inland side of the harbor promenade; a small marina foots the bulwarks, whose arena steps invariably hold buskers seeking coins, First Nations carvers, and other vendors. There are almost always tall ships at dock here; floatplanes sail the skies in and out of the Aerodrome along Wharf Street. The Parliament Buildings anchor the south side of Belleville Street, and the Tourism Victoria Infocentre is along the promenade on the north corner of the harbor, where Government, Wharf, and Humboldt streets come together. Virtually all walking expeditions in Victoria begin or end here, and it's one of the great small harbors in North America.

Numerous for-hire **horse-drawn carriages** ply the promenade, and unlike such attractions in other tourist towns, here they blend artfully with the scene. Trotting past the Empress and Parliament Buildings, it's a pleasant if touristy thing to do. Tally-Ho (250-383-5067) and Victoria Carriage (250-383-2207) both operate here; expect to pay up to $200, including tip, for a one-hour tour good for up to four people. Although walk-up booking is often possible, if such a tour is a significant part of your itinerary for a visit, it's best to book ahead.

PARLIAMENT BUILDINGS
250-387-3046
www.leg.bc.ca
Government and Belleville streets, southwest corner
Daily guided tours; also self-guided tours
Admission free

This oft-photographed complex, now also formally known as the BC Legislative Buildings, was designed by seminal architect Francis X. Rattenbury, who also designed the Empress Hotel. Its copper dome, stained glass, gold and silver leaf, plaster moldings, and marble all add flair to the stolid granite stone of the exterior. Guided tours take visitors through the building seven days a week in summer, Monday through Friday the rest of the year. When the legislature is in session, tours may include a glimpse of the proceedings. Each night building is outlined by the glow of more than 3,000 lights outlining the complex; photographers of every skill level line up to attempt pictures as dusk descends.

ROYAL BC MUSEUM
250-356-7226 or 1-888-447-7977
royalbcmuseum.bc.ca
675 Belleville St., Victoria, BC V8W 9W2
Open: Daily 10 AM–5 PM, except Christmas and New Year's
Admission: Adults $15, students and seniors $9

One of Canada's most popular museums is also one of its most significant. The core of the RBCM is one of the world's greatest collections of **North Pacific Coast indigenous art and culture**, likely second only to the Museum of Anthropology in Vancouver. Huge historic totems stand tall both inside the museum, in its hallways and across the street at **Thunderbird Park**, which holds what used to be the world's tallest totem. Much of the

Hall of totems, Royal BC Museum   Leslie Forsberg

work here was created by master carver Mungo Martin, a Kwakwaka'wakw chief.

Nearby, **Helmcken House** is the home of Victoria pioneer Dr. John Sebastian Helmcken, an HBC surgeon and son-in-law of Territorial Governor James Douglas. It's one of the oldest houses (1852) still on its original site in BC.

Inside, the bounty continues in large exhibit halls devoted to smaller totems, bentwood boxes, and especially carved **ceremonial masks**. One of the museum's greatest treasures is an elaborate, carved cedar panel by **Bill Reid**, the Haida artist who led the resurgence of First Nations art in the second half of the 20th century. Nearby, an exhibit created by Reid depicts the appalling effects a **smallpox epidemic** had on his people in 1862. A vast second-floor room holds an elegant reproduction of a **chief's longhouse** created by a Kwakwaka'wakw family.

The museum's **Modern History Gallery** gives an able and evenhanded recounting of the European settlement of British Columbia, from the early days of the fur trade to the 2010 Winter Olympics. The **Natural History Gallery** depicts the province's many ecosystems, ranging from the Salish Sea shoreline to the subarctic tundra of the northern mountains, as well as the threats to these natural habitats. Another highlight in the main lobby is a vast **relief map** of British Columbia that gives viewers a better sense of how big the province really is (larger than Washington, Oregon, and California combined).

The museum has an IMAX theater (admission is extra) with the usual big-screen shows available around the world, such as National Geographic films. It also brings in visiting exhibitions that sometimes are big enough deals to prompt visits to Victoria for these alone, such as the traveling show of *Titanic* artifacts that came through in 2007. Something like half a million people visit the RBCM a year; aside from all the tourists, school groups are regular visitors Tuesday through Friday. The best times for a contemplative visit are thus Sunday morning and all day Monday.

Also on the museum grounds, at the corner of Belleville and Government streets, is the **Netherlands Centennial Carillon**, whose 62 bells produce an astounding melody when activated. Recitals take place Saturday and Sunday afternoons in summer, and Sundays the rest of the year. The carillon, housed in an 88-foot (27 m) tower, was a gift from the Dutch community in BC.

A half-block east from the museum's Thunderbird Park, at Blanshard and Humboldt, is **St. Ann's Academy**, a huge former girls' school now a national historic site (835 Humboldt, www.stannsacademy.com). This late 19th-/early 20th-century landmark has extensive grounds and gardens worth wandering; self-guided tours of the historic building are available Tuesday through Sunday.

VICTORIA BUG ZOO
250-384-2847
www.bugzoo.bc.ca
631 Courtney St., Victoria, BC V8W 1B8
Open: Daily 10 AM–5 PM
Admission: Adults $9, children to 11, $6

This novel attraction caters to kids and adults both—the human fascination with the insect and arachnid world is boundless. Visitors get a close-up introduction to tarantulas, praying mantids, scorpions, and many other creatures. A huge ant farm reveals the complex social structure of these colonies. Of course there's a shop—for just $100 you could bring home a red-legged tarantula. Better practice your speech explaining that to the customs inspectors.

RECREATION

The centerpiece of outdoor activity in the Victoria area is the recreation trail system, whose showpiece is the 34-mile (55 km) Galloping Goose Trail. This abandoned rail bed leads from downtown (the northwest end of the Blue Bridge) all the way through the western suburbs and into the Sooke foothills, from whence it carried passengers, mail, and commercial goods back and forth between Sooke and Victoria. Opened as a bike, pedestrian, and horse path in 1992, it exemplifies the Victoria affection for outdoor recreation.

Victoria is also an excellent place for **wildlife watching**, both in and around the city. Bald eagles are a common sight, especially in Beacon Hill Park along the shoreline. Orcas are periodically seen from the same locale; the largest Salish Sea killer whale pod plies the channel between Victoria and San Juan Island much of the year. Waterfowl of all kinds are common in and around the Inner Harbour, from the exotic puffins to everyday mallards. Raptors such as red-tailed hawks and osprey frequent the waters and prairies around the city, especially on the Saanich Peninsula.

And, believe it or not, bears and cougars are occasionally sighted. Vancouver Island is the world capital of mountain lions, and sometimes they encroach on the city—in one famous incident, a young male cougar got trapped in the Empress Hotel parking garage in 1992. Captured by wildlife officials, he was returned to the wild, and all involved repaired upstairs for high tea.

Kayaking (or canoeing) the Inner Harbour is a lovely way to gain a different perspective on the city, watch for waterfowl and marine mammals such as harbor seals, and get some fresh-air exercise. Island Boat Rentals (250-995-1661) is on the Inner Harbour and offers three-hour kayak rentals for $35, canoes $45.

BEACON HILL PARK
250-385-5711
www.victoria.ca or www.friendsofbeaconhillpark.ca
East of Douglas Street, south of the Inner Harbour

Victoria's signature park anchors a small rise south of the Empress. A classic European-style park space, the 200-acre preserve features massive old rhododendrons and azaleas framing flower beds set beside winding paths, with playfields, swards of green lawn, and conifers framing views of the Salish Sea, Olympic Mountains, and San Juan Islands. Despite the intensive historic park development, much of the land still holds native habitat such as oak prairie, arbutus and fir woodland, and cottonwood lowlands. Long beaches invite strolling, and a water-play park provides warm-day splashing. A children's farm offers kids the chance to learn about (and pet) goats, chickens, sheep, and such. The famous totem here, carved by Chief Mungo Martin in 1956, stands 128 feet (39 m) high and is the fourth-tallest in the world.

BEAR MOUNTAIN RESORT
250-391-7160 or 1-888-533-2327
http://bearmountain.ca
1999 Country Club Way, Victoria, BC V9B 6R3
Golf course fees $149 summer, $69 winter

This California-style purpose-built development hugs the slopes of its namesake mountain northwest of Victoria proper. While it's mostly residential subdivision, there is a large, Northwest-lodge style Westin hotel that offers lodging and the usual resort amenities such as swimming pools, tennis courts, a spa, and a good West Coast cuisine restaurant, Black Rock.

The centerpiece of Bear Mountain, however, is a pair of high-profile Jack Nicklaus–designed **golf courses** that are among the most challenging, and entertaining, in Western Canada (250-744-2327). The signature hole on the older, **Mountain Course**, #14, is a 509-yard uphill masterpiece that crests at a saddle green with views of Mount Baker, the Olympic Mountains, the Strait of Juan de Fuca, and the city of Victoria, all spread below. The 18th hole is also a 500-yarder that features a long, narrow target green guarded by six bunkers, two ponds, and a rock gully. Not for the faint-hearted, but memorable nonetheless! The newer **Valley Course** is a more user-friendly, shorter track with wider fairways, fewer bunkers, and larger greens.

GALLOPING GOOSE TRAIL
www.crd.ba.ca/parks/galloping-goose
Starting point just west of Johnson Street Bridge (Blue Bridge) in downtown Victoria

One of the finest recreation trails in Western North America wends its way from downtown Victoria 34 miles (55 km) westward through city, suburb, farm, and forest into the foothills of the Sooke Mountains. A former railroad line that carried mail and passengers in the 1920s, it begins as a paved path in central Victoria, crosses an old trestle over the Gorge Waterway, wends its way into the suburbs, then into farm country and the Sooke foothills, switching to gravel at about 9 miles (15 km). Farms, fields, and forests await those who venture out into the countryside; dedicated riders can make it all the way to Sooke Potholes Provincial Park (see p. 71) at 31 miles (50 km), have a picnic and a refreshing swim, and return to the city for a most memorable century ride. Road crossings are occasional, with only a few requiring great caution on the part of trail users. Be sure to bring along ample water, as fountains are rare.

At 2½ miles (4 km), the trail branches north into the **Lochside Regional Trail**, a 20½-mile (33 km) route that traverses the Saanich Peninsula, through Sidney, all the way to Swartz Bay and the BC Ferries terminal. This trail, too, follows and old rail bed, though in some sections it detours onto back roads in farm country.

Several B&Bs along the Goose offer overnight lodging for cyclists; visit www.the gallopinggoosetrail.com.

SWAN LAKE NATURE SANCTUARY
250-479-0211
www.swanlake.bc.ca
3873 Swan Lake Rd. V8X 3W1
Park open dusk to dawn daily
Nature House interpretive center open 8:30 AM–4 PM weekdays, noon–4 PM weekends

This lovely urban preserve holds a small lake that does indeed usually have its namesake birds gliding gracefully across its waters. The lake is surrounded by wetlands popular with innumerable other waterfowl, and a park that reaches up the hillsides around the lake. The latter, known as Christmas Hill, hold a Garry oak ecosystem preserve that's one of the best left in the Victoria area. Strolling the park's trails allows you to watch for hawks and osprey, listen for the bell song of red-wing blackbirds and the chitter of chickadees, and observe swallows snatching insects from midair. Easiest way to reach Swan Lake from downtown is to hop on a bike, head out the Galloping Goose Trail, take the Lochside Trail turnoff, and veer north 1¼ miles (2 m).

SHOPPING

The main commercial strip in downtown Victoria is **Government Street**, between the Empress Hotel (Humboldt Street side) and the end of Old Town at Pembroke. **Fort Street**, which runs east–west from Wharf Street uphill to Rockland Hill, is an antiques row, though many of the old-line antique stores have closed down in the new century. The nearest thing to a mall is the **Bay Centre**, a square block between Government, Fort, Douglas, and View streets which is anchored by the Bay Company—direct corporate descendant of the Hudson's Bay Company that, as much as any government, explored and settled Canada in the late 18th and early 19th century. **Trounce Alley**, a half-block north of the Bay Centre, has a charming collection of small shops, jewelers, and galleries. **Fan Tan Alley** in Chinatown holds several interesting stores, including the Turntable, a

Whale Watching in the Salish Sea

Whales are gentle beings that inhabit the food-rich waters of the Pacific Coast. Humans are not-so-gentle beings who, when they desire something, sometimes thrust aside all manner of compassion and common sense. The result is the troubling phenomenon of natural systems being loved to death, and so it is with whales in many spots around the world. The whale-watching industry has ballooned into a massive, billion-dollar global enterprise that, while it introduces travelers to the beauty and wonder of these creatures, also can make their lives miserable. Imagine if you spent your days, dusk to dawn, with the sound of hundreds of helicopters directly overhead: That's what life is like for inland orcas and other whales in the Salish Sea, where hundreds of Zodiacs and other boats chase and hound marine mammals every summer day. One university researcher who studied the noise these animals are subjected to likens it to a rocket taking off overhead.

I do not recommend taking part in whale-watching "tours" (chases, I call them), but visitors who do choose to patronize these services should at least take responsibility for selecting whale-watching operators who subscribe to the industry's code of ethics, such as it is. These include observing decent distances from their "quarry" (more than 330 feet [100 m]), not chasing after the whales, and putting safety and environmental respect ahead of guaranteeing sightings. There are no guarantees in nature, and that's as it should be. If you buy a "guaranteed sighting," you are in effect purchasing a transient thrill that's akin to treating wild animals as human amusement livestock. If you do go out whale watching, I charge thoughtful travelers with a responsibility to speak up when and if your boat violates the guidelines . . . chasing a whale pod, drifting too close, and so on. And, please, choose larger boats with inboard diesel engines over the Zodiacs, which create the most noise and havoc.

Land-based whale watching is often productive along Beach Drive in Oak Bay and Cordova Bay Road northward. Keep your eyes peeled on ferry passage in and out of the city and you may be rewarded, too—ship's crew will announce sightings when they notice them, but they're not perfect.

warren of old records. All are eminently walkable and easily reached from most central hotels and inns.

The following stores are among my favorites, but any visit to Victoria demands the traveler put on good shoes and wander along Government Street, down through Chinatown, up Fort Street and back, at least once.

ALCHERINGA GALLERY
250-383-8224
www.alcheringa-gallery.com
665 Fort St., Victoria, BC V8W 1G7

The wide range and astounding similarities of Pacific Rim indigenous art are on display here at one of Canada's finest galleries. What Alcheringa calls "tribal art" ranges from masks from Papua New Guinea to bentwood boxes from the BC coastal peoples. Most of the art here is new, and exquisite, and expensive—up to $10,000, though there are more modest pieces priced in the hundreds. Among the artists represented are modern First Nations masters Tony Hunt, Richard Sumner and Susan Point. A visit here is more like a jaunt into a very fine small museum than a commercial gallery . . . until you notice the price tags. I can't resist stopping in, though, every time I go by.

BERNARD CALLEBAUT CHOCOLATIER
250-380-1515
www.bernardcallebaut.com
621 Broughton St., Victoria, BC V8W 3J2

When the scion of this famous Belgian chocolate family was looking for a New World location to strike out on his own, where did he settle? Calgary, believe it or not. The founder sold the business a while back, but its dedication to finer, flavorful chocolate remains. The Victoria location is a satellite store, and its products are the antithesis of traditional British creams—Callebaut's chocolate is generally darker, less sweetened, more robust. You won't find any pink frosting here.

CAPITAL IRON
250-385-9703
www.williesbakery.com
1900 Store St., Victoria, BC V8T 4R4

Is there actually iron here at this utterly unique hardware/housewares/variety store housed in an old warehouse along the Gorge Waterway? Heaps of iron, ranging from outdoor furniture to tools to immense marine buoys out back. There are also Chinese antiques, camping supplies, barbecues, fishing gear, sewing fabrics, Carhartt work jeans, garden fountains, and, of course, cast-iron casserole dishes. The slogan, "There's no store like it," is demonstrably true. Even though visitors will find few items here they'd be interested in lugging home, it's a most entertaining place to wander for a half-hour. Ask yourself: I wonder if they could possibly have *this*? Then go exploring.

FORT STREET
Between Wharf Street and Rockland Hill; most stores are between Douglas and Cook streets.

Even if it isn't actually true that the shelves of the antiques and collectibles stores here hold old Empire items that came to the island on clipper ships flying the Union Jack, it can seem like it. Some of the stores are chock-a-block with chotchkes one wonders why they were ever made. But others hold lovely treasures, and I suppose one man's kitsch is another's jewel. Several recession-caused store closures have thinned the density of shops here, but one long morning or afternoon (fueled by breakfast or lunch at Blue Fox, or dinner at Café Brio) can still be admirably devoted to browsing among the trinkets of history.

Among the more notable stores are **Lunds Auctioneers** (926 Fort, 250-386-3308, www.lunds.com), whose building is crammed with Old World furniture, housewares, china, and decorative objects that are priced in thousands as often as hundreds. **Pacific Antiques** (829 Fort, 250-388-5311, www.pacificantiques.com) offers sterling silver, porcelain and glass, Asian ceramics, and small decorative objects.

The entire street isn't devoted to just musty antiques. While other bookstores are struggling, **Russell Books** (734 Fort, 250-361-4447, www.russellbooks.com) recently expanded and is now Canada's largest, with hundreds of thousands of titles, used and new. **Roger's Jukebox** offers a vast selection of CDs, vinyl records, and music memorabilia. **Pacific Editions** offers both rare and new prints by West Coast indigenous artists (942 Fort, 250-388-5233, www.pacificeditions.ca).Perhaps my favorite Fort Street store, **Chronicles of**

Crime (1057 Fort, 250-721-2665, chroniclesofcrime.com) is devoted exclusively to mysteries and thrillers, and aside from its innumerable titles, the best thing on offer here is the encyclopedic knowledge of the staff—tell them an author you like, and they'll recommend similar writers.

HILL'S NATIVE ART
250-385-3911
www.hillsnativeart.com
1008 Government St., Victoria, BC
V8W 1X7

The island's longstanding First Nations art dealership dates back to a small store opened in Duncan in 1946. The company specializes in Inuit sculpture, Cowichan sweaters, argillite from Haida Gwaii, and numerous other artworks and crafts ranging from moccasins to baskets. Quality varies between excellent and medium, and it's much more touristy than BC's better indigenous art galleries, such as Alcheringa. But major artists such as Robert Charlie and Fred Baker are represented here, and this is the place for a moderately priced First Nations keepsake.

Totem pole, Duncan   Leslie Forsberg

Hill's also has stores in Duncan, Nanaimo, and Vancouver.

IRISH LINEN
250-383-6812
www.irishlinenvictoria.com
1019 Government St., Victoria, BC V8W 1X6

This business dates back to the early 20th century, and has been in its current location, an 1884 Italianate commercial building, since 1917. Linens here run the gamut from small handkerchiefs to tea towels to sheets, table runners, and tablecloths. The store also carries embroidered items from Belgium and Madeira, and very handsome linen clothing for those who really like ironing.

KISS AND TELL
250-380-6995
www.kissandtell.ca
531 Herald St., Victoria, BC V8W 1S6

Yes, this is an adult store—a very different sort of one. Clerks aren't tattooed slackers who smirk at anyone over 30. The wares on sale are designed for what the store advertises as "relationship enhancement," but won't much embarrass anyone under 80. I'll ignore the store's name and invite visitors to find out for themselves what the bungee harness does, exactly.

MUNRO'S BOOKS
250-381-8414
munrobooks.com
1108 Government St., Victoria, BC V8W 1Y2

Located right next to Murchie's, and housed in a 1909, column-fronted stone edifice that used to be a bank, Munro's is a classic bookstore with high shelves, even higher ceilings (24 feet) and especially large sections devoted to Canadian authors and Canadiana. Here you can find a biography of Francis X. Rattenbury, the nonpareil architect responsible for Victoria's Parliament Buildings and Empress Hotel. Here are guides to the locales, people, animals, and geography of Western Canada; here are Canadian, American, and British bestsellers galore. The children's book section is especially large, and after making a purchase the whole family can repair next door for tea at Murchie's.

MURCHIE'S TEA & COFFEE
250-383-3112
www.murchies.com
1110 Government St., Victoria, BC V8W 1Y2

Founded in 1894 here in Victoria, Murchie's is synonymous with the classic empire tea business that was stock in trade for the clipper ships that sailed into the Inner Harbour. Although the Government Street store is a large, recently expanded complex with a tea room, pastry counter, coffee shop (and a pass-through interior doorway into Munro's Books next door), the heart of the company remains its vast selection of traditional teas, from black to green to oolong to pekoe. Here are moderately priced everyday breakfast blends, loose or in bags; here are rare teas that surpass $100 a pound, such as the Darjeeling silver tips, carefully separated from the main harvest by hand each spring. Of course, one need not buy a pound to sample an exquisite, exotic tea—several times I've left with a 1-ounce envelope of some rarity, invariably worth the $15 price.

OUT OF IRELAND
250-389-0886
irishshopvictoria.com
1000 Government St., Victoria, BC V8W 1X7

One in a long line of Irish woolens stores that have occupied heritage storefronts on Government Street, this incarnation ranges the gamut from Guinness-branded clothing and rugby wear to hangings with Celtic symbols and classic throws, sweaters, and capes.

PLENTY EPICUREAN PANTRY
250-380-7654
www.epicureanpantry.com
1034 Fort St., Victoria, BC V8V 3K4

According to Epicuris, even wisdom and culture derive from "the pleasure of the stomach," which this store attends to delightfully. Hundreds of products associate with the pleasure of the stomach, and it's amazing just how many different things this relatively small shop packs into its space. (Diversity is one of its core values.) One year we picked up a wonderful hand-carved Christmas tree ornament from Peru; plus some island artisan cheese and island sea salt. The store is devoted to sustainability, and its gadgets section has some one-of-a kind items that will entertain kitchenware devotees.

ROGER'S CHOCOLATES
250-381-8414
www.williesbakery.com
537 Johnson St., Victoria, BC V8W 1M2

Victoria's classic chocolate-maker is a longstanding destination for many of the city's repeat visitors. Roger's signature confection is a traditional British-style cream, made with hazelnuts and lots of sugar, called the Victoria Cream. Almond brittle and milk chocolate round out the majority of the inventory here. It's the sort of chocolatier in which truffles feature swirls of pink or yellow frosting on top. Opened in 1885, Roger's has since grown to a vast industry whose 200,000-square-foot factory ships confections to 50 countries. Sometimes it looks like half the people boarding ferries to return to the States from Victoria are clutching Roger's sacks!

SILK ROAD
250-704-2688
www.silkroadtea.com
624 Government St., Victoria, BC V8W 1M2

Poised by the entrance to Chinatown, this now-seminal tea, unguents, and aromatherapy store is as much an herbalist as a beverage purveyor. Yes, there are green, white, and black teas—dozens of them, virtually all of which are varietals with exotic names and flavor profiles, such as Golden Treasure, a high-altitude Yunnan tea. Herbal concoctions abound, and the vast universe of lotions, oils, potions, and salves led Silk Road to open its own spa, with a menu of services focusing on massages, skin treatments, and wraps.

WEST END GALLERY
250-388-0009
www.westendgalleryltd.com
1203 Broad St., Victoria, BC V8W 2A4

This expansive, airy gallery on the north side of the Bay Centre is Victoria's best for fine mainstream artwork by regional artists. Most of the paintings depict the landscapes and people of Western Canada; if you'd like to take home a good canvas that captures the moody, vivid colors of an arbutus tree leaning from a rocky headland over an island cove, this is the place. There are also extensive collections of glasswork and sculpture.

Sooke and West Coast

Head west from Victoria and the mountains climb down toward the shore, farms start to give way to forest, and rocky headlands divide sandy beaches that front the increasingly open ocean as you leave the Strait of Juan de Fuca behind. Rainfall increases apace, and by the time you reach Port Renfrew, 49⅔ (80 km, or three hours' drive time) west, you are completely out of the Olympic rain shadow and into marine rainforest, with towering Sitka spruce and Western red cedar dominating the landscape. Here, powerful waves thrash the coast during powerful storms, and the clouds that pile up on the mountains drop torrents of rain—12 feet (3.6 m) a year in Port Renfrew.

Sooke is about 18½ miles (30 km) west of Victoria; the drive takes 30 to 45 minutes, depending on traffic leaving the city. Be alert to signage on Highway 1 as you head west, as the turnoff comes up suddenly. In Sooke you'll find a smattering of small shops and galleries; the **Sooke Region Museum** provides a concise but interesting view of the region's logging and farming history, as well as the ecology of this area at the edge of the sea. This is also the area's visitor infocentre, a good place to pick up local maps and tide tables (www.soookeregionmuseum.com). **Port Renfrew** is a quiet fishing village with uncertain visitor services (inns and cafés here come and go regularly), a small campground, and good hiking, kayaking, and wildlife watching. It's also the end of the highway, and those planning to venture onward from here into the maze of logging roads that ply the mountains north of Renfrew must have good tires, full gas tanks, good maps, and high-clearance vehicles.

LODGING

Two of the island's best-known and most beloved resorts lie out here on the coast, each quite different from the other. Sooke Harbour House is a world-renowned center for sustainability and slow food; Point-no-Point is a traditional family-getaway cluster of cabins on the shore at which some fans book next year's vacation as they check out of this year's. A couple dozen small inns and B&Bs offer rooms in the area; visit the **Sooke Bed and Breakfast Association** at sookebnb.com for a comprehensive rundown and to make reservations.

OCEAN WILDERNESS INN
250-646-2116 or 1-800-323-2116
www.oceanwildernessinn.com
stay@oceanwildernessinn.com
9171 West Coast Rd. (Hwy. 14), Sooke, BC
V9Z 1G3
8⅔ miles (14 km) west of Sooke
Price: Moderate
Credit cards: Yes
Handicapped Access: Partial
Special Features: Pets welcome in some rooms, free WiFi

This seven-room small inn is distinguished by its exceptional location—on a promontory near Muir Creek Beach, facing the ocean amid cedars and spruces—and its amenities, such as a huge garden, a hot tub, and a communal kitchen. Rooms are bed and bath, with unfussy décor (virtually no doilies, the hosts promise) and some soaking tubs; the main lodge room has a fireplace, and the beach trail leads down to tide pools. Room rates include a hot breakfast. The innkeepers practice sustainable hospitality (for instance, eschewing chemical cleaning products) and are active in local environmental conservation efforts.

POINT-NO-POINT RESORT
250-646-2020
www.pointnopointresort.com
10829 West Coast Rd. (Hwy. 14), Shirley,
BC V9Z 1G9
On Hwy. 14, 15½ miles (25 km) west of Sooke
Price: Moderate to Expensive
Credit cards: Yes
Handicapped Access: Some units
Special Features: Pets welcome (in some cabins)

Consisting of a variety of cabins, cottages, and small houses tucked into the trees on a rocky slope above the water west of Sooke, this comfortable old-line family resort is the sort whose adherents book year after year, on down through generations. One reason is the relative economy of the place, for what you get—most cabins have full kitchens, fireplaces, soaking tubs, water views, and room for four to eight occupants. For instance, Grace's Cabin offers sleeping quarters for four, a wood-burning rock fireplace, water views, a hot tub on the deck, full kitchen, and living room, for $280 a night in high season. The new Bridge House is a Japanese-style post-and-beam four-bedroom accommodation on its own 2.5-acre parcel. The 40-acre resort property includes hiking trails to the namesake point, two beaches, and a creek. "Point no point," by the way, is a marine surveying term.

The resort's **restaurant** is well known for its simple fine-dining menu, devoted to local seafood such as salmon, halibut, and spot prawns, and melding modern West Coast cuisine with such traditional fare as iceberg lettuce.

SOOKE HARBOUR HOUSE
250-642-3421 or 1-800-889-9688
www.sookeharbourhouse.com
info@sookeharbourhouse.com
1528 Whiffen Spit Rd., Sooke, BC V9Z 0T4
On Sooke Harbour bay, 1⅞ miles (3 km)
south of Hwy. 14
Price: Expensive
Credit cards: Yes
Handicapped Access: Full
Special Features: Pets welcome, free WiFi, in-room breakfast available

Poised on a sunny slope just above its namesake small bay, Sooke Harbour House is simultaneously a divine small inn, a restaurant famed around the world, and one of the pillars of the slow food and sustainability movements on the island. (For a description of the restaurant, see Dining.) The inn's main buildings and out-building suites are all different evocations of a country inn ethos that blends comfort,

style, and luxury in equal proportions. The 1929 clapboard farmhouse holds five smaller rooms; various additions over the years have added an additional 23 generally larger rooms and suites. Each is different, ranging from cozy cubbyholes under the gabled farmhouse roof, to deluxe suites with fireplaces, hot tubs, sitting areas, and country pine furnishings. Room rates include breakfast, and numerous packages add dinner—a highly advisable approach to a visit here. Activities range from admiring the gardens to strolling the nearby beach spit watching for seals. But really it's a place for relaxation and contemplation, and savoring some of the best food on the continent. The inn is also quite a gallery for the work of local artists, much of which is on sale.

DINING

SOOKE HARBOUR HOUSE
250-642-3421 or 1-800-889-9688
www.sookeharbourhouse.com
1528 Whiffen Spit Rd., Sooke, BC V9Z 0T4
On Sooke Harbour bay, 1⅞ miles (3 km)
south of Hwy. 14
Price: Expensive
Credit cards: Yes
Serving: L, D

Often reckoned the most famous restaurant in Canada, this now-legendary dining room is known for the quality and inventiveness of its regional cuisine, and for its unswerving commitment to sustainability and the slow-food philosophy. Proprietors Frederique and Philip Sinclair met in France, where they conceived a plan to bring the local-food ethos to Canada. When they bought an existing old-line inn in 1977, the concepts they adopted were then unheard-of here. "Gourmet" cuisine meant lobster (flow 2,500 miles to Vancouver Island), sirloin steak, and baked Alaska. And here were two visionaries serving

European greens grown in the garden outside the restaurant, introducing octopus, sea cucumber, and barnacles to the island seafood lexicon, commissioning foragers to bring seaweed and wild mushrooms to their kitchen. What was radical has since become, while not commonplace, at least mainstream—although the Sinclairs continue to push the envelope: Philip has only half-jokingly proposed to banish coffee and bananas from the inn, as they must be shipped thousands of miles. Chefs here rely heavily on island growers, fishers and gatherers, and most of the herbs used come from the expansive gardens just outside.

Gourmands literally make pilgrimages here from other continents to sample menus that remain astounding. It's not cheap—a chef's menu with wine can be $120 per person. But the culinary experience is like no other. A bisque might combine kelp and spot prawns; octopus aspic could be an appetizer; rabbit is marinated in red wine and juniper berries, then pan-seared; dessert could be salmonberry, honeydew, and sage sorbet. The dining room overlooks the gardens and water, the service is expert but unfussy, and the wine list includes the best of the island and BC, as well as selected European vintages. Yes, those are shipped thousands of miles—and coffee remains on the menu. So far!

RECREATION

The coast turns ever wilder as you head west, then north, from Victoria to Sooke and then on to Port Renfrew. The latter is the southern trailhead for the legendary **West Coast Trail** (see p. 178), which winds along the coast between there and Bamfield. That's only for very experienced wilderness travelers—as a friend of mine put it after she hiked it, "Your opinion of the experience will depend on your opinion of knee-deep mud." The more accessible provincial parks near Sooke offer a thoroughly engaging opportunity to experience this marvelous coast, and Botanical Beach is one of the island's greatest natural wonders.

BOTANICAL BEACH
1¼ miles (2 km) west of Port Renfrew on well-marked gravel road
www.env.gov.bc.ca/bcparks
Admission: $1 day use parking fee

Although this is now technically part of Juan de Fuca Provincial Park, it is a long-famous coastal attraction that's misnamed in two aspects—it's not a beach at all, and its natural appeal derives from marine biology rather than botany. The rock-bordered **tide pools** here are among the best on the entire West Coast, if not the best, period. Although the Northwest Coast can seem a universe of cloud gray and forest green, the vivid colors of tidal zone life paint a much different picture. Brilliant orange and purple seastars; glistening ivory-white nudibranchs; chartreuse anemones—all shimmer beneath the topaz waters of the rock pools that stretch a quarter-mile along the coast here. The pools are accessible and easily seen whenever there is a 1-foot or lower tide; minus tides (common around midsummer) are best. The infocentre in Sooke usually has tide schedules, as do most hotels in the region. An excursion here is a full daytrip from Victoria; plan to bring a picnic lunch and stop at one of the other beaches in Juan de Fuca Provincial Park along the way.

EAST SOOKE REGIONAL PARK

www.eastsookepark.com

1¼ miles (2 km) south of Hwy. 14 on East Sooke Road

This 3,500-acre park straddles the inland, drier ecosystem that shifts to a wetter, cooler regime along the open ocean. Beautiful amber-bark arbutus trees cling to rocky headlands, bigger Douglas firs strive skyward, and numerous pocket beaches and rocky coves invite poking about. Six and an eighth miles (10 km) of trail hug the shore (a challenging six-hour day hike), and 32 miles (51 km) of trail plunge through the woods. Wildlife watching—for seals, river otters, waterfowl, hawks and eagles, deer, and whales offshore—adds interest to hiking and picnicking.

JUAN DE FUCA PROVINCIAL PARK

Starts 24⅞ miles (40 km) west of Victoria on Hwy. 14

www.env.gov.bc.ca/bcparks

Open: Daily dawn-dusk

Admission: $1 day use parking fee

One of BC's newer parks is composed of several parcels along the coast west of Sooke, between the shore and Highway 14. Much of the park is wilderness, and in fact includes a shoreline trail with wilderness camping, the **Juan de Fuca Trail**, that is a kinder, gentler version of the famous West Coast Trail (see p. 178). Day users can access Juan de Fuca park at several points. **China Beach**, the major day-use area 21 miles (34 km) west of Sooke, has a pleasant ⅔-mile (1 km) trail leading through mature Sitka spruce forest down to a lovely sand beach. Another trail leads from the China Beach campground to **Second Beach**, reaching a more remote beach through impressive old-growth timber. Several other access points along the highway include **Sombrio Beach**, a scenic pebble-and-cobble beach popular with surfers and windsurfers.

SOOKE POTHOLES PROVINCIAL PARK

www.env.gov.bc.ca/bcparks

Admission: $1 day use parking fee

3 miles (5 km) north of Sooke on Sooke River Road

These rock formations in the Sooke River form perfect swimming holes, and the river itself moderates from icy torrent in winter to burbling, clear stream by midsummer. Although it's never really warm, by most people's standards, it is pleasantly refreshing late June through early September, and for dedicated bike riders, the fact it's near the end of the Galloping Goose Trail (see p. 61) makes it a worthy and ambitious early afternoon goal. Aside from swimming, the park affords a great place to watch spawning salmon in autumn.

Saanich Peninsula

Once considered the farm-basket of Victoria, this lightly wooded expanse of pastoral rolling hills north of Victoria is pleasantly scenic and offers several attractions to draw visitors. It's also the last major stand of the Garry oak prairie, the historic ecosystem here that consists of spare grasslands dotted with stands of Garry oak (known as Oregon white oak in the States) and crusted with rock outcrops. Farmers had long run cattle in tidy pastures; row crops were grown wherever better soil lay; picturesque red-trunked arbutus (madrona) trees leaned out over quiet coves from rocky headlands. Then suburban development began galloping north from the capital, and the Garry oak habitat has been described by several conservation groups as the most threatened in Canada.

The peninsula is also the transportation locus for the Victoria region. Here is the city's airport, directly east of Sidney. BC Ferries main terminal is at Swartz Bay, at the northern tip of the peninsula; from here ships depart for Vancouver (Tsawassen) and the southern Gulf Islands of Salt Spring, Pender, Mayne, and Saturna. Washington State Ferries service from Anacortes and the San Juan Islands docks in Sidney. For literally thousands of visitors a day, the sum total of their Saanich experience is zipping north or south along Hwy. 17 for a half-hour.

That overlooks the peninsula's many virtues. It's a great place for a Sunday drive, any Sunday, popping in to a couple of the little farm stands that dot the back roads, overnighting at one of the new hotels, visiting a couple of the attractions here. A full circle takes a full day, roughly, with three or so stops, including a few hours in Sidney, the main town here. Perhaps, the more it is visited, the more bottles of wine bought at local vineyards, the more sacks of fresh lettuce picked up from farm stands, the less the beautiful landscape will be transformed into paved cul de sacs.

Amber arbutus limbs   Leslie Forsberg

Brentwood Bay Harbour   Leslie Forsberg

One of the island's most delightful excursions departs from the peninsula's Brentwood Bay. The **Mill Bay ferry** is a small boat that trundles back and forth from here to the Cowichan Valley; it's a lovely, scenic 25-minute ride, and an excellent choice for those heading north on the island, as an alternative to returning to Victoria and crossing Malahat Mountain on Highway 1. Passage is about $20 for the nine daily departures, roughly one per hour (www.bcferries.com).

LODGING

Until a decade or so ago, lodging north of Victoria consisted of a few motels and a half-dozen of the sort of small B&Bs that consist of a spare bedroom in an old farmhouse. Brentwood Bay Lodge upped the ante considerably, and the arrival of two other modern, upscale hotels has boosted the area's appeal a lot.

BEACON INN
250-665-3288 or 1-877-420-5499
www.thebeaconinn.com
reservations@thebeaconinn.com

9724 Third St., Sidney, BC V8L 3A2
Price: Moderate
Credit cards: Yes
Handicapped Access: Partial
Special Features: Free WiFi, breakfast included, free afternoon sherry service

Tucked into a back street in Sidney, the peninsula's "Booktown," this charming small inn is steps from the bookstores, about a 10-minute walk to the Shaw aquarium, and 15 minutes' drive from Butchart Gardens. Although the décor is sort of neo-Edwardian—lots of lace, doilies, flowered fabrics, and such—the inn was purpose-built in 2001. Most of the rooms have fireplaces, and even the spacious standard rooms here, with large bathrooms and a sitting area, would be called "junior suites" at a mainstream hotel, yet they go for just $150 in peak season.

BRENTWOOD BAY RESORT
250-725-3100 or 1-800-333-4604
www.brentwoodbayresort.com
info@ brentwoodbayresort.com
849 Verdier Ave., Brentwood Bay, BC
V8M 1C5
About 5 miles (8 km) west of Sidney, by the Mill Bay
Price: Expensive
Credit cards: Yes
Handicapped Access: Full

Featuring New Age Northwest lodge design based on an elegant melding of warm-toned wood, metal, and glass, this boutique getaway destination overlooks its namesake bay with all the aplomb of a resort hotel, though it's really rather compact and began life as Brentwood Bay Lodge. The setting is gorgeous—in the distance the mountains rise into misty heights, in the middle ground the delightful Mill Bay ferry chugs back and forth over the sapphire waters of Saanich Inlet, and in the foreground small boats bob in the marina framed by arbutus trees. Aside from visiting nearby Butchart Gardens, relaxing by the pool and paddling kayaks in the bay, there's not a lot to do, which is why the lodge has established an identity as a romantic couples-weekend destination (and changed its name to "resort"). The dining in SeaGrille restaurant is a fine rendition of West Coast cuisine, with everything from spot prawn risotto to braised bison short ribs and pan-fried Arctic char. As the menu indicates, though, the restaurant's dedication is to Western Canada rather than Vancouver Island ingredients.

The resort's 33 suites are spacious, modern and spare, with earth tones such as sage, bark and sand setting the atmosphere. The lavish spa focuses on Asian treatments such as a body wrap derived from Japanese bathing rituals. Butchart Gardens is about five minutes by car. Room prices drop dramatically in winter, almost half. That's coincidentally one of the best times to visit Butchart Gardens.

The resort's top-notch restaurant, **SeaGrille**, is housed in a splashy high-ceilinged-room with a vantage on the harbor; its West Coast menu focuses on seafood and BC wine.

COMPASS ROSE CABINS & MARINA
250-544-1441
www.members.shaw.ca/compassrosecabins
compassrosecabins @shaw.ca
799 Verdier Ave., Brentwood Bay, BC
V8M 1C5
Price: Moderate
Credit cards: Yes
Handicapped Access: Partial

Poised above the waters of Brentwood Bay, these delightful cabins are airy and spacious, trimmed in light woods, and feature full kitchens and gas fireplaces. The squeak of boat riggings and squawk of sea gulls are the most prevalent sounds, and you've a great view of the boats at dock and the charming Mill Bay ferry as it plies Saanich Inlet. Kayak rentals are available on site; Butchart Gardens is 10 minutes away.

LATCH INN
250-656-4015
www.latchinn.ca
info@latchinn.ca
2328 Harbour Rd., Sidney, BC V8L 2P8
Price: Budget to Moderate
Credit cards: Yes
Handicapped Access: Partial

Historic in look and in fact, this wood-slab-sided inn on the waterfront just outside Sidney was the summer residence of a BC lieutenant-governor, and was designed by Victoria architect Samuel Maclure. Maclure's instructions were to make his design unusual, and use lots of the province's wood, and the 1926 building still testifies today to his faithful interpretation of this commission. Wood beams, wood paneling, wood siding, wood shingles—stone foundations, chimney, and steps relieve the hegemony of wood. The six deluxe guest rooms are all cozy and outfitted with antiques such as glistening brass beds and Edwardian hanging lamps. Room rates include breakfast. The inn's restaurant is a well-known, traditional fine dining room with an Italian inflection.

SIDNEY PIER HOTEL
250-655-9445 or 1-877-844-7873
www.sidneypier.com
reservations@sidneypier.com
9805 Seaport Place, Sidney, BC V8L 4X3
In Sidney proper
Price: Moderate to Expensive
Credit cards: Yes
Handicapped Access: Full
Special Features: Pets welcome, free WiFi and local phone calls

This glistening metal-and-glass midrise hotel is part of the new complex that holds Sidney's delightful small aquarium, the Shaw Ocean Discovery Centre. The hotel lobby is notable for its wall décor, featuring something you'd never expect to find in what's obviously a business hotel—the bow-plate of *Sea Shepherd*, the famous Greenpeace boat that saw long service harrying the world's industrial whaling fleet and nuclear-powered navy ships. The hotel, appropriately, is committed to sustainability, with refillable soap dispensers in guest rooms, hotel composting out back, and a heat pump that manages heating and cooling. Many of the spacious suites feature kitchen facilities, and the earth-

Shaw Ocean Discovery Centre Leslie Forsberg

tone décor melds sage, sand, and leaf colors soothingly.

The hotel's restaurant, **Haro's**, is a first-class practitioner of West Coast cuisine, with signature dishes that range from smoked seafood and bacon chowder to bison short ribs and simply sensational fish-and-chips made with lingcod.

DINING

Aside from the dining rooms at Brentwood Bay Resort and Sidney Pier Hotel, there are few notable restaurants on the peninsula. The pastoral countryside is the home of numerous **farm stands** offering fresh vegetables, fruits, and berries in spring, summer, and fall. For a guide to these, visit www.islandfarmfresh.com. **The Roost** is a country bakery that uses house-ground grains for some of its breads, muffins, pastries, and such; it's at the corner of McTavish and East Saanich roads, not far from Victoria International Airport (250-656-1819).

DOCKSIDE GRILL
250-725-2341
www.docksidegrillsidney.com
2320 Harbour Rd., Sidney, BC V8L 2P6
Open: Daily 11 AM–9 PM
Price: Moderate
Credit cards: Yes
Cuisine: West Coast
Serving: L, D
Handicapped Access: Yes

Perched on a wharf in Sidney Harbour, this charming restaurant has a lovely setting overlooking the town's marina, and a West Coast cuisine café menu that deals out staple food favorites made with (mostly) fresh, local ingredients. The splendid fried calamari with garlic aioli is a favorite, and among the best anywhere; so are fried artichokes and rock-crab cakes with shrimp. The simple, changing weekly menu focuses on fresh seafood steak and poultry.

THIRD STREET CAFÉ
250-656-3035
www.weighwest.com

2466 Beacon Ave., Sidney, BC V8L 1X8
Open: Daily 7 AM–2 PM
Price: Moderate
Credit cards: Yes
Cuisine: Café
Serving: B, L
Handicapped Access: Yes

Scott Keanie abandoned a career as a fine dining chef to open this small (20-seat) breakfast and lunch café just off the main drag in Sidney, the Booktown. The ebullient proprietor is usually on hand to explain his no-frills approach to café dining. The highlight of the menu is the inventory of eggs Benedict—six different kinds, ranging from sausage and avocado to Mexican. All are splendid; so is the French toast, which is a hearty rendition made with real French bread. You might have to wait for a table here, but it's a worthy start to a morning browsing the nearby bookshelves. Lunch shifts to burgers and sandwiches, but breakfasts are the foundation of the menu.

CULTURE

Cultural attractions on the peninsula north of Victoria used to be pretty much limited to one big megillah, the world-famous Butchart Gardens. The opening of the new aquarium in Sidney (see below) and expansion of the Centre of the Universe astronomical observatory have combined with the growth of a small but distinctive local wine industry to make the area worth at least a day trip, or better a weekend.

Saanich wineries number about a half-dozen, and are small operations that focus on cool-climate vintages such as Ortega, pinot noir, and Marechal Foch; as well as blackberries and kiwis. For a touring map, visit www.wineislands.ca/saanich-peninsula.

BUTCHART GARDENS
250-652-4422, 1-866-652-4422
www.butchartgardens.org
email@butchartgardens.org
800 Benvenuto Ave., Brentwood Bay, BC V8M 1J8
14¼ miles (23 km) north of Victoria—allow 40 minutes—on west side of Saanich Peninsula; free parking
Open: Daily 9 AM–dusk, extended hours in summer and Christmas season
Admission: Adults $34, youths $17

Butchart Gardens, one of the best-known tourist attractions on the continent, strains the writer's ability to provide a thoughtful description. Butchart vies with Versailles for title as the most famous gardens on earth, visited each year by throngs of tourists—a total of about 1 million here—many of whom arrive on huge tour buses that line up in a special bus-parking lot which is all by itself bigger than most gardens. The complex is big but not gargantuan: 55 acres including separately themed gardens (Italian, Japanese, Sunken, Mediterranean) along with 26 greenhouses totaling 1 acre. A staff of 55 full-time gardeners oversees the complex, aided by more than 500 other workers in peak season. And these are among the most deliberately composed gardens you'll ever see, arranged and tended and tidied to the point that it seems arranged down to the molecular level. As at Disneyland, one struggles to find anything out of place or, heaven forbid, littered. The history is charming—Jennie Butchart, wife of the owner of what was once a gaping quarry, decided to turn it into an aesthetic attraction in 1904. Her descendants still operate the garden, and Butchart celebrated its centennial in 2004 with a designation as a Canadian National Historic Site.

Many are the wonders here, including unbelievable color zones achieved by masses of blooming annuals; ranks of rhododendrons, azaleas, and other flowering shrubs; pathways and ponds, embankments and bridges, gazebos and arches, and fountains and more. A particular favorite of mine is the winter fragrance garden, whose witch hazels, daphnes, mahonias, and jasmines demonstrate the marvels possible in the Pacific Maritime climate. It's best visited in early to mid-February, which coincides with low-crowd season.

There are some drawbacks to fame. Summertime visits often bring the necessity of breasting implacable crowds of tour groups whose members clump up like seaweed. Although smoking is barred, the ban is poorly enforced and I've never escaped cigarette smoke. And garden connoisseurs often consider Butchart overly composed, nature framed too tightly.

But the latter facet is exactly what most visitors adore. The color masses! The exquisitely tended lawns—weeds dare not venture here! The graceful curve of pathway and pond edge, like a painting! Whether you like formal gardens or not, this is the best place in the Western Hemisphere to form an opinion.

SHAW OCEAN DISCOVERY CENTRE
250-665-7511
www.oceandiscovery.ca
9811 Seaport Place, Sidney V8L 4X3
Open: Daily 10 AM–4 PM
Admission: adults $12, youths $8

Although fairly small as aquariums go, this lovely facility on the waterfront in Sidney does an admirable job of introducing visitors to the rich and colorful life beneath the waves that surrounds the island. Compact tanks brimming with life hold kelp, seaweed, shellfish, and fish galore; extensive interpretive information explains the delicate ecological interactions between land and sea that the whole ecosystem depends on. Touch pools allow kids (and adults) to caress starfish and urchins.

RECREATION

CENTRE OF THE UNIVERSE

250-363-8262

www.nrc-cnrc.gc.ca

5071 West Saanich Rd., Victoria V9E 2E7

Admission: Adults $10.25 daytime, $13.50 evenings

Open 11 AM—10 PM May—October

This observatory is poised atop a rocky hill, little Saanich Mountain, on the Saanich Peninsula about 20 minutes north of Victoria. Its highlight, a 65-inch telescope, was the largest in the world when it was installed here in 1918. Nighttime tour visitors get to turn

Jellyfish tank, Shaw Ocean Discovery Centre   Leslie Forsberg

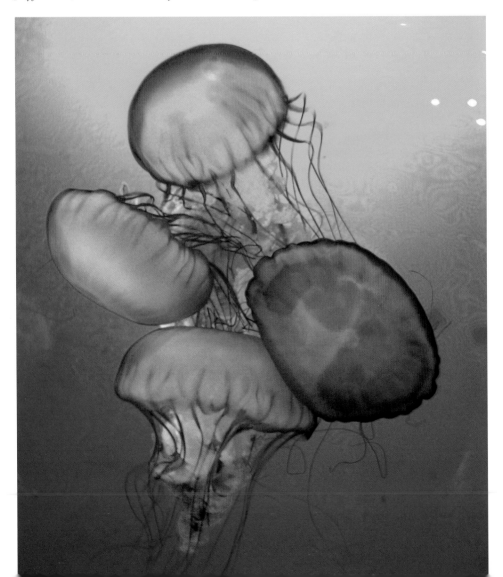

the massive, still-operating, and still-sharp instrument. The interpretive center (this facility is the actual Centre of the Universe) offers engaging exhibits on astronomy, space exploration, and Canada's part in it.

ELK/BEAVER LAKE PARK
250-478-3344
www.crd.bc.ca/parks/elkbeaver
Just west of Hwy. 17, 15 minutes north of Victoria; watch for exit signs

A rowing center, two swimming beaches, water-skiing, equestrian trails and canoeing and kayaking occupy visitors to this huge park in the middle of the Saanich Peninsula. Picnic facilities, bathhouses, and a nature center supplement the activity venues. The grounds offer hiking trails through pleasant woods, by wetlands that hold lots of migratory birds, and along the lakeshore.

GOLDSTREAM PROVINCIAL PARK
Starts 10 miles (16 km) west of Victoria on Hwy. 1
www.env.gov.bc.ca/bcparks
Open: Daily dawn–dusk
Admission: $1/hour day use parking fee

Strung along each side of Highway 1 in the valley formed by Goldstream Creek, this busy park is famed as a site to watch spawning salmon in the low, clear waters of late autumn. While the name of the creek (and thus park) derives from a brief gold rush here in the mid-19th century, it might as well apply to the colors of autumn in the creekside cotton-woods and hillside bigleaf maples. Hiking trails wend their way into the woods from numerous roadside parking lots, leading to old-growth Douglas fir groves more than half a century old. A highlight is 135-foot (47 m) Niagara Falls, so named as it's the same height as its more famous East Coast cousin (though infinitely smaller). The park's Freeman King Visitor Centre often has naturalists on hand to explain the complex ecosystem that supports the trees, waters, and salmon that make the park a natural marvel.

GULF ISLANDS

Moored in the west side of the Salish sea like water-borne parks, washed by balmy breezes, inhabited by people who want and practice a more contemplative, low-key lifestyle, Canada's Gulf Islands comprise a semimythical travel destination. Here are small coves with rocky points, and arbutus trees leaning over emerald waters in which purple seastars cling to barnacled rocks. Here are Garry oak meadows leaning down grassy headlands fringed by salal and gnarled old Douglas firs. Here small bayside harbor towns sport tidy inns, bustling cafés, local coffee roasters, art galleries, and bookstores, ringed by marinas at which sailing boats from around the world tie up. Warm inland lakes draw vacationing families; morning mists burn away to sun-warmed summer afternoons; sea lions, seals, and orcas ply the channels; and artisans in woodsy studios craft everything from blue cheese to granite sculpture. Life slows down the moment you step on a ferry bound for Salt Spring, Galiano, Gabriola, Pender, Mayne, or Saturna—yes, the pace of living here is even more soothing than the mild metaphysical climes of Vancouver Island itself. The visitor cannot help but enjoy the same ease of days that islanders do. At least until you, alas, leave. If you do.

TRANSPORTATION

As small islands subsidiary to a bigger island, the Gulf Islands are so dependent on public ferry services that in many cases the average visitor must ship on at least two ferries (sometimes three!) to reach them. Even veteran ferry travelers must consult the daily schedules to keep track of how to get somewhere, especially if you are contemplating a visit to two or more of the islands. Virtually all have at least one direct sailing a day from Swartz Bay (Victoria); a couple, such as Mayne and Galiano, also have a daily trip from Tsawassen (south Vancouver). Gabriola,

BC ferry outbound from Swartz Bay Leslie Forsberg

LEFT: *Hiking the headlands* Leslie Forsberg

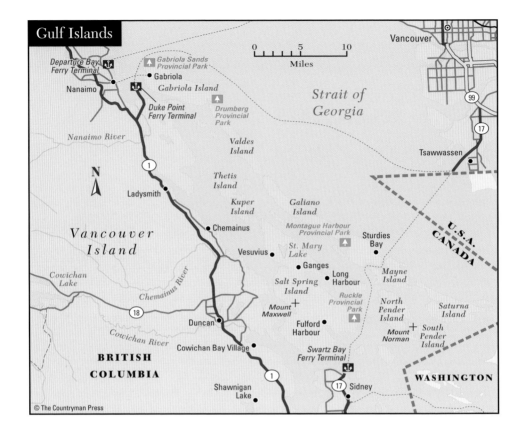

meanwhile, can be reached only from Nanaimo. Complex as the logistics may be, the ferry rides are all lovely scenic excursions as well as wildlife-watching cruises; in all my travels around the world, one of my favorite sensations remains sailing out of Swartz Bay on a small ferry bound for Salt Spring.

Gulf Islands visitors must bear two things in mind: Weekends and holidays bring increased ferry loads. Lines can be long and personal schedules upended; allow plenty of flex time during high-traffic periods. Also, residents of several of the islands commute to work in Victoria, so morning "rush hour" ferries can attract crowds as well. For routes, schedules and information, visit www.bcferries.com.

In addition, Harbour Air offers scheduled floatplane service to Ganges, on Salt Spring, from Vancouver and Victoria (250-384-2215, 1-800-665-0212, www.harbour-air.com).

Aside from BC Ferries and Harbour Air, the islands have their own airline, **Salt Spring Island Air**, which operates four scheduled floatplane flights a day between Ganges on Salt Spring, and Vancouver International Airport, the downtown Vancouver floatplane base at Canada Place. Other routes reach most other Gulf Islands seasonally (www.salt springair.com).

Car-free travelers face greater logistical challenges on the Gulf Islands. Because ferries follow routes that make the most sense on the water, only one of the islands' ferry terminals is in or near the major town (on Galiano, and it's a very modest little town). But at the least every island has a taxi service to provide transportation from ferry to the town

Onboard a BC ferry in the Gulf Islands   Leslie Forsberg

Ferry Terminal, Gulf Islands   Leslie Forsberg

Ganges Harbour, Salt Spring   Leslie Forsberg

or major resort area, and once you are there, all the islands can support a fine vacation without a car.

Many bike travelers happily wend their way around the islands in summer; though the roads are usually fairly narrow, with little or no shoulder, islanders are moderate drivers—if you are brushed by a speeding car, it's probably someone from off-island.

Salt Spring Island

The biggest, most populated and most developed of the Gulf Islands nonetheless retains a small-town atmosphere and sense of country charm that have made it famous across Canada. Salt Spring has lovely small resorts; innumerable B&Bs, cottages, and inns; one of BC's most popular parks; and a wonderful small main town, Ganges. Its balmy climate is often labeled "Mediterranean," though that's not quite so. (Try growing olives here—there isn't enough summer heat.) An almost impossibly idyllic harbor-side hamlet toward the north end of the island, Ganges faces southeast from the upper end of a long bay, and is often likened to a New England coastal village, a comparison that makes some sense visually and topologically, but overlooks the distinctive nature of life here.

Just over 10,000 people live on the island—about as many as all the other islands combined. Seems like a large number, but Salt Spring is quite big, largest of the Gulf Islands at 114 square miles (183 square km), so it remains largely pastoral and undeveloped. Quite a few sheep live here, too: The island was first settled by ex-slaves from the States in 1858, who came here to escape slavery and prejudice and to raise sheep. The sheep herding tradition lives on at a number of small family farms, and **Salt Spring lamb** is a famous dinner menu item throughout BC. Ironically, dunderheaded federal slaughtering regulations mean the sheep must be shipped off-island in most cases, and Salt Spring lamb is thus more often found on menus in Victoria and the mainland. Ironically, a century after it was a refuge for slaves escaping the United States, it served as a refuge for more Americans, this time escaping the draft for the war in Vietnam.

The island's **Saturday Market**, held in Ganges April through October, is one of the largest and longest running in BC, and draws food producers and vendors, and artists and crafters of every sort (www.saltspringmarket.com). The annual **Folk Dance Festival** in May is a spirited celebration of dance styles from around the world (www.members .shaw.ca/ssfdf). The **Jazz Festival** in mid-August brings a large roster of performers to cafés and parks in Ganges for a weekend (www.saltspringjazzfest.org). By late summer, attention turns to the island's farming tradition. In September, the **Fall Fair** (http://ssifi .org/fall-fair) focuses on all the products of island farmers. In early October, the **Apple Festival** (www.saltspringmarket.com/apples) celebrates the 350 varieties of apples grown organically on the island; visitors enjoy the opportunity to taste dozens of kinds, and kids are offered the chance to pick their own apples off the tree.

For complete travel information on the island, visit www.saltspringtourism.com.

By the way, is it Salt Spring or Saltspring? Canadian geographers and islanders have wrestled with this for years, and finally reached a de facto conclusion that either one is fine. How's that for a relaxed attitude?

In Ganges, Salt Spring   Leslie Forsberg

LODGING

Quite a collection of small inns and B&Bs welcomes Salt Spring travelers, ranging from sleeping rooms in family homes to one of BC's most elegant heritage hotels. Alas for budget travelers, the island's various versions of hostels are all closed now.

BETWEEN THE COVERS B&B
250-537-2440
www.betweenthecoversbandb.com
info@betweenthecoversbandb.com
160 Sharp Rd., Salt Spring Island, BC
V8K 2P6
⅔ mile (1 km) north of Ganges
Price: Budget to Moderate
Credit cards: Yes
Handicapped Access: Full
Special Features: Free WiFi, guest shuttle available for extra fee

Overlooking a pastoral valley scene north of Ganges, this personable two-unit B&B is operated by a children's book author, and the suites are lavishly stocked with books of all types. Both suites have decks looking out on forest and field, and the quiet is only broken by the sounds of waterfowl and the hosts' chickens. The hot tub is admirably situated to take advantage of the serene surroundings.

CUSHEON LAKE RESORT
250-537-9629 or 1-866-899-0017
www.cusheonlake.com
resort@ cusheonlake.com
171 Natalie Lane, Salt Spring Island,
BC V8K 2C6
Mid-island, between Ganges and Fulford Harbour
Price: Moderate; three-night minimum July and August and long weekends
Credit cards: Yes
Handicapped Access: Full
Special Features: No pets

Warm lake waters, sandy beaches, and sunshine draw guests (including many repeat visitors on family vacations) to this 4-acre mid-island resort's log cabins and cedar chalets. The cabins offer numerous different configurations, but all feature virtually uninterrupted wood décor, full kitchens, living rooms, and decks overlooking the lake. Activities are innumerable and include canoeing, swimming, rafting, badminton, volleyball, picnicking, and relaxing in the small hot tub. Reservations for summer stays must be made far ahead.

FOXGLOVE FARM
250-537-1989
www.foxglovefarmbc.ca
accommodations@foxglovefarmbc.ca
1200 Mount Maxwell Rd., Salt Spring Island, BC V8K 2H7
On the lower slopes of Mount Maxwell, southwest of Ganges
Price: Moderate to Expensive
Credit cards: Yes
Handicapped Access: No
Special Features: Pets welcome (extra fee); meals not included, but farm produce is available for purchase

Located on a sustainable working farm southwest of Ganges, Foxglove's accommodations consist of a remarkable heritage log cabin (chinked walls and all), and two smaller heritage farm cottages. All are newly refurbished; feature antique furnishings, full kitchens, and decks or porches; and can house 4 to 10 guests, depending on the cottage. Surrounded by fields, garden plots and heritage orchard trees, the setting is memorably peaceful. The farm itself is also a teaching center for sustainable farming, and is a CSA serving the Salt Spring community.

HASTINGS HOUSE
250-537-2362 or 1-800-661-9255
www.hastingshouse.com

info@hastingshouse.com
160 Upper Ganges Rd., Salt Spring Island,
BC V8K 2S2
⅔ mile (1 km) north of the center of Ganges
Price: Expensive to Very Expensive
Credit cards: Yes
Handicapped Access: Full
Special Features: No pets, free WiFi; morn-
ing coffee, full breakfast, and afternoon
tea included

The estate that now comprises this high-
profile luxury resort was built in the early
20th century as a faithful rendition of a
Sussex manor back in Warren Hastings's
English birthplace. An expatriate British
naval architect, Hastings and his wife settled in this small vale adjacent to Ganges
because they found the area's beauty and
climate irresistible. Dark, dense timbers,
gabled roofs, and stone fireplaces mark the
design; Edwardian antiques provide the
décor. In an early episode of (unintended)
sustainability, the stones for the massive
manor fireplace were quarried on-site, the
floors are of BC end-grain fir, and much of
the iron hardware was made by the local
blacksmith.

Sold to lodging entrepreneurs in 1980,
the hotel today pursues the ambience of an
English country inn. Suites are scattered
around the 22-acre property, whose peaceful vale runs down to a tiny cove on Ganges
Harbour. Heritage fruit trees shade walkways, pastures, and patios; old maples and
firs line the edge of the forest. Of the 18
suites, 11 were fashioned from the manor
house and various farm buildings, including an old barn. These are all elegant,
spacious, and comfortable, with sunny
colors and warm wood trim. The new-
construction Hillside Suites, in the woods
overlooking Ganges, are spacious but not
nearly as charming as the rest of the
accommodations.

The hotel's dining room is one of the
best fine-dining venues in the islands. The
fresh-sheet menu almost always includes
Salt Spring lamb, local seafood, and foraged
island ingredients such as fiddleheads.
Desserts rely on island fruits such as
quince, plum, and apple. Leaded glass windows overlook the harbor and the farm, and
this is one of the few BC restaurants that
expects diners to show up in appropriate
garb—"smart casual," which does not mean
sandals and cargo shorts.

SALT SPRING SPA RESORT
250-537-4111 or 1-800-665-0039
www.saltspringspa.com
info@saltspringspa.com
1460 North Beach Rd., Salt Spring Island,
BC V8K 1J4
10 minutes north of Ganges on the northeast shore of the island
Price: Moderate to Expensive
Credit cards: Yes
Handicapped Access: Full
Special Features: Pets welcome, free WiFi

Yes, there really are mineral salt springs on
the island—cold, not hot; and calling them
"springs" overlooks the fact the supply
actually comes from wells. The waters here
at this somewhat quirky retreat are heated
for bathing use by guests; their beneficial
mineral content is similar to that at most
hot springs, with potassium, manganese,
magnesium, barium and other trace ele-
ments present. The 13 Quonset hut–shape
cottages, which the resort colorfully calls
"rustic gothic arch pine chalets," are comfortable if unappealing from outside;
inside, all is warm-toned wood, hardwood
floors, woodstoves, kitchens, and soaking
tubs that fill with the resort's mineral
water. Just across the road from the shore,
the resort's rowboat and crab trap are available for use by guests, as are laundry facilities, barbecues, bikes, and a badminton
court. Yoga, Ayurvedic treatments, and
classic body work are all on offer in the
spa's separate spa facility.

St. Mary Lake Resort

250-537-2832 or 1-888-329-5651
www.stmarylakeresort.com
stmarylakeresort @shaw.ca
1170 North End Rd., Salt Spring Island, BC
V8K 1M1
Mid-island 3 miles (5 km) north of Ganges
Price: Moderate; multinight minimums
apply certain high-demand periods
Credit cards: Yes
Handicapped Access: Full
Special Features: No pets

Like Cusheon Lake Resort, only smaller, St. Mary Lake is another longstanding family vacation complex that has been drawing repeat guests for decades. The lake itself is bigger (biggest on the island); the resort's grounds are more open, with grassy lawns shaded by arbutus trees; and the nine cottages have a wide range of configurations, some with fireplaces, some with showers only, one with a soaking tub. All have full kitchens, barbecues, and decks overlooking the lake. Canoeing, rowing, swimming, fishing, and relaxing pass the time for guests.

DINING

Many are the small cafés, pubs, and bakeries around the island—more than any other of the Gulf Islands. The Salt Spring sustainability ethos reigns strong here; it would be difficult if not impossible to find a restaurant that does not rely on local products, naturally grown. Aside from the notable venues below, the island's several pubs offer reliable if not inspired food at moderate prices, with nice outdoor seating in good weather. **Oystercatcher** is right in central Ganges overlooking the marina, and concentrates on seafood such as fish-and-chips, salmon and oysters (100 Manson Rd., 250-537-5041). **Moby's Marine Pub** is right on the water in Ganges, prides itself on its tap-beer selection, offers pub-food

favorites (oysters are a specialty), and often presents live music (124 Upper Ganges Rd., 250-537-5559). The legendary Vesuvius Inn pub, alas, is now closed, its most recent owner having run afoul of legal authorities.

Barb's Bakery

250-725-3444
121 McPhillips Ave., Salt Spring Island, BC
V8K 2T6
Open: Daily 7 AM–5 PM, 10 AM–2 PM Sunday
Price: Moderate
Credit cards: Yes
Cuisine: Bakery and deli
Serving: B, L
Handicapped Access: Yes

One of the biggest and busiest bakery cafés you'll find anywhere, Barb's draws crowds, especially mornings, for a wide range of breads, pastries, muffins, cookies, cakes, and such. At lunch, soups, sandwiches, pizzas, pastas and salads round out the menu, and never a customer leaves hungry. It's all wholesome, hearty, and economical. It used to be Barb's Buns, but is now evidently seeking a more serious aura.

House Piccolo

250-537-1844
www.housepiccolo.com
108 Hereford Ave., Salt Spring Island, BC
V8K 2V9
Open: Daily 11 AM–9:30 PM
Price: Expensive
Credit cards: Yes
Cuisine: West Coast
Serving: D
Handicapped Access: Yes

Special Features: In summertime, the outside patio adds space for 16 more diners. One of the pioneers of West Coast cuisine is housed in a charming, blue-sided heritage home in Ganges that is fairly small—space for just 32 diners, so reservations are essential during peak travel times. Hastings House's only competition for fine dining supremacy on Salt Spring, Piccolo's menu is continental in style, relying on local ingredients for such dishes as pan-fried sablefish meunière, prawn and scallop risotto, roast venison, and peppercorn beef tenderloin.

MORNINGSIDE CAFÉ AND BAKERY
250-653-4414
http://morningsideorganic.com
107 Morningside Rd., Salt Spring Island, BC V8K 1X6
Open: Daily 7 AM–3:30 PM
Price: Budget
Credit cards: Yes
Cuisine: Bakery and deli
Serving: B, L
Handicapped Access: Yes

Looking ever so much like a Hobbiton café, with a New Age atmosphere that even surpasses the norm on Salt Spring, this long-term establishment near the Fulford ferry terminal produces hearty muffins, pastries, breads, and sandwiches for morning and afternoon travelers. Vegan foods, veggie burgers, organic coffee, and a socially conscious small bookstore complete the ambience; free WiFi is the newest modern update.

ROCK SALT RESTAURANT
250-653-4833
www.rocksaltrestaurant.com
2961 Fulford-Ganges Rd., Salt Spring Island, BC V8K 1X6
Open: Daily 8 AM–9 PM
Price: Moderate
Credit cards: Yes
Cuisine: West Coast
Serving: B, L, D
Handicapped Access: Yes
Special Features: Thursday nights kids dine for $2

Everything from morning muffins (the coffee bar opens at 7 AM) to full-on evening repasts are on offer at this bustling, popular restaurant by the ferry terminal in Fulford Harbour. Rock Salt fans are voraciously loyal to the eatery, which has won several popularity contests. The bustling atmosphere and constant crowds do not hamper the good service and excellent food, which ranges from steaks to burritos and features a slew of Asian-style dishes. Salt Spring lamb here is in a cumin and bean stew, for example. The owners are longtime Salt Spring restaurateurs and the chefs emigrated from Mexico City, so the menu diversity reflects that of the operators.

SALT SPRING COFFEE
250-537-1211
www.sobo.ca
109 McPhillips Ave., Salt Spring Island, BC V8K 2T5
Open: Daily 7 AM–4 PM
Price: Budget
Credit cards: Yes
Cuisine: Coffeehouse
Serving: B, L
Handicapped Access: Yes

Better known around much of the Northwest simply for its hand-roasted organic coffees, which are sold widely, this island-born company has a great little café in downtown Ganges at which you can pick up dandy muffins, croissants, butter tarts, and other delights that serve handsomely for breakfast. But the chief draw is the coffee, which is among the freshest and best you'll ever find, and prepared expertly.

TREE HOUSE CAFÉ
250-537-5379
www.treehousecafé.ca
106 Purvis Lane, Salt Spring Island, BC V8K 2S5
Open: Daily 8 AM–9:30 PM
Price: Budget
Credit cards: Yes
Cuisine: Café
Serving: L, D

Tree House Café, Ganges   Leslie Forsberg

Handicapped Access: Yes
Special Features: Listen to past live performances on the café's Web site.

Only on Salt Spring could such a small café be such an institution. Actual tables inside the ramshackle wooden building near the Ganges waterfront are few—no matter, as customers all want to eat outside on the various lawn-furniture setups scattered about beneath the namesake gnarled old plum tree. The heated patio extends the outdoor dining season into the winter, and that's great for both customers and the steady roster of performers who offer live music here several nights a week. The fare is largely what you might call natural-food Mexican, with numerous burritos and quesadillas, lots of black beans, cilantro, and chicken. Service can get a tad stressed during high-traffic times, but the atmosphere is quintessentially Salt Spring, and if you came to the island to hurry . . . wrong island.

CULTURE

As the largest and most populous of the islands, Salt Spring enjoys an active cultural scene that includes local theater, musical groups and venues that host visiting performers. **ArtSpring Theatre** in central Ganges is the key performance venue, a 265-seat hall that hosts a remarkably diverse range of performances year-round. Opera, symphony, folk music, dance, theater—even live-in-HD broadcasts of Metropolitan Opera performances—all are on the calendar here (250-537-2125, artspring.ca). Live music is almost always found at the Saturday Market in Ganges (www.saltspringmarket.com); other common performance venues include the **Tree House Café** (see Dining), a couple of the island's vine-yards, local churches, and community halls. Consult the tourism bureau for an events calendar at saltspringtourism.com.

RECREATION

The centerpiece of recreation on Salt Spring is one of BC's most popular (and unique) provincial parks, Ruckle. Aside from the many trails at Ruckle, a network of paths traverses **Mount Maxwell**, the provincial park that surrounds the island's highest point at 1,930 feet (588 m), Baynes Peak. A rough gravel road leads to a viewpoint and picnic ground at the top, from which views encompass almost all the Gulf Islands, Vancouver Island, the mainland of BC and Washington State, and innumerable snowy peaks in the distance. Aside from vistas, the park holds old-growth Douglas fir and Garry oak forest.

Biking is popular but challenging on the many country roads of the island; elevation gains are numerous, and roads are mostly narrow. Rentals are available in Ganges at **Salt Spring Adventure Company** (250-537-2764, www.saltspringadventures.com). The island's new indoor pool at the edge of Ganges is open to all (262 Rainbow Rd., 250-537-1402).

Fulford Harbour and Long Harbour (Ganges) are excellent kayaking locations; rentals are offered by several operators at marinas in both harbors.

BLACKBURN MEADOWS GOLF CLUB
250-537-1707
www.blackburnmeadows.com
269 Blackburn Rd., Salt Spring Island, BC V8K 2B8

Canada's first fully organic golf course is a lovely 9-hole links-style layout that wanders amid forest and field north of Ganges. No pesticides or fertilizers are used here to maintain the course, whose sustainable ethos is quintessentially Salt Spring. The course borders a small lake, thus adding wildlife watching to the pleasures of a round here. Greens fees are remarkably economical—less than $30 for 18 holes.

RUCKLE PROVINCIAL PARK
250-539-2115
www.env.gov.bc.ca/bcparks
At the end of Beaver Point Road, east of the Fulford Harbour ferry terminal

One of the greatest and most popular gems of the BC parks system is both scenic and historic—it's the site of the 1872 Ruckle family farm founded by Irish immigrant Henry Ruckle, whose descendants still raise sheep nearby. Heritage farm buildings and orchards are open for touring by visitors.

Farm stand on Salt Spring Leslie Forsberg

However, the key attractions are the enchanting open woodlands and meadows overlooking quiet coves and rocky shores. There are eight vehicle campsites, but these are

Meadow flowers, Gulf Islands   Leslie Forsberg

set in dark woods by the parking lot and are not as appealing as the 78 walk-in sites spread along the bluff above the water. Few if any other opportunities exist in all the islands, U.S. or Canadian, to pitch a tent in such a setting, in or next to an open meadow facing the sun, with the sound of the waves splashing the shoreline below. No reservations are taken for campsites here; best to arrive early in the day on summer weekends, and have a backup plan if the place is full. Yes, it happens, even with 78 sites.

Elsewhere in the park, a delightful trail leads along the shore and through the woods north of the picnic area, which is itself shaded by old maple trees, just above a lovely cove.

SHOPPING

Aside from a plethora of galleries and artists' studios, Salt Spring is known for its foods. And these include the ultimate in local foods—island tradition is that small growers scattered around the countryside set **produce and flower stands** along the road by their driveway. These are honor-pay operations, with coin jars in which customers drop their money. So, driving around the island (chiefly May–October), one finds innumerable opportunities to buy vegetables, fruit, flowers, even fresh-baked breads and muffins. It's one of the island's most cherished, most distinctive, and most user-friendly traditions.

Cheese-making is the standout here in commercial food production, with two major, regionally famous producers. **Salt Spring Island Cheese** (www.saltspringcheese.com) is mid-island, and has a full-service store at which you can buy any of a dozen handmade cheeses, ranging from mild fresh types to salty blues with hefty flavors. The tasting room is almost sufficient for a lunch all by itself; yes, you should feel guilty if you leave without buying any cheese, but that's almost impossible. At **Moonstruck Organic Cheese**, the varietal cheese ethos is taken so seriously that the cheese makers produce, package, and sell cheeses crafted from individual cows—Blossom's Blue, for instance; (www.moonstruck cheese.com). **Salt Spring Island Bread** is baked and sold daily at a woodsy facility perched atop a rocky point at 251 Forest Ridge Rd. (250-653-4809).

There are literally dozens of artists, weavers, crafters, jewelers, sculptors, painters, woodcrafters, potters, and such who live and work on the island. Some have full-service studios open regularly; some offer opening hours only during scheduled art tours and such; some sell only at commercial galleries in Ganges. A comprehensive **touring catalog** of three dozen such artists, with a touring map, is available at www.saltspringstudiotour .com. In Ganges, **Pegasus Gallery** is the major dealer and art showroom, with a large selection of First Nations art, as well as painting, sculpture, and glass by island artists (www .pegasusgallery.ca).

Pender Island

Actually, this is two islands joined amidships by a tide flat; purists (and some maps) say "Pender Islands," or, locally, "the Penders." Like several other Gulf Islands such as Salt Spring, a large central mountain hoists the land and forests skyward in a park preserve, Mount Norman, with a short but steep hiking trail that leads to a spectacular westward view

Artisan starts here—goats on Salt Spring   Leslie Forsberg

Gulf Islands National Park Reserve

250-654-4000

www.pc.gc.ca

One of Canada's newest national parks is also one of its, well, most diffuse—it consists of literally dozens of parcels spread across the Gulf Islands. Some are reached by road, some by foot, some by boat only; some islands have large portions, such as Saturna; some only a few bits and pieces, such as Mayne Island. The parcels range from entire undeveloped islands to small coves to secluded forest groves. One very popular segment is **Sidney Spit,** a long strand of sand on an undeveloped island; summer passenger ferries bring visitors back and forth between the park and Sidney. Sidney Spit is for wilderness camping or day use only. Round-trip passage is $19 (www.alpinegroup.ca).

The park has two vehicle campgrounds, McDonald, near Sidney on the main island (open mid-March through October); and Prior Centennial, on North Pender Island (open mid-May through October). Both are in high demand and reservations are highly advisable, through the Parks Canada reservations Web site, www.pccamping.ca, or by calling 1-877-737-3783.

The park's main office is in Sidney, north of Victoria; but very few of the properties within the park are on the main island.

from the top. Aside from a couple other small parks, a mid-island campground, and a few B&Bs and boutique inns, the big draw on the island is the large, upgraded marina resort, Poets Cove (see Lodging). For complete travel information, consult www.penderisland chamber.com.

LODGING

There are a half-dozen B&Bs on Pender. As well, two small boutique inns offer relaxed, quiet getaway lodging. **The Inn on Pender Island** is a mid-north-island lodging amid 7 acres of forested seclusion, with cozy budget rooms in the main lodge, and two moderately priced private cabins, one with a private hot tub (www.innonpender.com). **Oceanside Inn** enjoys its own low-bank bluff vantage point on the north island, with two queen-size-bed rooms and one small suite, a hot tub, and stairs down to the rocky beach; open May through September only (www.penderisland.com).

POETS COVE RESORT

250-629-2100 or 1-888-512-7638

www.poetscove.com

info@ poetscove.com

9801 Spalding Rd., South Pender Island, BC V0N 2M3

On South Pender, 8⅔ miles (14 km) south of the BC Ferries Otter Bay Terminal

Price: Expensive to Very Expensive

Credit cards: Yes

Handicapped Access: Full

Special Features: Free WiFi

Simultaneously the largest, and one of the oldest, resorts in the Gulf Islands, Poets Cove is centered around a small harbor and marina that have been welcoming travelers since the late 19th century. Long just a small marina and hotel, a $42 million rede-velopment in 2004 transformed it into a full-scale luxury resort, with 22 rooms in the main lodge, 9 villas, and 15 cottages. All are constructed Northwest resort style, with lots of visible wood beams, stone facings, bay windows, and fireplaces. The lodge is an Arts and Crafts heritage building. The villas and cottages have kitchenettes and multiple bedrooms. What truly sets the resort apart from others in the islands is the range of activities: there's a heated outdoor pool, a full spa and fitness center, tennis court, beach, and kids' playground. Activities include kayaking and canoeing, hiking, biking, windsurfing, sailing, and fishing. Other facilities include two restaurants, a huge marina, customs entry, floatplane dock (obviating that pesky multistop ferry ride), and on-site store. Although the resort is quite pricey in summer, off-season last-minute specials sometimes bring rates below $100.

DINING

With less than 1,000 residents, and few resorts to draw visitors, Pender Island has just a few places to eat. **Birdie's Bistro** is in the clubhouse at Pender Island Golf and Country Club (www.penderislandgolf.com) and offers breakfast and lunch café-style items—omelets, sandwiches, soups. **Pender Island Bakery** (www.penderislandbakery.com) has excellent fresh-baked bread and sandwiches, as well as pizzas and panini, pot pies, and such. **Hope Bay Café** is in a refurbished building on the wharf at its

Artisan cheese on Salt Spring   Leslie Forsberg

namesake harbor, with stunning views east over the water to Mount Baker in the distance. The food ranges from soups and salads to West Coast dinner specials such as salmon and venison (www.hopebaycafé.com).

RECREATION

The centerpiece of recreation on the Penders is also the highest point. **Mount Norman Park** is a forested preserve that rises to its namesake pinnacle, an 800-foot -high (244 m) ridge whose west face drops away precipitously to Bedwell Harbour below. A steep but well-maintained trail leads to the top; needless to say, the views are jaw-dropping. **Roe Lake Park** offers hiking paths through woods and fields to its namesake lake. Formerly a separate provincial park near the south end of North Pender, **Prior Centennial Campground** is now part of Gulf Islands National Park (p. 94) (www.pc.gc.ca).

Bedwell Harbour, a long narrow inlet with Mount Norman on one side, is an ideal locale for kayaking, though afternoon winds can rise; rentals are available at Poets Cove Resort (www.poetscove.com).

Island flowers Leslie Forsberg

Galiano Island

A long, narrow northwest–southeast-running ridge that forms the northeast verge of the Gulf Islands, Galiano is 16¾ miles (27 km) long and only 3¾ miles (6 km) across at its widest point. Reached by direct passage from Tsawassen, south of Vancouver, it is thus a popular weekend getaway for residents of the Lower Mainland metropolis, only an hour away by ferry. Virtually all the visitor services and attractions are in the little village by the ferry terminal, Sturdies Bay; and up-island about 6⅛ miles (10 km) at a west-facing bay, Montague Harbour.

In Sturdies Bay, **Galiano Island Books** is one of the largest independent booksellers in the province, with 25,000 titles that include a strong focus on children's books and Western Canada nature and travel (www.galianoislandbooks.com). Between Sturdies Bay and Montague Harbour, **Trincomali Farms** offers island-grown produce, flowers, and handmade soaps, as well as horseback rides (www.trincomalifarms.com). Montague is one of the most protected harbors in the islands, and ideal for paddling; rentals are available at the marina from **Galiano Kayaks** (www.seakayak.ca). The west-side channel between Galiano and Salt Spring is a good locale to see marine mammals, including orcas.

Aside from the deluxe and wonderful Galiano Inn, a fairly large number of small B&Bs and rental cottages serve visitors. For complete travel information, visit www.galiano island.com.

LODGING

GALIANO INN

250-539-3388 or 1-877-530-3939
www.galianoinn.com
info@ galianoinn.com
134 Madrona Dr., Galiano Island,
BC V0N 1P0
In Sturdies Bay, just west of the ferry
terminal
Price: Expensive
Credit cards: Yes
Handicapped Access: Full
Special Features: Pets welcome in two
units, free WiFi, bicycles available nearby,
Smart Cars on property for guest rental

One of the Gulf Islands' best-known lodgings is a hugely popular getaway destination for Vancouver residents—it's just a short walk from the ferry dock (the only such resort in the islands) and there is direct ferry service between Galiano and Tsawwassen in south Vancouver. So, while the inn describes itself as "best-kept secret" in the islands . . . not really. But it is perhaps overlooked as one of the finest luxury inns in the islands—the 20 newly built or refurbished suites and villas all overlook the water, and the entire inn is decked out in sunny Mediterranean colors, with warm wood trim enhancing the stucco construction. Some units have delightful outdoor patios with a fireplace and soaking tub; a grassy verge sets off the inn from the beach. The main lobby is the home of a massive floor-to-ceiling mural, *Kunamokst,* composed of 231 individual small paintings hung as one to create and overall depiction of undersea life in the islands. Elsewhere in the lodge are priceless Bill Reid carvings and prints. The spa features such exotic treatments as a "Blueberry Smoothie" body wrap, a BC seaweed salt scrub, and a chocolate pedicure. The dining room's seasonal soups and salads are prelude to West Coast main dishes such as halibut cheeks with olives, artichokes, and pine nuts. Wednesday through Sunday in summer, handmade pizzas are served on the sunny patio after baking in a wood-fired oven. Although the inn is expensive during summer high season, it's much more economical November through mid-May, and late April and early May can bring delightful weather to Galiano.

Galiano Island Leslie Forsberg

Bill Reid panel, Galiano Inn   Leslie Forsberg

DINING

As it is so reachable from Vancouver, Galiano has a small number of cafés and dining spots worthy of a visit by themselves. **Sturdies Bay Bakery** is about ¼ mile (a few hundred meters uphill from the ferry terminal, and specializes in pizzas, samosas, soups, salads, and sandwiches; free WiFi adds to the appeal (2450 Sturdies Bay Rd., 250-539-2004).

Halfway between Sturdies Bay and Montague Harbour, **Hummingbird Pub** is a regionally famed institution whose pub food includes all the standards (yes, *poutine*, too) and is even better known for its own bus service. In summer, the Hummingbird bus shuttles visitors between Montague's park and harbor and the pub throughout the evening. Sequestered in a small clearing on the road to Montague Harbour (and within a short walk of the harbor and the provincial park), **La Berengerie** is a French restaurant whose owner emigrated here from Avignon (250-539-5392, www.galianoisland.com/laberengerie). Note: It's a laidback island, but it would be rude to ask the Hummingbird bus to drop you at La Berengerie.

Right by the Sturdies Bay ferry dock—in fact, trading largely on travelers waiting for a boat—**Max and Moritz Spicy Island Food** is a delightful fast-food stand whose Indonesian plates are filling and flavorful, and quite economical.

RECREATION

Galiano's heights reach their pinnacles at the very south end of the island within two large regional parks. West of Sturdies, **Mount Galiano**, at 1,033 feet (315 m), is the highest point on the island; a steep and stiff hiking trail leads to the top where spectacular views await of the other islands and the narrow passage below. Between Mount Galiano and Sturdies Bay,

The Bluffs Preserve is much more accessible, with a gravel road through deep forest reaching almost to the highest point and a parking spot from which inspiring, cliff-top views also reward the journey.

MONTAGUE HARBOUR PROVINCIAL PARK

250-539-2115
www.env.gov.bc.ca/bcparks
Montague Park Road, 6⅛ miles (10 km) northwest of Sturdies Bay

One of the most popular parks in the islands, behind only Ruckle, Montague encompasses a tongue of land that is the north side of its namesake bay. There's a lovely grassy play area, a public boat dock, a small headland with mature forest, and hiking trails that lead up the nearby hillside. But the park is best known for a distinctive and very lovely white shell beach on whose smooth expanse visitors might see minks fishing in tide pools beneath the ruddy, smooth trunks of arbutus trees. The 14 car campsites and 15 walk-in sites here are very, very popular. Campsite reservations for summer visits can be made (with a private concessionaire) through the park Web site, or by calling 1-800-689-9025. Best to reserve as far ahead as possible for summer travel.

Saturna Island

One of the least populated, least developed and most remote of the Gulf Islands, Saturna forms the southeast toe of the island chain, pointing directly across to Bellingham, Washington, in the States. No direct ferries sail here; one must stop at Pender and Mayne islands on your way to Saturna from Victoria. It is thus a very quiet, pastoral, and uncrowded isle on which one large vineyard, several small lodges, curving sand beaches, and serene parks draw visitors. A small collection of B&Bs, pubs, and cafés provide visitor services; for travel information, consult www.saturnatourism.com.

Almost half the island is now part of the new **Gulf Islands National Park** (p. 94); the island's biggest event, its annual **Canada Day lamb barbecue** July 1 is an old-fashioned country-fair event with Scottish bagpipes, local artisans selling wares, live entertainment, and of course island-grown lamb roasted over an open firepit (saturnalambbarbeque.com).

The chief commercial attraction on the island is **Saturna Island Estate Winery**, a

Relaxing on the sand   Leslie Forsberg

large (60-acre) estate vineyard that specializes in pinot gris, Chardonnay, pinot noir, Merlot, and Gewürztraminer (www.satrunavineyards.com). The winery's bistro is one of the better dining spots on the island, with a compact menu of local seafood, cheeses, and breads. The best-known accommodation is **Saturna Lodge**, a six-room inn on a terraced hillside above a small cove (www.saturna.ca).

Mayne Island

Wedged in between Galiano and Saturna, Mayne enjoys direct ferry service to Vancouver, and thus holds a large number of weekend homes owned by urbanites. There's a central hill, **Mount Parke**, a regional park with hiking trails that lead to viewpoint picnic spots. A most attractive heritage lighthouse at **Georgina Point** marks the narrow passage between Mayne and Galiano islands; watching BC Ferries' massive Vancouver–Victoria boats thread this channel is quite a sight. A **Japanese Garden** at Dinner Bay Park honors the islanders who were forcibly removed to internment camps during World War II. Island artisans offer everything from farm products to artwork.

Like Saturna, Mayne's visitor infrastructure consists of small B&Bs, pubs, cafés, and one newly upgraded small resort. **Mayne Island Resort**, centered around an old oceanside hotel, has spiffy new kitchen cottages, a spa, and modern amenities such as free WiFi (www.mayneislandresort.com). The island prides itself on its system of 25 **"Car Stops"** where residents and visitors hitchhike, in effect, to reduce traffic and resource consumption. For complete travel information, visit www.mayneisland.com.

Gabriola Island

Northernmost of the Gulf Islands and easily reached with a short ferry ride from Nanaimo Harbour, Gabriola has a long history as a family summer vacation retreat and is the second most developed in the chain. Its many small coves and harbors hold tidy sand beaches tucked in between rocky headlands; the island's famous rock formations are much photographed. Several provincial and regional parks preserve the best of the coves and headlands; a large community of small inns, old-line resorts and B&Bs serves visitors.

Although it has a large residential population (about 5,000), many of whom commute to work in Nanaimo, it remains a simple place: The two main highways that traverse the island lengthwise are called North Road and South Road.

Drumbeg Provincial Park, Gabriola Leslie Forsberg

Gabriola Sands Provincial Park is a small day-use preserve with two beaches along a narrow tongue of land between Taylor Bay (the warmer west side) and Pilot Bay (the cooler northeast side). Nearby, **Malaspina Galleries Community Park** holds Gabriola's best-known and most photographed feature, an eroded gallery cave along a side cliff in a tiny cove. **Descanso Bay Regional Park** is the

Harbour on Gabriola Leslie Forsberg

island's only public campground, leading down to another pocket cove. At the far southeast corner of the island, **Drumbeg Provincial Park** is an oak prairie preserve on a small headland overlooking rocky tidal channels in which currents are constantly swirling.

At the far northeast corner of the island near the end of Berry Point Road, vistas emerge of the Salish Sea, snowy Coast Mountains and, in the near distance, the scenic offshore **Entrance Island Lighthouse**, which guides ships into Nanaimo Harbour. The island's rocky-ledge shoreline here is much sculpted by wind and wave into swirling shapes that invite careful poking about.

For complete travel information, visit www.gabriolaisland.org.

LODGING

Gabriola lacks anything resembling a major resort, or even a small inn. About a dozen B&Bs and old-fashioned family-cabin clusters serve visitors; there's one sizeable campground (32 sites) at Descanso Bay Park, a small marina motel, Silva Bay Inn, and a personal growth retreat center, the **Haven Resort and Institute** (www.haven .ca), which concentrates on melding Eastern wellness disciplines with interpersonal dynamics and communication. The classic, decades-old family resort on the island, **Surf Lodge**, offers cabins at moderate rates, but is fairly rundown. Many of the island's lodgings have two-night minimums in summer and on holiday weekends.

JUPITER RANCH

250-247-2051
www.jupiterranch.com
jupiterranch@shaw.ca
2220 Shaw Rd., Gabriola Island,
BC V0R 1X7
Just off South Road, 10 minutes east of the BC Ferries terminal
Price: Moderate
Credit cards: Yes
Handicapped Access: Full
Special Features: Free WiFi, breakfast included, fridge and microwave in rooms

Built and operated by an artist who emigrated to the islands from Quebec, this strikingly modern small inn is a distinct contrast to the islands' usual B&B style. Highly sustainable construction and operation strategies reflect the inn's environmental philosophy—passive solar heating, fans rather than air-conditioning, Xeriscape landscaping, and water conservation. From the two guest suites, vast expanses of glass overlook a broad, grassy meadow on the sunny south side of the island. The suites are sparely decorated but include long clawfoot tubs in the spacious bathrooms and gas fireplaces by the windows. Artists' retreats and workshops are often offered in the adjoining studio; excellent biking, hiking, and beachcombing are nearby. Yes, you can often see Jupiter from the open meadow.

THREE GATES FARM

250-725-3100 or 1-800-333-4604
www.threegatesfarm.com
info@threegatesfarm.com
1830 South Rd., Gabriola Island,
BC V0R 1X0
15 minutes east of the BC Ferries terminal
Price: Moderate
Credit cards: Yes
Handicapped Access: Partial

Georgina Point Lighthouse on Mayne Island, one of the Gulf Islands, at the entrance to Active Pass.
IStockphoto/Maxvis

Special Features: No pets, free WiFi, breakfast included

Aside from the lovely country setting on a 20-acre working farm, this three-room inn is distinguished by the heated pool by which guests can soak up the sun on the south side of the island and wake up with a morning dip. Two rooms overlook the water, one has a pasture view, all have private bath. The farmhouse breakfast relies heavily on Three Gates' own products, such as eggs and sheep's milk. Excellent biking, hiking, and beachcombing are nearby.

DINING

Restaurants, alas, come and go on Gabriola, and few are reliably good and reliably, well, reliable. **Raspberry's Jazz Restaurant** is in the Folklife Village Shopping Centre and, aside from serving up respectable soups, salads, sandwiches, and other café food, it schedules periodic live jazz performances (www.gabriola.org/raspberry). **Robert's Place**, perhaps the island's best restaurant, is a comfortable dining room with great service and a comfort food menu that ranges from a chef's salad to amazingly good Southern fried chicken. (No, not southern Canada.) *Poutine,* onion rings, burgers, pizza, and even liver and onions are on the expansive menu (www.roberts placegabriola.com). **Woodfire Pizza & Pasta** is a brand-new spot that, aside from its namesake dishes, offers appetizers ranging from soufflés to classic antipasto; risottos and wood-fired meats; and a full slate of desserts (www.woodfirepizza.ca).

3

Mid-Island from Cowichan to Campbell River

The long, mostly developed strip of land along the island's east coast stretches from the Cowichan Valley almost 125 miles (200 km) north to Campbell River—the area I am calling "mid-island" for this book. It's both psychologically and geographically separate from the Capital region around Victoria. The demarcation takes place on the shoulder of a huge mountain, Malahat, which Highway 1 crests at a narrow pass about 15½ miles (25 km) northwest of Victoria. Residents of the rest of the island subscribe to the same amiable sense of distinction that differentiates residents of interior BC from those who live in the Vancouver metropolitan area—different perspectives, lifestyles, and outlooks. Victoria residents can thrive without cars, for example; that would be impossible anywhere else on Vancouver Island.

Much similarity binds the mid-island region: Small cities and towns front the coast on flat shelves of land, with wild forest starting barely 6 miles (10 km) inland. Well, sort of wild—it's all been logged, and is mostly second- or third-growth outside the various parks. Travelers taking the high-speed Highway 19 between Nanaimo and Campbell River will occasionally be greeted by the spectacle of a "leave tree," an old-growth Douglas fir snag along the road, towering over a clear-cut—a sight both impressive and discouraging and, often, holding a bald eagle impassively watching the traffic roar by.

Along the shoreline, pleasant gray-sand beaches face the islands in the Strait of Georgia, or the towering snowy peaks of the mainland's Coast Range. Quiet coves and bays pock the coastline; famously, Fanny Bay, between Qualicum and Courtenay, is a producer of much-sought oysters.

Here, between the Malahat and Campbell River, Vancouver Island's own central mountain range fends off much of the Pacific's wild weather, and sunnier, drier climes bless the shores, with many famed beach resorts that draw throngs of sun-seeking families in July and August.

North of Campbell River, the island veers westward, the land turns wilder, the towns are farther apart, residents far fewer, clouds and rain far more common. I have often

LEFT: *Breakfast in the garden* Leslie Forsberg

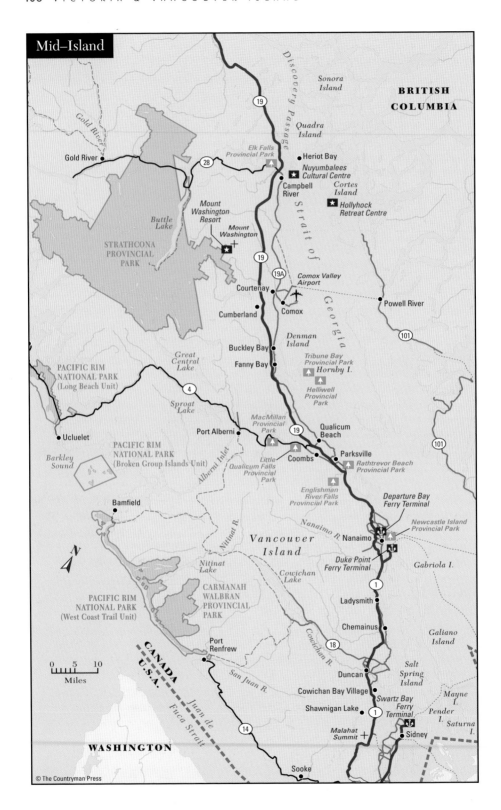

Mid–Island

BRITISH
COLUMBIA

Discovery Passage

Sonora
Island

Quadra
Island

Gold River

Gold River

19

28

Elk Falls
Provincial Park

Heriot Bay

Nuyumbalees
Cultural Centre

Campbell
River

Cortes
Island

Hollyhock
Retreat Centre

Mount
Washington
Resort

Mount
Washington

Buttle
Lake

STRATHCONA
PROVINCIAL
PARK

Strait of

19

19A

Comox Valley
Airport

Courtenay

Comox

Powell River

Georgia

Cumberland

101

Great
Central
Lake

Denman
Island

Buckley Bay

Fanny Bay

Tribune Bay
Provincial Park

Hornby I.

Helliwell
Provincial
Park

PACIFIC RIM
NATIONAL PARK
(Long Beach Unit)

4

Sproat
Lake

MacMillan
Provincial
Park

Ucluelet

PACIFIC RIM
NATIONAL PARK
(Broken Group Islands Unit)

Barkley
Sound

Port Alberni

19

Qualicum
Beach

Little
Qualicum Falls
Provincial
Park

Coombs

101

Parksville

Rathtrevor Beach
Provincial Park

Alberni Inlet

Englishman
River Falls
Provincial Park

Bamfield

Departure Bay
Ferry Terminal

Nitinat R.

Nanaimo R.

Vancouver
Island

Nanaimo

Newcastle Island
Provincial Park

N

Nitinat
Lake

Cowichan
Lake

Duke Point
Ferry Terminal

Gabriola I.

PACIFIC RIM
NATIONAL PARK
(West Coast Trail Unit)

CARMANAH
WALBRAN
PROVINCIAL
PARK

1

Ladysmith

Chemainus

Galiano
Island

CANADA
U.S.A.

Port
Renfrew

Cowichan R.

18

Salt
Spring
Island

0   5   10
Miles

San Juan R.

Duncan

Cowichan Bay Village

Shawnigan Lake

Swartz Bay
Ferry
Terminal

1

Mayne
I.

Pender
I.

Saturna
I.

Juan de Fuca Strait

14

Malahat
Summit

Sidney

WASHINGTON

Sooke

© The Countryman Press

Tribune Bay Provincial Park, Hornby Island Leslie Forsberg

driven to Campbell River in sunshine, turned northwest from there, and soon encountered rain. Coincidentally, the four-lane high-speed road that eases this journey, the Inter-Island Highway, diminishes back to two lanes north of Campbell River as well, reinforcing the sense of passing into a different land.

Mid-island is a place of verdant farms—it's a dairying center—shore-hugging resorts, oyster farms, clear-cuts visible in the near distance and snowy peaks farther off. It boasts a major ski resort, several huge vacation-destination (for campers) provincial parks, surging rivers with famous falls, teeming salmon runs, old-school family resorts with funky waterfront cottages, deluxe modern resorts with massive spas, and charming country-house B&Bs whose hosts are both hospitable and knowledgeable about their territory.

For comprehensive travel information, visit www.vancouverisland.travel or the various local tourism Web sites listed in each section that follows.

HISTORY

The present-day Salish Sea, including the eastern shore of Vancouver Island, was generally the territory of **Salish** language group peoples, while from Quadra Island north were bands in the **Kwakwaka'wakw** peoples (formerly this language group name was rendered Kwagiulth or Kwakiutl). All enjoyed a fairly prosperous lifestyle based on the abundance of salmon, shellfish, and wild game. All built large longhouses of cedar as living quarters. And all celebrated the periodic feast ceremonies known as the **potlatch**.

The latter became the fiercest bone of contention between the area's indigenous people and the European settlers who began arriving in the mid-19th century. The Hudson's Bay

Company established an outpost at Nanaimo in 1853; the **bastion** (fort) still stands and is now the city's compact history museum. The area's timber resources were obvious, and small mills began to process lumber as settlers arrived from Europe. More important, **coal seams** in the area (ironically, a local Salish chief showed these to HBC factors) were utilized to supply the growing populations in Victoria and on the mainland. Scottish immigrant Robert Dunsmuir built a huge family fortune on the coal mines and a rail line between Nanaimo and Victoria. Then as now, coal mining was a dangerous business: The **1887 Nanaimo Mine explosion** killed 150 miners and was ranked the largest man-made explosion in history to that point.

Meanwhile, efforts to "civilize" the First Nations people of the area focused on erasing indigenous languages and customs, such as the potlatch. A federal ban on potlatches, first enacted in 1885, proved difficult to enforce and was widely ignored, especially by Kwakwaka'wakw bands. The controversy came to a head in 1921 with a notorious seizure of potlatch regalia (see p. 187) at an "outlaw" gathering. The ban was formally repealed in 1951, and potlatch has enjoyed a resurgence among the indigenous peoples of the island.

Coal mining largely ended in the area around the mid-20th century; timber processing continues. Reliably sunny summer weather helped the island's shore from Nanaimo north become a popular vacation area, and the same mild climate and ample recreation availability has boosted the region as a retirement center in the new millennium.

TRANSPORTATION

Nanaimo is the main transportation center for the entire island north of Victoria, by virtue of its two big BC Ferries terminals. The one at the north end of Nanaimo harbor, **Departure Bay**, serves Horseshoe Bay north of Vancouver. The huge new **Duke Point** terminal south of Nanaimo has routes to Tsawwassen, south of Vancouver. In addition, a smaller terminal at the south end of Nanaimo harbor serves Gabriola Island, northernmost of the Gulf Islands (see p. 100). The two mainland routes are high-traffic corridors, and travelers are best advised to make reservations to ensure a spot on a particular sailing, *especially on weekends and holidays.* **Comox** is the departure point for ferries to Powell River, on the Sunshine Coast; **Campbell River** is the terminal for ferries to Quadra and Cortes islands. For schedules, fares, and reservations, visit www.bcferries.com.

The compact and very user-friendly **Nanaimo Airport** (YCD; www.nanaimoairport .com) has a dozen daily flights between here and Vancouver International Airport, Victoria, and Abbotsford. The much bigger **Comox Valley Airport** (YQQ; www.comox airport.com) offers daily service to and from Vancouver International, Calgary, Edmonton, and Victoria.

Train service between Victoria and the up-island cities of Nanaimo and Courtenay is offered daily by **Via Rail** (www.viarail.ca). Bus service is provided by **Greyhound Canada**, but their Web site and customer service are dicey at best (1-800-661-8747, www.greyhound.ca).

Drivers traversing the length of this coast begin on **Highway 1** in Victoria, and follow this four-lane route to Nanaimo, where it magically turns and crosses the Strait of Georgia (on a BC ferry!) to Horseshoe Bay, there picking up asphalt again and continuing on 4,971 miles (8,000 km) to the Atlantic coast and Newfoundland. It's the world's longest national highway; Milepost Zero is in downtown Victoria. From Nanaimo north, the same road becomes **Highway 19**—still a four-lane, now largely controlled access freeway that runs

BC ferry arriving at Comox Leslie Forsberg

along a shelf above the water ⅔ to 6 miles (1 to 10 km) inland and is thus called the Inland Island Highway. The opening of this road in the late '90s revolutionized life on the island, cutting several hours off the drive time northward. Today, it's less than two hours from Nanaimo to Campbell River; allow at least four hours from Victoria to Campbell River, not counting traffic getting out of Victoria. One of BC's most notorious speed traps is at Nanoose Bay, about 12½ miles (20 km) north of Nanaimo; be sure to slow down for the signaled intersection here.

The old island highway hugs the shoreline, and now provides access to the resorts and small town centers along the coast north of Nanaimo. Generally marked 19A, and mysteriously called the **West Island Highway**, it's a more scenic and definitely slower-paced drive.

Cowichan Valley

"Warm land" is the usual interpretation of this valley's Native name, now transliterated as Quw'utsun' by the First Nations band here. Facing southeast into the sun, shielded from Pacific storms by mountains, it is a balmy eden of small farms and wooded dales, vineyards, and quiet country lanes that wind across the valley.

Duncan is the main town in the valley, a mostly uninteresting small city whose most visible aspect, along Highway 1 through town, is a dispiriting string of small strip malls,

Modern totem poles, Duncan Leslie Forsberg

fast-food restaurants, and cheap motels. Off-highway, though, the city sports a collection of 80 hand-carved **First Nations totems**, scattered about town at plazas and street corners; you can find a map delineating the "Trail of Totems" at the city's in-town visitor centre (381 Highway 1, V9L 3R5, 250-746-4636).

Chemainus, an old-fashioned water-front town 12½ miles (20 km) north of Duncan, about 3 miles (5 km) east of Highway 1, is globally famous as the "Mural City" for the three dozen hand-painted historic scenes that decorate the sides of almost every available building in the town. Conceived as a tactic in 1981 to bring visitors to the town, it has since been copied by many other cities around the world (www .chemainus.com). Chemainus is also the terminal for ferries to **Thetis Island**, a small, pastoral and notably laid-back community where visitors might discover the best food to be found on a day trip is the weekly community lunch at the fire hall (www.thetisisland.net).

The chief present-day draw for many visitors to the Cowichan valley is the dozen or so wineries whose **estate vineyards** rely on the area's reliably warm, dry summer weather. Cool-climate varietals—Ortega, Gewürztraminer, pinot noir, pinot gris, and sparkling wines—dominate the scene here. Venturi-Schulze (www.venturi-schulze.com), Blue Grouse, often rated the valley's best (www.bluegrousevineyards.com), Zanatta (www .zanatta.ca), Cherry Point, with a wonderful facility and setting (www.cherrypointestate wines.com), and Glenterra (www.glenterravineyards.com), are among the more established estate wineries. All operate sustainably or organically, all have tasting rooms open seasonally; some such as Zanatta have food as well. Virtually all the wineries are in the valley south of Duncan. The road network here is complex, to say the least, and it's imperative to consult each winery's Web site before setting off; or visit the island vintners' association at www.wineislands.ca. Google Maps and MapQuest do not always yield reliable results here.

LODGING

A scattering of small inns, B&Bs, and highway motels compose the lodging community in the Cowichan Valley; like its wine region counterparts in Washington state and Oregon, lack of true destination resorts has been a hindrance to full development of this as a visitor destination, compared to Northern California or BC's own resort-rich Okanagan Valley in the interior. But there are charming small inns a-plenty, and a one-night stay is sufficient for all but the most serious wine-touring zealots.

FAIRBURN FARM
250-746-4637
http://fairburnfarm.bc.ca
info@fairburnfarm.bc.ca
3310 Jackson Rd., Duncan, BC V9L 6N7
Price: Moderate
Credit cards: Yes
Handicapped Access: Partial

The late 19th-century red-roofed manor house at Fairburn houses a comfortable small inn whose upstairs rooms lie somewhere between guesthouse and hotel. A broad front porch overlooks the 130-acre farms' fields and forests, including the resident water buffalo herd. The hearty farm-style breakfasts focus on ingredients from the farm itself, including mozzarella made from the water buffalo milk. The setting, with a small creek meandering through the valley, is unfailingly serene; yoga, walking, biking, and other meditative pursuits fill the time.

OLD FARM INN
250-748-6410 or 1-888-240-1482
www.oldfarminncowichan.com
stay@ oldfarminncowichan.com
2075 Cowichan Bay Rd., Cowichan Bay, BC
V0R 1N1
⅔ mile (1 km) north of Cowichan Bay
Village
Price: Moderate
Credit cards: Yes
Handicapped Access: Full
Special Features: Free Internet access in
library, breakfast included

Designed in 1908 by island architect Samuel Maclure, this large yet graceful, green-gabled farmhouse anchors a bluff above the tidal estuary on 2 lovely acres of gardens. The three suites are furnished in Laura Ashley florals, with brass beds and wicker chairs; one, in a separate building, has a kitchenette and soaking tub. The village is just a 10-minute stroll away.

PENFOLD FARM
250-746-6678
www.penfoldfarm.com
penfoldfarm@shaw.ca
1444 Maple Bay Rd., Duncan, BC V9L 5L9
Price: Moderate
Credit cards: Yes
Handicapped Access: Full
Special Features: Free WiFi

This early 20th-century former dairy farm has, as its centerpiece lodging, a delightful small stucco cottage that fronts a huge flower garden. Period furniture and cottage

Cottage at Penfold Farm Leslie Forsberg

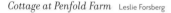

artwork complete the atmosphere; breakfast is served on a small patio amid the flowers when weather permits. The garden's collection of antique fragrant roses is extensive. The main building, a former barn, has a large upstairs suite carved from a hay loft; outside, a massive old growth Garry oak spreads its branches almost 131 feet (40 m) over the backyard. The country setting is blissfully peaceful.

DINING

Despite its fame as a lovely, pastoral valley dotted with vineyards and farms, restaurants in the Cowichan area tend more toward traditional neighborhood cafés than gourmet destinations. Foodies from around the world make pilgrimages to Cowichan Bay Village (p. 117), but they are coming for its cheese, baked goods, and ice cream. Oddly enough, there are two gourmet destination restaurants in Shawnigan Lake, an old resort village in the foothills overlooking Cowichan Valley, Amuse, a French-style bistro (www.amusebistro.com) and Steeples.

BISTRO LA POMMERAIE
250-743-4293 or 1-800-998-9908
www.merridalecide.com/bistro
1230 Merridale Rd., Cobble Hill,
BC V0R 2Z0 (consult maps on the Web site)
Open: Lunch–dinner, May–September; abridged hours fall, winter, and spring
Price: Moderate
Credit cards: Yes
Cuisine: West Coast
Serving: L, D
Handicapped Access: Yes

Merridale Cidery's on-site restaurant is the Cowichan Valley's premier fine dining purveyor of local cuisine. The ambience, in a new, light-filled, purpose-built "farmhouse" rich with structural wood and trim, is memorably warm. The wood-fired brick oven renders splendid artisan breads and pizzas. The wide-ranging menu might feature chili with local pork, a traditional British-style beef pot pie, seafood chowder, and lamb roast. Naturally, the highlight at dessert is classic deep-dish apple pie, a splendid rendition also baked in the brick oven.

GENOA BAY CAFÉ
250-746-7621
www.genoabaycafé.com
5000 Genoa Bay Rd., Duncan, BC V9L 5Y8
Open: Lunch and dinner Friday and Saturday, brunch Sunday, dinner only Wednesday and Thursday
Price: Moderate to Expensive
Credit cards: Yes
Cuisine: West Coast Seafood
Serving: L, D
Handicapped Access: Yes
Special Features: Reservations by phone only

Hugely popular, this splendid marina café deftly navigates between classic marine pub food and West Coast modern cuisine. Prime rib, rack of lamb, and burgers are perennial favorites; wild salmon is touched up with rhubarb and scallop-leavened sticky rice. The waterside setting is hugely appealing—one of few such locations in the area—and reservations are essential as far ahead as possible, especially if you hope for an outside table on a warm summer evening.

ROCK COD CAFÉ
250-746-1550
www.rockcodcafé.com
1759 Cowichan Bay Rd., Cowichan Bay, BC V0R 1N0
Open: Daily 11 AM–9 PM
Price: Moderate
Credit cards: Yes
Cuisine: Seafood, burgers
Serving: L, D
Handicapped Access: Yes

Special Features: Monday–Friday dinner specials are economical choices.

The ambience is Formica tables and waitresses named Esther at this old-fashioned seafood restaurant on the water in Cowichan Bay Village, but the food is surprisingly good and the service is down-home friendly. Yes, there are fish-and-chips of various sorts (cod, halibut, and prawns), but you'll do much better with the excellent wild sockeye salmon burger, halibut burger, or oyster burger; the calamari is the best appetizer.

STEEPLES
250-743-1887
www.steeplesrestaurant.ca
2744 E. Shawnigan Lake Rd., Shawnigan Lake, BC V0R 2W0
Open: Daily 11 AM–9:30 PM, for brunch weekends at 10 AM
Price: Moderate to Expensive
Credit cards: Yes
Cuisine: West Coast
Serving: L, D
Handicapped Access: Yes
Special Features: Lunch and dinner both feature economical three-course fixed menus

The name derives from the heritage church in which this locally famed bistro is housed, in the middle of an old-line foothills lakeside resort village. Although the menu is distinctly West Coast, classic fine dining touches are the hallmark here, such as the traditional tableside Caesar salad service for two. The menu is heavy on seafood and steaks, from flash-fried calamari to Alberta beef sirloin and sesame-crusted seared tuna. The house wines-by-the-glass feature a dozen local Cowichan Valley vintages.

STONE SOUP INN
250-749-3848
www.stonesoupinn.ca
6755 Cowichan Lake Rd., Cowichan Lake, BC V0R 2G0
Open: 5 PM–10 PM Thursday–Saturday; closed in January
Price: Moderate to Expensive
Credit cards: Yes
Cuisine: West Coast
Serving: D
Handicapped Access: Yes
Special Features: Nightly five-course chef's menu

Although quite small (barely a half-dozen tables) this sustainably operated gourmet restaurant draws diners from afar for chef Brock Windsor's inventive and unflinchingly local menus. Windsor incorporates wild weeds in his salads, acquires his beef, chicken, greens, and oddments such as hazelnuts from local farms, and prepares only what the season's provender allows. Dishes range from a bisque made with local shrimp to local chicken roasted with fresh morels. More than any other valley restaurant, Stone Soup blends the slow food ethos with gourmet dining. The inn has two comfortable, modern **B&B suites** upstairs with a shared kitchenette—though the best food by far is downstairs.

VIGNETI ZANATTA
250-748-2338
www.zanatta.ca
5039 Marshall Rd., Duncan, BC V9L 6S3 (consult the Web site map)
Open: For lunch and early dinner, Wednesday–Sunday, April–November
Price: Moderate
Credit cards: Yes
Cuisine: Italian
Serving: L, D
Handicapped Access: Yes
Special Features: The winery's wine shop and tasting room is adjacent to the restaurant.

Taking up most of the first floor of a heritage 1903 clapboard farmhouse, this

Italian bistro, Vinoteca, is operated by one of the Cowichan Valley's oldest estate wineries. Handmade pastas, rustic-bread sandwiches, panini, and seafood specials such as steamed island mussels highlight the compact bistro menu. The tables on the farmhouse porch, overlooking the 120-acre farm's pastures and the forested ridge beyond, enjoy one of the finest settings on the entire island.

CULTURE

The waters and the trees of the valley are the focus of its cultural offerings. All the attractions below incorporate each of those two aspects—new and old.

BC FOREST DISCOVERY CENTRE

250-715-1113
www.bcforestmuseum.com
2892 Drinkwater Rd., Duncan, BC V9L 6C2 (just off Hwy. 1)
Open: Daily 10 AM—4 PM in summer, Thursday–Sunday spring and fall
Admission: Adults $15, students and seniors $13

Visitors here discover what European settlers did 150 years ago—big trees that make lots of good timber grow on the slopes of Vancouver Island. Although this complex asserts a broad-based perspective that theoretically looks at the forest as an ecosystem as well as an industrial resource, most exhibits glorify the logging past rather than the more thoughtful present. Within are huge old pieces of logging machinery, the bones of long-dead ancient

BC Forest Discovery Centre, Duncan Leslie Forsberg

Maritime Centre, Cowichan Bay Village   Leslie Forsberg

trees, pictures of downed forest giants, and so on. One room makes a passing attempt at explaining the forest as a biological community, and describing new, more sustainable approaches to what Canadians call "forestry," but it's a modest part of the still industrially oriented whole.

The complex hosts a most worthy local event each February, the **Bigleaf Maple Syrup Festival,** at which area residents and producers show off the results of tapping bigleaf maples and birches for sap in the spring, an art little known outside the area.

COWICHAN BAY MARITIME CENTRE

250-746-4955
www.classicboats.org
1761 Cowichan Bay Rd., Cowichan Bay, BC V0R 1N0
Open: Daily 9 AM–dusk
Admission: Donation urged

Solely and lovingly devoted to wooden boats, their history, beauty, and manufacture, this small bayside attraction rests on wharves above the water. Small exhibits illustrate the history of hand-built boats in the area; a shop redolent of wood shavings and spar varnish usually holds a couple boats under construction or renovation, and the craftsmen here will be happy to explain what they're doing. Strolling the long wharf to its end 262 feet (80 m) out in the bay affords a great view of the harbor and numerous boats at dock within it.

MERRIDALE CIDERY

250-743-4293 or 1-800-998-9908
www.merridalecide.com
1230 Merridale Rd., Cobble Hill, BC V0R 2Z0 (consult maps on the Web site)
Open: Daily 10:30 AM–5 PM
Admission: Free

Although it's a commercial venture, this now-famed local institution is as much an attraction as it is an orchard. Twenty years ago, Western Canada's largest cidery pioneered what has now become a growing Western industry. The extensive farm store offers numerous local agricultural products; the acres of heritage European cider apples are a wonderful locale for a stroll; the ciderhouse is open for tours daily; the tasting room introduces visitors to the farm's dozen varieties of hard cider, soft cider, and fruit brandy; the Merridale spa offers a full range of treatments. The visitor facilities serve as a gallery for local artists, and the farmhouse restaurant (Bistro La Pommeraie; see Dining) is an outstanding practitioner of sustainable valley cuisine. This is a wonderful place to spend an afternoon and evening, whether you like hard cider or not—and a great place to find out whether you do.

QUW'UTSUN' CULTURAL CENTRE

250-745-8119 or 1-877-746-8119
www.quwutsun.ca
200 Cowichan Way, Duncan, BC V9L 6P4
Open: Daily 10 AM–4 PM June–September, abridged hours fall and spring
Admission: Adults $13, students and seniors $10

Sheltered by tall old-growth cottonwoods along the bank of the burbling amber Cowichan River, this fine First Nations interpretive center offers visitors a glimpse into the traditional lifestyle of BC's now-largest First Nation (3,900 members). Visitors learn the

Suspension bridge, Cowichan River   Leslie Forsberg

Cowichan Bay Village

Tucked against a slope on the upper end of the complicated channel between Vancouver Island and Salt Spring Island, this tiny village is about a half-mile long, and has a half-dozen restaurants, a couple small inns, and a smattering of shops. Hard to imagine it is the center of international attention, but this is a world capital of the sustainability-oriented slow food movement, and in 2008 earned designation as the first "cittaslow" in North America. Chefs and producers in the area are committed to sustainable, natural production and preparation of food, and an afternoon visit here allows visitors to sample some of the best food on the island—and the most meaningful. No chemicals boost the growth or marketability of the breads,

True Grain Bakery, Cowichan Bay Leslie Forsberg

cheeses, meats, fish, and desserts on offer here. As little hydrocarbon fuel as possible is expended to bring the food here. The ingredients are created and the producers all operate largely within the 60-mile (100 km) radius often mentioned as a sustainability goal.

Within reason, of course. You can't grow coconuts on Vancouver Island, so coconut is shipped to the **Udder Guys** factory, where they flake it into ice cream made with milk and cream from local dairies; the result is some of the best ice cream on the continent (www.udderguysicecream.com). Although some grain is grown on the island (including the fabulously robust Red Fife heritage wheat), much of what master baker Bruce Stewart uses comes from organic farms in Saskatchewan; the breads, rolls, pastries, and other baked goods at **True Grain** are superb and never dull (www.true grain.ca). Literally next door, at **Hilary's Cheese and Deli**, milk from local sheep, cows, and goats is

continued next page

Pottery shop, Cowichan Bay Village Leslie Forsberg

continued from previous page

used for the savory chèvre, blue, Brie, Camembert, and other robust cheeses on offer here, along with excellent sandwiches (www.hilarycheese.com). All three of these slow food shrines are on the water, with cozy fireside seating in Hilary's, and a fine little deck out back of Udder Guys that overlooks the harbor. It's a great place to wind up a visit with an ice-cream cone . . . or two.

The boat-dotted harbor and bird-rich bay are superlative locales for a **kayak expedition**; Cowichan Bay Kayaks offers rentals and guidance (250-748-2333, www.cowichanbaykayak.com). Several midrange B&Bs offer rooms right on the water in the village, where there is also a midsize convention hotel. For complete travel information, visit www.cowichanbay.com or www.slow cowichan.com.

Kayaking near Nanaimo   Tourism Nanaimo

stories the center's totems tell, watch traditional dances and chants, and can enjoy a midday salmon fire-pit barbecue (additional charge). The gift shop offers a fine selection of indigenous art, including Cowichan sweaters, and visitors can also craft dreamcatchers under the guidance of Quw'utsun' artisans.

Nanaimo

The "Harbour City" has long been more of a pass-through municipality than a destination, a fact changing lately as its downtown revitalizes, good restaurants proliferate, and accommodations increase. A new (2011) permanent cruise-ship wharf is expected to welcome up to 30 boats a year for stopovers on their way north along the Inside Passage.

The city's waterfront is now a delightful promenade of wharfs, shoreline paths, and pocket parks overlooking the bustling harbor, protected by two barrier islands and facing southeast into the sun. At the north end of the promenade, the entrance to Sutton Park, is a man-made but nonetheless intriguing **saltwater lagoon** in which you can watch the sea-stars, anemones, fish, and other intertidal creatures that make the area's waters so colorful.

The city is famous for two somewhat novel, and completely different distinctions. It is the birthplace of the famous **Nanaimo bar**, a chocolate confection about which, like key lime pie, arguments persist regarding its origins and "correct" preparation. Numerous local bakeries and restaurants offer their versions, and the local tourism folks have conjured up the "Nanaimo Bar Trail" for tourists to learn about and, most important, sample the local signature dish (www.tourismnanaimo.com/content/nanaimo-bar). Here you will also find the "official" recipe, the winner of a community-wide 1985 contest.

Nanaimo Harbour is also the home of the world-famed **bathtub races**, first conceived to celebrate the Canada centennial in 1967. Every year since, hundreds of "tubbers" have sailed what is now a 36-mile course that starts and ends in Nanaimo, and is the highlight of the Nanaimo Marine Festival in July. For more information about the Loyal Nanaimo Bathtub Society and its race, visit www.bathtubbing.com. Between the bathtub race, the city's hub status for BC Ferries, and the large number of pubs that historically served the coal-mining community, Nanaimo is sometimes called the "Hub, Tub, and Pub City." Complete travel information is at www.tourismnanaimo.com.

Nanaimo harbor offers the same sort of quirky **tub ferry** service available in Victoria's Inner Harbour and on False Creek in Vancouver, though on a much more limited basis. Ferries run between Sutton Park, at the north end of downtown, to the city's seaplane base

Harborfront, Nanaimo   Leslie Forsberg

and to Newcastle Island (see p. 124), on a half-hour basis, weekends in April, and then daily through mid-October. For more information, visit www.nanaimoharbourferry.com. Even if you don't disembark, it's a delightful way to tour the busy harbor.

On the way into Nanaimo northbound, keep your eyes open for Yellow Point Road, the turnoff to the wonderful **Yellow Point Cranberries** farm, a family operation in a lowland, lakeside bog whose products range from the usual dried berries and jam to excellent cranberry marmalade (www.yellowpointcranberries.com). The farm and store are about 10 minutes down the road from Highway 1. And, as you loop around Nanaimo, you'll twice cross Jingle Pot Road, named after a now-defunct coal mine. And why "Jingle Pot"? Theories range from the use of a pot filled with rocks to signal time to raise a lift in the mine, to the sound of miners' pay jingling in a teapot when they stashed it after payday.

LODGING

Mainstream chain hotels still dominate the central city in Nanaimo, but the area around the city holds several of the island's best family resorts. Aside from Yellow Point, Kiwi Cove Lodge (www.kiwicovelodge.com) and Mermaid Cove (mermaidcove.ca) offer cottages and suites in the countryside in waterfront settings.

INN THE ESTUARY
250-468-9983
www.inntheestuary.com
inntheestuary@shaw.ca
2991 NW Bay Rd., Nanoose Bay, BC V9P 9J9
On Nanoose Bay, 12½ miles (20 km) north of Nanaimo
Price: Moderate; three-night minimum
Credit cards: Yes
Handicapped Access: Full
Special Features: No pets, free WiFi

Carved carefully out of marshland at the north end of the Nanoose Bay tide flats, this upscale new property has two suites overlooking the wetland wildlife sanctuary. All are spacious accommodations with electric fireplaces, private patios with soaking tubs, full kitchens, and living rooms. Bird-watching is the top activity here, with more than 100 species in the marshes, and the song of red-winged blackbirds, chitter of kingfishers, and squawk of herons accompanying morning coffee or an after-dinner soak.

PAINTED TURTLE GUESTHOUSE
250-753-4432 or 1-866-309-4432
www.paintedturtle.ca
stay@paintedturtle.ca
121 Bastion St., Nanaimo, BC V9R 3A2
In downtown Nanaimo's Old City Quarter
Price: Budget
Credit cards: Yes
Handicapped Access: Full
Special Features: Free WiFi, laundry available for guest use

The 1875 hotel in which this sparkling hostel is located offers a sturdy brick envelope for the European-style hostel within. The 20-room lodging has both family and dorm-style rooms; all the common areas are new and generously outfitted, and the Australian owners keep the ethos at the Hostelling International level—quiet, family-friendly, low-key, and affordable. It's within walking distance of everything in Nanaimo, and close enough to the BC Ferries Departure Bay dock to walk back and forth there, too.

YELLOW POINT LODGE
250-725-3100 or 1-800-333-4604
www.yellowpointlodge.com
info@wickinn.com

Snow geese, Nanoose Bay Leslie Forsberg

3700 Yellow Point Rd., Ladysmith,
BC V9G 1E8
9⅓ miles (15 km) south of Nanaimo
Price: Moderate
Credit cards: Yes
Handicapped Access: Full
Special Features: Rates include all meals
plus tea and recreation activities; bicycles
and kayaks available for guest use

Like a half-dozen other resorts throughout
BC, this classic lodge has such a long-
established clientele (often spanning generations), it needs to do little to promote or
advertise its presence. Sitting astride a
rocky point overlooking the passage
between the main island and the Gulf
Islands, the self-advertised rustic retreat
has cozy, wood-paneled rooms, all with
private bath. Outside, set around the old-
growth-forest grounds, is an eclectic collection of cottages and cabins that range
from an old boathouse to "field cabins" that

hark back to early 20th-century camp-
resorts. There's a fire warming the library
and lodge lounge, the hot overlooks the
water, a tiny swimming cove warms nicely

Relaxation at Yellow Point Lodge Leslie Forsberg

in the sun, and marine mammals are often sighted in the channel offshore. Book far, far ahead if you are seeking a high-season (June through September) vacation here.

DINING

High-style gourmet restaurants are not in character in Nanaimo, but the following bistros and pubs do focus on using local ingredients, just as slow-food advocates in Victoria and Cowichan Bay do.

ACME

250-753-0042
www.acmefoodco.ca
14 Commercial St., Nanaimo, BC V9R 5G2
Open: Daily 11 AM–11 PM
Price: Moderate to Expensive
Credit cards: Yes
Cuisine: West Coast
Serving: L, D
Handicapped Access: Yes
Special Features: Live music on weekends

This ever-bustling joint in downtown Nanaimo is several grades above a sports pub, though it devotes its basement to big-screen TVs where city residents might occasionally watch a hockey game. Upstairs, the service is exceptional, the ambience is like a ski resort bistro, and the food is simple but very well executed. The mild Asian flair is reflected in the panko-crusted fried tuna rolls, the fresh tuna salad with wasabi-lime dressing is simply superb, and seared salmon and stir-fried prawns buttress the steaks and burgers. There's an extensive sushi menu, and the wine list includes a good roster of BC vintages and craft beers and ales.

CROW & GATE PUB

250-743-1887
www.crowandgate.com
2313 Yellow Point Rd., Cedar, BC V9X 1W5
Open: Daily 11 AM–11 PM
Price: Moderate
Credit cards: Yes
Cuisine: Pub
Serving: L, D
Handicapped Access: Yes
Special Features: Nightly dinner menu offers specials in addition to pub fare.

Sequestered in the farmland countryside south of Nanaimo, built to look exactly like a pub you'd find in the south English moors, Crow & Gate is historic mostly in the sense it was the first such institution opened in BC after rules prohibiting neighborhood pubs were relaxed in 1972. The neo-Tudor design evident outside holds true within as well, where dark wood, fireplaces, and nooks and crannies are spread throughout a modest warren of dining rooms. Pegged beams, plaster walls, wood trestle tables, stonework, and British pub memorabilia are found in each room. The classic pub food ranges from oyster stew to Scotch eggs to a Stilton ploughman's lunch and, yes, steak and kidney pie. The pecan pie dessert, though not any authentic pub standard, is darn good, too. It's about as close to an English pub experience as you can get on this continent.

DINGHY DOCK MARINE PUB

250-753-2373
www.dinghydockpub.com
On Protection Island in Nanaimo Harbour (#8 Pirates Lane) Nanaimo V9R 6R1
Open: Daily 11 AM–11 PM, closed Mondays
Price: Moderate to Expensive
Credit cards: Yes
Cuisine: West Coast
Serving: L, D
Handicapped Access: Partial
Special Features: Moor your kayak right at the restaurant.

This hugely popular pub is on floating docks at the corner of the island opposite Newcastle, guarding the entrance to Nanaimo Harbour. If you don't have your own boat (or kayak), the Harbour Ferry folks will drop you off for lunch or dinner, and the chief attraction is the setting—outdoor tables are highly prized—the amiable pub atmosphere and a menu that skates an inventive line between old-fashioned and West Coast. Where else can you find a grilled iceberg salad (yep, seriously) on the same menu page as sesame-crusted halibut with shiitake vinaigrette? The dinner menu ranges from peppercorn steak to pizza, pasta, halibut burger, and a wild mushroom burger.

Mon Petit Choux

250-753-6002
www.monpetitchoux.ca
101 Commercial St., Nanaimo, BC V9R 5J6
Open: Daily 7 AM–3 PM, open weekends at 8 AM
Price: Budget
Credit cards: Yes
Cuisine: Artisan bakery

Serving: B, L
Handicapped Access: Yes
Special features: Most items are organic.

The midcentury stucco building that houses this exceptional bakery looks ever so much like an old gas station, but what's inside is what pastry fans consider fuel for the soul. Although many are the delights one might find at a French bakery, from apricot tarts to olive bread, the measurement standard is the croissants, and these are exceptional, buttery, and light. Soups, salads, sandwiches, quiches, and even puff pastry meat pies compose the lunch menu. Yes, they do have Nanaimo bars, but the other delicacies on offer here are much better.

Troller's Fish and Chips

250-741-7994
104 Front St., Nanaimo, BC V9R 5H7 (at water level in the marina)
Open: Daily 11 AM–10 PM, closed in winter
Price: Budget

Fish-and-chips at Troller's, Nanaimo Leslie Forsberg

Credit cards: Yes
Cuisine: Seafood
Serving: L, D
Handicapped Access: Yes
Special Features: The restaurant buys much
of its seafood from Nanaimo fishers.

Oh, how the fish-and-chips fans avow their
loyalty to Troller's—you might hear someone 125 miles (200 km) from Nanaimo
swear they'd happily drive to the Harbour

City for a meal here. Indeed, the battered
halibut, shrimp, clams, oysters, and salmon
are quite good; the chips are savory; the
coleslaw is great. But perhaps best of all is
the setting, a shack perched on a small
barge moored at the marina walkway.
Diners sit outside on patio furniture surrounded by flower barrels in the sun. It can
be hard to find, but one need only ask a
passerby—everyone in Nanaimo knows of
Troller's.

CULTURE

History dominates the cultural attractions in the Nanaimo area. Luckily, it is history rendered most aesthetically—the new Nanaimo Museum is a spiffy but compact exhibit hall
next to the city's convention center. And historic Newcastle Island is one of the loveliest
places in all BC.

NANAIMO MUSEUM
250-753-1821
www.nanaimomuseum.ca
100 Museum Way, Nanaimo, BC V9R 5J8
Open: Daily 10 AM–5 PM; closed Sunday September–May
Admission: $2

Opened in 2008 adjacent to the city's conference venue, the Nanaimo Museum has a wealth
of concise but vivid exhibits conveying the area's colorful history. The highlight is the century of coal mining that ended in the 1960s—the city was one of North America's leading
producers of coal, and experienced both
the prosperity and trouble (labor strife,
mine accidents) that brought. Other
exhibits detail aboriginal life before the
Hudson's Bay Company arrived in 1853,
and what daily life has been like for
Nanaimo citizens since.

NEWCASTLE ISLAND
250-754-7893
www.newcastleisland.ca
In Nanaimo Harbour; access via Nanaimo
Harbour Ferries
Open: Daily; ferries run 9 AM–9 PM in
summer
Admission: free

This deliriously lovely small island was the
home of a popular early 20th-century

The author at Kanaka Bay, Newcastle Island
Leslie Forsberg

Newcastle Island shoreline   Leslie Forsberg

Canadian Pacific resort; when that fell into decline after World War II, the citizens of
Nanaimo had the foresight to buy it and preserve it as a park and 1955. It was turned over
to the province in 1961, and today is a marine park that provides an enchanting day-trip
idyll for Nanaimo residents and visitors. The south end of the island is a beautiful expanse
of meadow dotted with huge old Garry oaks, arbutus, bigleaf maples, and Douglas firs; it's
one of the best and largest such oak prairies this far north. A large walk-in campground
spreads through the woods next to the meadow. A bustling colony of colorful, musical purple martins, one of the largest in Western Canada, greets island visitors at the dock.
Inland a bit is a large event hall, the Pavilion, the last remnant of the old resort, with con-
cessions and modest visitor facilities. From here, broad paths lead off into interior copses
of old-growth forest, past a placid inland lake, and back around to a small cove, Kanaka
Bay, with tide pools, lovely wading, herons and cormorants, and outrageous vistas across
the Strait of Georgia to the mainland Coast Range's snowy peaks.

   Newcastle often is near the top of lists cataloging favorite BC parks. The quaint
Nanaimo Harbour Ferries provide access to the island for passengers (and bikes). Passage
is $9. Dogs ride free, but the island is a strictly on-leash area (www.nanaimoharbour
ferry.com).

RECREATION

New Zealand and Nanaimo fight for claim to the title of bungee-jumping birthplace. No matter who actually deserves credit, there's no doubt bungee jumping has been taking place here for decades and a bridge over the Nanaimo River built in 1990 expressly for the purpose was one of the first formal sites in North America, if not the first. Hiking, biking, and fishing are also all popular local recreation activities.

One worthy low-key adventure for travelers is renting kayaks in Nanaimo Harbour to paddle out to **Newcastle Island** (p. 124). Alberni Outpost offers rentals near the BC Ferries Departure Bay terminal at 1840 Stewart Ave. (250-754-6626, www.alberni outpost.com).

WILDPLAY ELEMENT PARK

250-755-1196 or 1-888-716-7374
www.wildplay.com/nanaimo
35 Nanaimo River Rd. Nanaimo, BC V9X 1S5

What began as a simple bungee jump has grown into a recreational complex that incorporates elements ranging from zip lines to ropes courses to a device they call the King Swing, a tandem ride that is

Monkido element, WildPlay Park   Boomer Jerritt/ Tourism Vancouver Island

advertised as an even more intense thrill than bungee jumping. The Monkido tree course is an obstacle course in the trees, designed to teach participants personal confidence while they have fun essaying various challenges in the forest canopy. The venue creators have carefully engineered their devices to rest gently in the trees, with cushioning to prevent damage. Activities range from $39 to $89 per person.

Parksville/Qualicum

Mid-island's longest-established vacation district, less than an hour north of Nanaimo, consists of a multitude of family resorts facing broad sand beaches. Lodgings range from funky log cabins to glistening new midrise buildings with condo-style rental apartments. One of Canada's highest-profile spas is here, as are half-century-old campgrounds, resorts whose dozen cabins are booked the same two weeks every year for generations by one family, and highway motels that have struggled to adapt to the opening of the Inland Island Highway a decade ago, which pulled travelers off the old shoreline highway. The two communities here, Parksville and Qualicum Beach, are known together as "Oceanside," an inarguable description. It's old school resort-land here, with a few modern enhancements. For complete travel information, visit www.visitparksvillequalicumbeach.com.

LODGING

Funky log-cabin resorts, highway motels, campgrounds, spiffy glass-and-steel condo complexes—Oceanside has it all these days, including a massive spa, Tigh-Na-Mara, which is famous across Canada. Aside from that, other major resorts, all of fairly comparable quality and character, are Beach Acres (www.beachacresresort.com); Pacific Shores, a newer condo development (www.pacific-shores.com); Ocean Sands (www.oceansandsresort.ca); and The Shorewater, another condo complex (www.shorewaterresort.com). All are comfortable, friendly, priced fairly, and sizeable; many are what is known in Canada as "strata" resorts, where specific units are owned by private individuals but available in a resort-wide rental pool. All of them rely on these virtues above all: warm sandy beaches, fresh salt breezes, and reliable summer sun.

FREE SPIRIT SPHERES

250-757-9445
www.freespiritspheres.com
tom@freespiritspheres.com
420 Horne Lake Rd., Qualicum Beach, BC
V9K 1Z7
On Qualicum Bay, 18⅔ miles (30 km) north
of Parksville
Price: Moderate to Expensive
Credit cards: Yes
Handicapped Access: No
Special Features: No pets, adults only
(16 and older)

From outside they look like large, wooden seed-pod orbs, hanging from the trees. Inside, they are much like compact staterooms in a small yacht, with fold-down tables and beds, trimmed with warm burnished wood. The spheres hang 10 to 15 feet (3 to 4.5 m) off the ground, reached by wooden stairs. Yes, you do have to clamber down if you need a restroom. The novelty of these lodgings has earned Free Spirit a lot

Hotel in the trees, Free Spirit Spheres   Leslie Forsberg

of notice, but they are obviously not for everyone. Guests at this "treehouse for adults" enjoy the sense of peace and tranquility that comes from sleeping within nature's surrounds, the spheres gently swaying in the breeze.

TIGH-NA-MARA

250-248-2072 or 1-800-663-7373
www.tigh-na-mara.com
info@tigh-na-mara.com
1155 Resort Dr., Parksville, BC V9P 2E3
Price: Moderate to Expensive
Credit cards: Yes
Handicapped Access: Full
Special Features: Pets welcome, free WiFi and local calls, bicycles available for guest use

Once this was an old-line family resort on the shores of Rathtrevor Beach, its rustic lodge cottages bustling with kids, parents, and grandparents from end of school in June to start of school in September. That atmosphere remains the foundation of this midcentury complex, but it added a completely new facet a decade ago when it opened one of Canada's largest and most comprehensive spas, along with newer cottages adjoining the latter. The Grotto Spa encompasses 20,000 square feet, with 18 treatment rooms, a spa-food tapas café, pedicure thrones (whatever those may be) and the pièce de résistance, the 2,500-square-foot namesake grotto, a manufactured stone soaking complex with a waterfall, atrium, huge mineral-water pool, cold plunge, and hot tub. The firelit relaxation lounge offers blissful meditation space for guests to recline following treatments that range from a hot chocolate hydro bath (seriously) to a peppermint oil pedicure. So today, while multigenerational families enjoy a classic sand-and-splash vacation in the now-heritage log cabins, urban office workers head north from Victoria or Vancouver simply to spend a day or two in the spa and relax in a suite next door. The resort restaurant features West Coast cuisine such as island pork chops with an apple cider–mustard glaze. There's an indoor (very noisy) pool; outdoor recreation ranges from volleyball and tennis to strolling the beach. Few places straddle old and new as expertly as Tigh-Na-Mara. By the way, the name is not indigenous at all—it means "house by the sea" in Gaelic.

DINING

There are few if any notable restaurants in the Oceanside region. The Cedar dining room at Tigh-Na-Mara focuses ably on sustainable West Coast cuisine. So does **The Landing Grill** at Pacific Shores (www.landinggrill.com); the restaurant's 7,133-gallon (27,000 L) aquarium, which contains salmon from the small resort hatchery, is one more among the "Seven Wonders of Oceanside." It's big, folks.

CULTURE

The Oceanside region has conjured up what it calls the "Seven Wonders of Oceanside," which range from a miniature golf complex, Paradise Fun Park (p. 132), to one of the best-known old-growth forest preserves on the West Coast, Cathedral Grove. That illustrates as well as anything the wide spectrum of the visitor attractions here—in the morning you can wander amid thousand-year-old forest giants, at noon you can putt a golf ball between windmill blades, and then in midafternoon you can head to the beach for sand castle–building.

CATHEDRAL GROVE/MACMILLAN PROVINCIAL PARK

250-474-1336
www.env.gov.bc.ca/bcparks
15½ miles (25 km) east of Qualicum Beach on Alberni Highway (Hwy. 4)
Open: Daily dawn–dusk
Admission: free

This magnificent old-growth forest is perhaps the best known in Canada, lying right along a major tourist highway and enjoying a memorable name. Cathedral-like it is indeed, though some of the ancient trees here were felled in a massive 1997 windstorm.

In the woods, Cathedral Grove Leslie Forsberg

Park managers have left many of the fallen giants to illustrate the authentic nature of old growth, which is far more diverse and changeable than the silent, eternal ranks of broad tree boles often imagined by the public. The huge Douglas firs, Western red cedars and Western hemlocks here range up to 800 years old; one measures more than 30 feet (9 m) in circumference. Filtered sun dapples the forest floor, and the corrugated bark of the firs is many inches thick. Although quiet paths lead back into the forest (especially on the north side), the situation near the road can approach pandemonium, especially on summer afternoons and weekends. The park's original 136 acres were donated to the province in 1944 by H. R. MacMillan, a BC timber magnate.

Parking is confined to a fairly narrow shoulder along the road, as they'd have to cut down old-growth trees to make more room for cars. Approach the area slowly, please; and for heaven's sake don't stop in the middle of the highway in the hope a parking space will come free. No smoking. I'll repeat that: *Do not smoke.*

HORNE LAKE CAVES PROVINCIAL PARK

250-248-7829
www.hornelake.com
info@tbgf.org
3900 Horne Lake Caves Rd., 7½ miles
(12 km) west of Highway 19 on Horne
Lake Road
Open: Daily 10 AM–5 PM late June–
September, abridged hours winter,
spring, and fall
Admission: $3 day use for park; cave
tour prices vary

True caverns are a rarity on the Pacific Coast, though there are hundreds of small caves on Vancouver Island. Unlike so many well-known tourist-attraction caverns, these are largely undeveloped—no huge spotlights hung on the cave ceilings, no poured concrete pathways and steps. The cave was protected as a provincial park in 1971 at the behest of island spelunking groups. Today most visitors join guided tours for which they are given spelunker headlamps and led through the caverns, which have a modest amount of cave

World Parrot Refuge

Long-lived, social, beautiful and intelligent, parrots are among the most sought and most mistreated of human-domesticated animals. They can also be demanding, noisy, expensive and cranky, and all too many humans who think they'd like one as a companion soon decide they can't be bothered. And then, like millions of dogs and cats, they are tossed aside as if so much pointless flotsam. Rescued by animal protection people, many of these abandoned birds have wound up here at a simultaneously heart-warming, and heart-breaking, facility that's one of the province's most memorable visitor attractions.

More than 800 parrots live in the buildings that compose the refuge, and were there room for them, no doubt hundreds or thousands more could be brought here. Gaily colored in vivid greens, reds, yellows, blues, and purples, they are among nature's most magnificent sights. Birds greet visitors amiably and vociferously, and as you wander amid the aviaries you quickly ascertain just how much personality these birds have—and how dependent they are on contact with their own kind, and people. Most of the birds live in free-flight enclosures within the 23,000-square-foot facility, and it's heartening to watch them move about freely.

Few visitor attractions in the world are as worthy as this one. Admission is $12, but few people visit without leaving an extra donation. The refuge is a few minutes off Highway 19 as it starts to climb through the mountains toward Port Alberni. It's open daily 10 AM–4 PM, at 2116 Alberni Highway, Coombs (250-248-5194; worldparrotrefuge.com).

Orphans at home, World Parrot Refuge
Leslie Forsberg

features such as stalactites. Tours, conducted by a private adventure company, range from a basic three-hour trip, to a five-hour adventure that includes rappelling inside the cave. Individual spelunking is permitted but is for experts only. The surrounding park has a small lake, picnic area and other facilities. Tour reservations are required fall, winter, and spring.

MILNER GARDENS
250-752-8573
www.viu.ca/milnergardens
2179 West Island Highway (Hwy. 19A), Qualicum Beach, BC V9K 1G1
Open: Daily 9 AM–dusk, May–September
Admission: Adults $10, students $6

Like Butchart near Victoria, this 70-acre seaside estate amply demonstrates the gardening potential of the island's balmy maritime climate. It was largely the mid-20th-century creation of a British aristocrat, Veronica Milner, wife of a prominent local lawyer. Mrs. Milner carefully blended horticultural plantings into an old-growth Douglas fir ecosystem, and the result today is 10 acres of garden and 60 acres of forest preserve. Azaleas, rhododendrons, and other flowering shrubs form the background for verdant lawns and perennial, annual, and bulb flower beds. In the distance, the snowy peaks of Coast Range present a wild backdrop. Bald eagles haunt the firs, blue herons hunt the shore; songbirds carol during their island summer visits. The magnificent Milner manor house is a shingled bungalow meant to mirror some aspects of a Ceylonese tea plantation house; its tearoom offers tea and pastries ($7.25) in the afternoon.

Mrs. Milner died in 1998 at her garden estate; it's now owned by Vancouver Island University and operated as a nonprofit local attraction.

RECREATION

Several of BC's most popular parks lie along the Oceanside strip; in summer months all those below offer an experience that can range from bustling to just plain crowded. If you're there during peak periods, best to plan your visit before noon, and midweek if possible. If you're camping . . . reserve far ahead.

ENGLISHMAN RIVER FALLS PROVINCIAL PARK
250-474-1336
www.env.gov.bc.ca/bcparks
8 miles (13 km) southwest of Parksville on Errington Road
$3 day-use fee

The two medium-size waterfalls here are visually striking for their setting in a deep canyon of old-growth forest. The lower falls plunge into a large pool that's a popular swimming hole in July and August; the campground serves as a de facto overflow facility for the huge but perennially full Rathtrevor Beach park. Campsite reservations can be made (with a private concessionaire) through the park Web site, or by calling 1-800-689-9025. It's best to reserve as far ahead as possible for summer travel.

LITTLE QUALICUM FALLS PROVINCIAL PARK
250-474-1336
www.env.gov.bc.ca/bcparks
11⅞ miles (19 km) west of Parksville on Highway 4, toward Port Alberni
$3 day-use fee

Little Qualicum Falls Provincial Park

Embracing the southern end of Cameron Lake and the outfall from it, this popular park's waterfall plunges into a rocky gorge west of Parksville. Swimming, fishing, and hiking occupy visitors; the lake is well known for windsurfing with the steady afternoon thermal breezes that sweep the water. Campsite reservations can be made (with a private concessionaire) through the park Web site, or by calling 1-800-689-9025. It's best to reserve as far ahead as possible for summer travel.

PARADISE FUN PARK
250-248-6612
www.paradisefunpark.net
375 West Island Hwy., Parksville, BC V9P 1A1
Open 9:30 AM–10 PM, abridged hours spring and fall, closed October–March

Not one but two lavish miniature golf course layouts await visitors to this Qualicum Beach complex right on the old Island Highway. Yes, miniature golf is an old-school activity more aligned with station wagons than with modern travel, but these courses are reasonably inventive and just plain fun. The older, "Surf 'n' Turf" layout includes a Victorian mansion, waterwheel, church, and lighthouse. Its newer companion, Treasure Island, fulfills its pirate theme, with galleons, skeletons, a cave, and such. The complex also includes bumper boats and a café. It's, ahem, one among the "Seven Wonders of Oceanside." Really.

RATHTREVOR BEACH PROVINCIAL PARK
250-474-1336
www.env.gov.bc.ca/bcparks
1⅞ miles (3 km) south of Parksville on Highway 19A
$3 day-use fee

Sunrise near Rathtrevor Beach Leslie Forsberg

Islands in the Salish Sea Leslie Forsberg

Occupying an 860-acre portion of the point guarding its namesake bay, Rathtrevor Beach is a complete summer vacation park with beaches, playgrounds, hiking trails, old-growth woods, picnic facilities, hot showers, a nature center, and interpretive programs, all serving a massive campground and picnic area. Windsurfing, canoeing, swimming, and beach-combing occupy visitors, including strollers who wander over from nearby private resorts such as Tigh-Na-Mara. Campsite reservations can be made (with a private concessionaire) through the park Web site, or by calling 1-800-689-9025. Best to reserve as far ahead as possible for summer travel; reservations are required in July and August.

Comox Valley

Holding down the north end of the "banana belt" coast on the east shore of Vancouver Island, this area, composed of the twin cities of Comox and Courtenay, enjoys warm summers and generally mild winters. In Comox in late March, residents may be skiing in the morning at Mount Washington and teeing off at one of the valley's golf courses that afternoon. In Alberta in late March, residents might be . . . shoveling snow in the morning at minus 4°F (minus 20°C), and shoveling new wind-driven drifts that afternoon at 14°F (minus 10°C). So, when WestJet Airlines added direct service between Comox and Calgary and Edmonton, the region was transformed into a retirement center for prairie denizens looking for a second home to spend wheat or oil money on. The result is a burgeoning small metro area with an excellent airport, a pleasant setting, a wealth of recreational opportunities, surrounded by a fine community of resorts. Complete Comox Valley travel information is at www.discovercomoxvalley.com.

Just south of the Comox area, Fanny Bay is the ferry terminal affording access to **Denman Island** and **Hornby Island**, two of the most distinctive and memorable of the many islands in the Salish Sea.

Denman, first in line and far more accessible from Vancouver Island, is a haven for artists and food crafters; this is the home of regionally famed **Denman Island Chocolate**, a dandy gourmet product found on the shelves at natural food markets throughout the Pacific Northwest. Tours are available Saturday afternoons *by reservation only* online (www.denmanislandchocolate.com) or by calling 1-866-335-2418. Two small shoreline provincial parks, Fillongley and Boyle Point, offer hiking, beachcombing, wildlife watching, and limited camping. Travel information for the island is at www.denmanisland.com.

Hornby Island is unique unto itself, a remote but thoroughly settled haven in the Salish Sea which holds semimythical status among island aficionados and New Agers. The island is famous as one of the most recycling-conscious places on earth (see Culture), and hosts a hugely popular August music and arts festival for which lodging reservations must be made months in advance. It's the sort of place where roads detour around big old-growth trees and pastoral farms look like movie sets, tucked against the flanks of the island's 1,080-foot (330 m) central mountain, Mount Geoffrey. One midsize family resort, a popular provincial park, and a few lovely B&Bs provide lodging (www.hornbyisland.com).

Ferries depart roughly once an hour to Denman; every other hour from between Denman and Hornby. Passage to both islands is provided by BC Ferries (www.bcferries .com). While you're waiting on the big island, the seafood store by the ferry dock offers **Fanny Bay oysters**, a divine treat: buy a dozen, grab an oyster knife, head down to the shore, and shuck them open on the beach.

Chrome Island, Deep Bay Boomer Jerritt/Tourism Vancouver Island

LODGING

Accommodations in the Comox Valley range from small B&Bs to modern resort developments to classic collections of cottages along the waterfront, especially south of Courtenay along the old Island Highway, now 19A. Complete lodging information is at the tourism Web site, www.discover comoxvalley.com.

KINGFISHER RESORT
250-338-0058 or 1-800-663-7929
www.kingfisherspa.com
info@kingfisherspa.com
4330 Island Highway South, Courtenay, BC V9N 9R9
On Hwy. 19A, 2½ miles (4 km) south of Courtenay
Price: Moderate to Expensive
Credit cards: Yes
Handicapped Access: Full
Special Features: Pets welcome; free WiFi; rates include access to spa pool, sauna, and hot tub

While it's certainly a lovely enough waterfront resort, with elegantly furnished rooms, suites, and villas overlooking the water south of Courtenay, what distinguishes this classic resort is its spa—in particular, the spa's unique **Pacific Mist Hydropath**, a glorious venue in which guests experience hot and cold waterfalls, therapy baths, steam rooms, and more during a half-hour "stroll" through the path, which melds local materials such as driftwood and beach stone into its construction. There's nothing quite like it in North America; the spa also offers a full range of ordinary treatments, and there is no extra charge for lodge guests to use the public spa facilities such as the hot tub. The resort's dining room is one of the premier practitioners of West Coast cuisine in the Comox Valley, with a lovely vantage point overlooking the Strait of Georgia. Chef Troy

Fogarty's creations include savory variations on local seafood, such as spot prawns, scallops, and Dungeness crab with lobster oil, and seared halibut with tomato and fennel. By all means avail yourself of a package that includes a trip through the Hydropath and dinner at the restaurant. Kingfisher also offers ski packages for winter visitors—trust me, an hour in the spa after a day on the slopes at Mount Washington is divine.

LA PAUSE B&B
250-703-4725 or 1-866-703-4725
www.lapausebb.com
info@lapausebb.com
540 Salisbury Rd., Courtenay, BC V9N 9M2
2½ miles (4 km) from downtown Courtenay
Price: Moderate; discounts for multi-night stays
Credit cards: Yes
Handicapped Access: Partial
Special Features: No pets, free WiFi

With a swimming pool, fireplace-warmed library, and hot and infrared sauna, this seems more like a small inn than a B&B. The three rooms are decorated in Southwest or Mediterranean colors, with vivid colors such as mustard and teal providing a welcome relief from the timber-lodge theme so prevalent on the island. Hearty breakfasts include such creations as bacon and Cheddar scones; an art gallery on the grounds features the splendid photographs of host David Innes.

OLD HOUSE VILLAGE HOTEL
250-703-0202 or 1-888-703-0202
www.oldhousevillage.com
reservations@oldhousevillage.com
1730 Riverside Lane, Courtenay, BC V9N 8C7
Price: Moderate

Credit cards: Yes
Handicapped Access: Full
Special Features: Pets welcome, free WiFi, bicycles available for guest use

Despite the name, there's nothing old about this immensely handsome, newly built complex of suites along the river in central Courtenay. Extensive use of Douglas fir timber and trim lends a warm air to the décor; subtle earth tones such as sage and sand mellow the atmosphere. All the suites have fireplaces and kitchens. The spa, outdoor pool, and fitness center offer big-hotel amenities. The location is handy to downtown dining and shopping, about 20 minutes from the airport, and a half-hour from Mount Washington; the resort offers ski packages in winter.

OUTER ISLAND R&R
250-335-2379
www.outerisland.bc.ca
retreat@outerisland.bc.ca
4785 DePape Rd., Hornby Island,
BC V0R 1Z0
Near Tribune Bay
Price: Expensive; weekly stays only in summer
Credit cards: Yes
Handicapped Access: Partial
Special Features: No pets; horseshoes, tennis, and croquet on site

This delightful small inn is part of a compact, 14-acre family farm on Hornby Island, which the indigenous people called Outer Island. Guests stay in one of two farm cottages, each with two bedrooms, kitchenettes, sitting rooms, and porches. The heritage orchards spread blossom scent across the property in spring; in summer, the swimming pool lends a resort air. In summer, guests are offered hearty breakfasts that rely heavily on the farm's own eggs, fruit, vegetables, and other provender. Kids are welcome to visit the livestock barns to pet the resident sheep and goats.

Visits between early September and late June are almost half the price of those July through Labor Day.

RIDING FOOL HOSTEL
250-336-8250 or 1-888-323-FOOL
www.ridingfool.com
info@ridingfool.com
2705 Dunsmuir St., Cumberland,
BC V0R 1S0
In "downtown" Cumberland
Price: Very Economical
Credit cards: Yes
Handicapped Access: Partial
Special Features: No pets, free WiFi, cruiser bicycles available for guest use

Riding Fool doesn't fool around—the basic dorm-room bunk beds are just $29 a night. (Private rooms are $60.) Housed in an 1895 building that was a hardware store, it's unequivocally oriented to the mountain biking scene that comprises Cumberland's new identity. There is a large communal kitchen, a sitting room with a woodstove, and a knowledgeable staff up on all the latest trail information. The best local café, **Tarbell's** (breakfast and lunch till late afternoon, 250-336-8863), is in the same building, with good coffee, baked goods, sandwiches, and Mediterranean food. Also in the complex is **Dodge City Cycles** (250-336-2200, www.dodgecitycycles.com), offering rentals, maps, gear, and most important guidance for cycling visitors.

SEABREEZE LODGE
250-335-2321 or 1-888-516-2321
www.seabreezelodge.com
info@ seabreezelodge.com
Big Tree 3-2 (Fowler Road), Hornby Island,
BC V0R 1Z0
1⅞ miles (3 km) from the Co-op store
4-way stop
Price: Moderate
Credit cards: Yes
Handicapped Access: Full

Special Features: Pets welcome, summer rates include all meals

You couldn't ask for a more definitive example of a classic island family resort than Seabreeze. The complex rests quietly on a broad expanse of meadow atop a small bluff overlooking the Strait of Georgia. Dogs greet visitors, the clop of tennis balls sounds nearby, and sea breezes do indeed rustle the fir boughs on the bluff. The 16 cabins and cottages vary from funky to comfortable; some have kitchens, many have bunk beds, most have ocean views. Hiking, beachcombing, and biking the island occupy visitors. The resort has croquet, badminton (remember that?), volleyball, and a playground. High style is represented by the bluff-edge hot tub and infrared sauna. The lodge dining room is probably the best place for dinner on Hornby, and focuses on hearty natural foods such as pastas, salads, soups, roasts, and fish.

SHIPS POINT INN

250-335-1004 or 1-877-742-1004
www.shipspointinn.com
info@ shipspointinn.com
7584 Ships Point Rd., Fanny Bay,
BC V0R 1W0
On Fanny Bay, 1⅞ miles (3 km) south of the Denman Island ferry terminal
Price: Moderate
Credit cards: Yes
Handicapped Access: Partial
Special Features: No pets, free WiFi, breakfast included, evening suppers occasionally available

Aside from the marvelous setting, surrounded by water on three sides on a small point in the channel between the main island and Denman, this boutique inn offers guests lavish lodgings at less-lavish rates, with spacious suites in the waterfront main house. Cheery Mediterranean colors such as mustard and sunflower set the color theme in the rooms, all of which have sitting areas. The hot tub overlooks the water, oysters on the beach are available for the picking (be sure to check for safety), and the overall atmosphere combines elegance and relaxation. Hearty breakfasts often include Fanny Bay oysters, grown in the waters right outside the inn.

DINING

Growth in the Comox Valley hasn't yet brought any corollary development in the dining industry. The best local gourmet restaurants are likely the dining room at Kingfisher Resort (p. 135) and at Crown Isle (p. 139). Other popular eateries include the **Atlas Café** (250 6th St., 250-338-9838, atlascafé.ca) a downtown establishment known for large breakfast platters, a bustling atmosphere, and a broad bistro menu from pastas to steaks. **Blackfin Pub** has a waterfront location and offers pub classics ranging from fish-and-chips to barbecued ribs (132 Port August St., 250-339-5030, www.blackfinpub.com). **Zen Zero** is a fully committed vegan café and juice bar with daily curries and soups and an extensive raw-food menu (407 5th St., 250-338-0571, zenzero.ca).

CULTURE

The **Courtenay & District Museum** offers a compact look at the region's past, including an exhibit devoted to the surprise 1988 discovery of a major fossil deposit near the city by two local kids (207 Fourth Street, 250-334-0686, www.courtenaymuseum.ca). The **Comox Air Force Museum** displays the history of the huge Canadian Forces air base here (today sharing its grounds with the Comox Airport). Artifacts and exhibits depict the

Street scene, Courtenay, Comox Glacier in distance   Boomer Jerritt/Tourism Vancouver Island

base's importance during World War II, and a dozen heritage aircraft please old-plane buffs (www.comoxairforcemuseum.ca).

HORNBY ISLAND RECYCLING DEPOT

250-335-0550
www.hirra.ca/Recycle
On Central Road, mid-island about 4⅓ miles (7 km) from the ferry terminal
Open: Daily 9 AM–1 PM Thursday–Sunday
Admission: free

Where else but on Hornby Island would the community recycling facility be a visitor attraction? Because it is so expensive to ship things (especially garbage) on or off the island, Hornby's 900 or so residents gleefully embrace what TV producers would call extreme reuse. The actual containers devoted to recycling are the lesser part of this center. The bulk of the facility is devoted to a huge storehouse to which islanders bring unwanted goods—clothing, furniture, books, tools, bicycles, appliances, sewing supplies, cookware, whatever—available to reacquisition by fellow residents. The island recycles or reuses more than 70 percent of its waste stream (the North American average is well below 50 percent). That success has brought the depot international attention from news organizations and other communities wanting to know how it works. It's worth a visit not only to marvel at the social consciousness that has made it so successful, but to imagine what might be possible in your community.

RECREATION

The tiny town of **Cumberland**, a former coal-mining center nicknamed Dodge City, has transformed itself into a mountain-bike riding capital. Hundreds of miles of single-track trail wind through the foothills around the town, which has a healthy helping of bike shops, small cafés, and coffee shops to serve the riders. Fans of the village's new persona pledge featly to the "Republic of Cumberland" and adorn themselves with T-shirts avowing their loyalty. Many, but not all, of the trails—"Bucket of Blood," "Black Hole," "Buggered," and so on—are for serious riders only. But kinder, gentler routes have been plotted along decommissioned logging roads, and hiking and swimming in local lakes also offers summer respite. In winter, some of the trails switch over to Nordic uses. In town, **Dodge City Cycles** (250-336-2200, www.dodgecitycycles.com) offers rentals, maps, gear, and most important guidance for cycling visitors. The **Cumberland Museum** offers a colorful look at the town's coal-mining history, including its once-huge Chinatown, in the middle of town (www.cumberlandmuseum.ca).

For information on Cumberland's visitor services, visit cumberlandbc.org. The Comox Valley mountain biking community offers complete information on trails and such at www.cvmtb.com.

CROWN ISLE RESORT GOLF AND COUNTRY CLUB
250-703-5000 or 1-888-338-8439
www.crownisle.com
399 Clubhouse Dr., Courtenay, BC V9N 9G3

This huge development (831 acres) near the Comox Airport wraps a championship golf course around a condo development in which 90 of the units are in a public rental pool.

Mountain biking near Cumberland   Boomer Jerritt/Tourism Vancouver Island

One- and two-bedroom and loft suites have full kitchenettes; the resort dining room, Silverado Grill, offers excellent West Coast cuisine featuring local oysters and seafood, as well as steaks. The course is a challenging but user-friendly layout wending its way through tall firs; water is in play on 8 of the 18 holes. Crown Isle collaborates with Mount Washington to offer late-spring ski-and-golf packages that test the ambition and energy of even the most dedicated amateur athletes.

HELLIWELL PROVINCIAL PARK
250-474-1336
www.env.gov.bc.ca/bcparks
On Hornby Island at the end of St. John's Point Road
$3 day-use fee

A 7,000-acre preserve that embraces the rocky headland east of Tribune Bay, this gorgeous park holds one of the rarest ecosystems in British Columbia. Here Douglas firs grown in poor soil and arid conditions are centuries old but barely 100 feet tall. Here are grassy swales beneath the trees that look like European parklands. Here are wave-tossed pebble bluffs with erosion pockets that look sculpted by pastry chefs. The day-use-only park has a 3-mile (5 km) loop trail that begins in thick, young woods, takes hikers to the old growth and past a rocky point, then back along the bluffs past red-trunked arbutus groves. Sea lions bark at a rookery about 330 feet (100 m) offshore at the southernmost point. The Coast Range's snowy mainland peaks shimmer in the distance. Not often visited by off-islanders, this park is one of BC's greatest treasures.

Helliwell Provincial Park, Hornby Island   Leslie Forsberg

Island Range peaks Leslie Forsberg

MOUNT WASHINGTON ALPINE RESORT
250-338-1386 or 1-888-231-1499
www.mountwashington.ca
11 miles (18 km) west of Highway 19 on Strathcona Parkway

One of the West Cost's very finest winter sports resorts hugs a mountain outside Comox, in sight of the Vancouver Island Range but separate from it. Here, the weather is better than on the island's west side, but snowfalls are prodigious—Mount Washington often wins the North American ski resort annual snowfall title with more than 3,000 cm (1,000 inches) of powder each season. And, yes, it is powder—the resort's relatively high base elevation and more northerly latitude bring it drier snow than other coastal ski areas, such as those outside Vancouver or down in Washington state. While there is ample expert territory here on the far side of the resort in the Outback, the highlights for most families are the broad and forgiving novice territory on the southwest side of the mountain, and the vast intermediate terrain beneath the Hawk and Eagle Express chairs. At the base of the ski mountain is a sensational network of scenic Nordic trails stretching into Strathcona Provincial Park. Views throughout the resort are amazing, with several spots from which one can see both the nearby peaks of the Vancouver Island Range and the distant spires of the mainland's Coast Range. The season ends in early April, more for lack of interest than lack of snow.

Ample on-the-mountain accommodations range from hostel rooms to kitchenette studios and suites to vacation home rentals; most are available through the resort's Web site booking engine. Several dining rooms (notably in the Raven Lodge, at the Nordic area) offer hearty food, with fondue dinners on weekends. Mount Washington collaborates with

Chairlift, Mount Washington

Crown Isle to offer late-spring ski-and-golf packages that test the ambition and energy of even the most dedicated amateur athletes. Several other Comox Valley resorts offer ski-and-lodging packages that include a shuttle ride to the mountain.

TRIBUNE BAY PROVINCIAL PARK
250-474-1336
www.env.gov.bc.ca/bcparks
Hornby Island, on Central Road past the Island Co-op
$3 day-use fee

The half-mile curve of broad white sand that is this park's central feature is nicknamed "Little Hawaii"—a jest that is half-true in July and August when the south-facing bay's shallow, emerald waters warm into near-balmy temperatures, the sands heat up, and hundreds of families flock here to swim, sunbathe, play in the sand and generally act as if they were 2,000 miles south. Tall cottonwoods back the park, with a small picnic area and, just to enhance the resort ambience, a tennis court. No palm trees, though. No camping, either.

"Little Hawaii"—Tribune Bay beach, Hornby Island   Leslie Forsberg

Cedar plank salmon roast, Cortes Island Boomer Jerritt/ Tourism Vancouver Island

Campbell River

The self-declared "salmon capital of the world" has competition for that title—Ketchikan, Alaska, for one—but a valid claim to it. Anglers have been streaming here since the early 20th century to ply the waters of the nearby Discovery Passage and Discovery Islands for big fish. All five species of Pacific salmonids spawn in the Campbell River: chinook (king), coho (silver), pink and chum salmon, and steelhead trout. Sockeye (red) salmon are plentiful as well. Waterfront resorts that started as tent complexes in the Roaring Twenties now are spiffy lodges or cabin collections to which wealthy vacationers fly in on floatplanes from Vancouver, Victoria, or Seattle. The city's downtown has a collection of mainstream chain hotels for travelers just passing through; a number of old-line family resorts line the water south of town.

Complete travel information for the city and the region is at www.northcentral island.com.

LODGING

The major resorts in the Campbell River area are first and foremost fishing lodges, though the best of these have added facilities and amenities to appeal to nonangling travelers (such as spouses).

DOLPHINS RESORT
250-287-3066 or 1-800-891-0287
www.dolphinsresort.com
fish@dolphinsresort.com
4125 Discovery Dr., Campbell River, BC V9W 4X6
Just off Hwy. 19, 1¼ miles (2 km) north of Campbell River
Price: Expensive
Credit cards: Yes
Handicapped Access: Full
Special Features: Pets welcome, free WiFi, breakfast included

Fronting the same Discovery Passage waterfront as the bigger and better-known Painter's Lodge next door, this small, low-key resort consists of lovely cedar cottages and a heritage timber lodge facing the water. Although Dolphins, too, is devoted to fishing, it has a more intimate atmosphere, and many couples repair here for a quiet getaway in a cabin with a private hot tub. The cottages are cedar cabins with antique lodge-style furnishings, the on-deck private hot tubs a modern enhancement. Lodging and fishing packages are good bargains, as is the package that rolls in salmon snorkeling (p. 146) for those who'd rather look than hook.

PAINTER'S LODGE
250-286-1102 or 1-800-663-7090
www.painterslodge.com
info@painterslodge.com
1625 McDonald Rd., Campbell River, BC
V9W 4S5
Just off Hwy. 19, 1¼ miles (2 km) north of Campbell River
Price: Moderate
Credit cards: Yes
Handicapped Access: Full
Special Features: Pets welcome, free WiFi, children under 12 free

The premier fishing lodge in Campbell River is just north of the city, poised right along the Discovery Passage in which so many millions of salmon have been caught over the decades. The lodge itself is a handsome timber structure whose rooms, suites, and cabins all feature light pastel colors, warm wood trim, and fir and spruce furniture. Artwork, naturally, focuses on fish and fishing and, yes, the lodge décor includes antique rods, creels, and such. The ambience does retain the flavor, for good or ill, of the era when wealthy fishing buddies from the States and the Prairie provinces repaired here for days designed to catch as many big fish as possible and then drink the night away. For those not fishing, Painter's has tennis courts, a spa, pool and hot tubs, fitness center, and business facilities. Accommodations and activities such as fishing can be booked separately (and the rooms are surprisingly economical) but virtually all visitors take advantage of packages that roll in lodging, fishing, golf, and such. Late summer and early autumn are prime time for fishing. The dining room focuses, naturally, on fish and steaks. The same Victoria-based company that owns Painter's Lodge, Oak Bay Marine Group, also operates a similarly deluxe boat- or plane-access-only remote lodge on the north end of Quadra Island, **April Point Lodge** (www.aprilpoint.com). *Lodge closed in winter.*

RODERICK HAIG-BROWN HOUSE
250-286-6646
www.haig-brown.bc.ca
haig.brown@crmuseum.ca
2250 Campbell River Rd., BC V9W 4N7
Price: Budget
Credit cards: Yes
Handicapped Access: Partial
Open: May 1–October 31

One of the first internationally prominent naturalist-writers, Roderick Haig-Brown was an angling devotee who used that as a fulcrum to promote habitat conservation, recognizing early on that fish populations depend on environmental protection. Now owned by the Campbell River Museum, his lovely home on the banks of the Campbell River offers a unique bed-and-breakfast accommodation in the summer, with three bedrooms sufficient for seven guests. The house is impeccably kept in the fashion as when Haig-Brown lived here; bedrooms are small but very comfortable, with pastel walls reflecting the natural beauty just outside. The author's library, with thousands of books on the shelves, is where he wrote famous works such as *A River Never Sleeps* and *Bright Waters, Bright Fish*. The grounds hold peaceful gardens, with tall cottonwoods lining the riverbanks about 5 yards (a few meters) away—exactly where Haig-Brown often waded into the waters to cast a streamer in the murmuring current.

STRATHCONA PARK LODGE
250-286-3122 or 1-800-333-4604
www.strathcona.bc.ca
info@strathcona.bc.ca
41040 Gold River Highway (Hwy. 28), Strathcona Park, BC V0R 2Z0
On Upper Campbell Lake, 26 miles (42 km) west of Campbell River
Price: Moderate (Lodging rates do not include meals.)
Credit cards: Yes
Handicapped Access: Partial

The motley collection (the resort calls it "eclectic") of cabins, cottages, lodge buildings, and such spread along the lakeshore here is exactly what you'd expect of an adventure lodge at the edge of the wilderness. The fact a paved highway goes right by only makes access easier; while the accommodations are certainly comfortable and atmospheric (lots of log structures with wood-paneled rooms), the many outdoor recreation programs are what draw travelers here. A brief list includes canoeing, hiking, volleyball, wilderness travel, life-saving education, climbing, orienteering, wildlife watching, a zip-line, and more. The lodge is the base for many wilderness programs in Strathcona Park itself, including survival skills courses. There's a wood-fired sauna on the beach; yes, the lake waters warm up in late summer, some.

DINING

Aside from the dining rooms at the various lodges, Campbell River is in the land of neighborhood pubs, funky Asian restaurants (beware places that advertise "Chinese and Canadian cuisine") and fast-food outlets. One of the better pubs, and a great place for lunch or dinner while waiting for a ferry, is **Riptide Marine Pub**, in a shopping plaza (1340 Island Highway, 250-830-0044). **Blue Water Bistro** is a nice, compact fine dining place downtown focusing on local foods (969 Alder Street, 250-287-8051). Sushi fans consider **Wasabiya** one of the best on the island (465 Merecroft Rd., 250-287-7711, www.wasabiyasushicafé.com). **Dick's Fish-and-chips** is a fast-food seafood fan favorite (1003 Island Highway, 250-286-0814). Downtown, **On Line Gourmet** is a great little sandwich shop with, of course, high-speed Internet (970 Shoppers Row, 250-286-6521).

CULTURE

Not surprisingly, the major local institution devoted to history is largely focused on the most famous local resource—salmon. Aside from the city museum in the summer, guided tours are available at **Roderick Haig-Brown House**, the riverside former home of the famous author; contact the museum at 250-287-3103.

MUSEUM AT CAMPBELL RIVER
250-287-3103
www.crmuseum.ca
470 Island Highway (Hwy. 19A), Campbell River, BC V9W 2B7
Open: Daily 10 AM–5 PM, May–September; winter noon–5 PM, Tuesday–Sunday
Admission: Adults $6, students $4

Aside from a large section devoted to the history of sport fishing in the area, this estimable local facility offers a look at the lifestyle of the aboriginal First Nations inhabitants, and at the salmon-canning and processing industry that once prospered here. In the early 20th century, there were 30 canneries along the BC coast between Campbell River and Bella Coola; today, there are none.

RECREATION

The centerpiece of outdoor recreation here at the north end of mid-island is Strathcona Provincial Park, one of BC's biggest, best and most significant. Aside from that, **salmon fishing** is the major attraction in the area. Traditionally arranged through the various fishing lodges around Campbell River, salmon charters can be booked from independent boat captains operating out of the city's marina; for a comprehensive listing of charter operators, visit www.northcentralisland.com.

A unique and most novel new adventure here is **salmon snorkeling**, the opportunity to float the Campbell River, in snorkel gear (and wet suits!), during its summer and early autumn salmon runs. All the major species of anadromous fish return to the Campbell River to spawn, and the spectacle is one of nature's most remarkable. Watching the colorful fish perform their courtship and mating rituals in the amber water of the spawning season is one of the most rewarding "soft adventure" activities one can undertake. The season is early July through early October. Destiny River Adventures offers raft-based snorkel excursions for $110 (www.destinyriver.com).

ELK FALLS PROVINCIAL PARK
250-474-1336
www.env.gov.bc.ca/bcparks
1850 Pacific Rim Highway, Tofino, BC
$3 day use fee

Northernmost among the three waterfall parks along the mid-island coast, Elk Falls may be the most appealing of them all. Two separate large cataracts plunge over rocky cliffs into a maelstrom below; the path that brings sightseers to the falls wends its way through forest and near cliff edges to create a memorable experience. Swimming holes become popular in July and August once the weather warms. The campground here is the largest in the immediate Campbell River vicinity. Campsite reservations can be made (with a private concessionaire) through the park Web site, or by calling 1-800-689-9025. It's best to reserve as far ahead as possible for summer travel.

STRATHCONA PROVINCIAL PARK
250-474-1336
www.env.gov.bc.ca/bcparks
30 miles (48 km) west of Campbell River on Hwy. 28, the Gold River highway

The oldest (1911) and one of the largest provincial parks in BC straddles more than 600,000 acres along the island's central mountain range from sea level on the West Coast to the foothills above Campbell River and the Comox Valley. It contains lakes, old-growth forest, glaciers, remote wilderness valleys, campgrounds, adventure lodges, forbidding alpine territory, and vast wilderness plateaus. Here is the island's highest peak, **Mount Golden Hinde**, at 7,207 feet (2,192 m). Here is BC's highest waterfall, 1,444-foot (440 m) **Della Falls**, one of the biggest in North America. Both are in deep wilderness, though Golden Hinde is visible from much of the north end of the mid-island. Buttle Lake, reached by road from Campbell River, is a 14¼-mile (23 km) natural lake in the park's main valley. Here are the two vehicle-access campgrounds in the park, and Strathcona Park Lodge (p. 145), one of the oldest adventure resorts in BC. The Forbidden Plateau, a famed backpacking destination, is in the southeast corner of the park (accessed from Courtenay).

Innumerable activities draw park visitors, with a partial list including swimming, sailing, windsurfing, fishing, camping, hiking, wildlife watching, mountain climbing, bike riding, waterskiing, canoeing and kayaking. The park is a hugely popular and thoroughly enjoyable **Nordic winter sports** destination—snowshoeing, cross-country skiing and winter camping—not only because of its stupendous winter snowfalls and great terrain, but because Provincial Parks authorities have made Strathcona one of the few major parks in North America where *snowmobiles are prohibited.* That's right, no howling noise and choking fumes. Just the peace and beauty of the forest in the snow.

Campsite reservations can be made (with a private concessionaire) through the park Web site, or by calling 1-800-689-9025. It's best to reserve as far ahead as possible for summer travel.

Discovery Islands

Although the general name "Discovery Islands" applies to dozens of land forms, from small skerries to large channel islands, between the north half of Vancouver Island and the BC mainland, only a few have scheduled ferry service. (For information on Alert Bay, in the north end of the island chain, see chapter 5.) The most commonly visited are **Quadra** and **Cortes**, opposite Campbell River, both relatively undeveloped, timbered tracts on which visitor services cluster along the south end. The ride from downtown Campbell River to Quadra is a brief 10 minutes; one must cross Quadra and take a second, 40-minute passage to reach Cortes, which gives it a remote, quirky flavor similar to Hornby farther south. For ferry information, visit www.bcferries.com. Aside from the notable lodges listed here, the visitor infrastructure is modest; visitor information for both islands is at www.northcentralisland.com.

About 20 minutes north of Campbell River along Highway 19 is a small overlook explaining what happened in the channel nearby, Seymour Narrows, to what used to be one of the smallest but most notorious land forms here. This passage is a major shipping lane that once held one of the worst navigation hazards in the world, **Ripple Rock**. At low tide, this twin-peaked rock was just 10 feet (3 m) underwater, ready and able to rip out the hull of any ship passing overhead. More than 100 vessels ran afoul of the rock; explorer George Vancouver called the passage "one of the vilest stretches of water in the world." All that ended in 1958 when Canadian demolition experts drilled shafts into the rock, placed more than 1,200 tons of explosives, and erased Ripple with one of the largest peacetime explosions in human history. Now the low-tide clearance in Seymour Narrows is 46 feet (14 m), enough for the many huge cruise ships and cargo ships that ply the passage.

LODGING

HERIOT BAY INN
250-285-3322 or 1-888-605-4545
www.heriotbayinn.com
info@heriotbayinn.com
Heriot Bay, Quadra Island, BC VoP 1Ho
On Quadra Island, 5 miles (8 km) east of
the BC ferries terminal at Quathiaski Cove
Price: Moderate to Expensive
Credit cards: Yes
Handicapped Access: Full

A classic marina resort on a pretty cove on
the east side of Quadra Island, Heriot Bay
offers comfortable, light-filled rooms in
a clapboard 1912 lodge building. Wood-
paneled cabins are tucked into the woods
beside the inn; they offer kitchens and
pull-out sofas. The inn's **Herons** pub/
restaurant is locally famed for its hearty
ambience (live music every weekend),
expertly prepared seafood, and sought-
after tables on the deck overlooking the
harbor.

SONORA RESORT
604-233-0460 or 1-888-576-6672
www.sonoraresort.com
info@sonoraresort.com
On Sonora Island, 21¾ miles (35 km) north
of Campbell River
Price: Very Expensive (Rates include all
meals and most activities.)
Credit cards: Yes
Handicapped Access: Partial

Accessible only by boat (from Campbell
River), helicopter (from Vancouver airport), or seaplane (from Seattle), this lavish self-contained complex is a high-end
wilderness resort with almost every con-
ceivable amenity, spread across a lovely
flange of land on a remote island. Here are
an outdoor swimming pool, a tennis court,
putting green, suites and lodge rooms and
cottages galore, two restaurants, hiking
trails, horseback riding, a golf simulator, a
theater, a full spa, a games room, and more.
Accommodations are invariably elegant,
with earth-tone décor setting off liberal use

Eagle Rock Lodge, Sonora Resort

Hollyhock, a Wonderful Retreat for the Soul

Getting to this famous New Age retreat center truly is a retreat from modern hustle and bustle—it takes most visitors three ferry rides to reach Cortes Island, the southeasternmost among the complicated chain known as the Discovery Islands. With its lodge, cottages, and other facilities spread out in old-growth woods on the southeast arm of the island, Hollyhock seems at first glance like one of the classic family summer resorts that dot the islands. Comfortable but somewhat spare accommodations range from bunk-bed dorms to spiffy private cottages—one has a kitchenette and private hot tub. New paint and renovations make the lodgings a cut above the "funky" description often applied to retreat centers. The grounds hold walking trails, gardens, a public hot tub, a main lodge with a sitting room, a dining room, a library, and a porch overlooking the Salish Sea. The spa facilities are set in separate cottages tucked into the woods.

All those features can be found at other resorts. Hollyhock's mission and philosophy are what truly set it apart. Dedicated to personal and spiritual growth and social improvement, it aligns itself with sustainability, social justice, natural health, and cultural diversity. World-renowned presenters include such luminaries as famed holistic health visionary Dr. Andrew Weil. The food is vegetarian (except for a weekly local seafood buffet); bodywork and yoga are key offerings; and almost every week includes a program nurturing some form of creativity—writing, painting, sculpting, singing, dancing. Biking and kayaking are the chief outdoor pursuits; Desolation Sound calls paddle adventurers to the east.

The gateway to Hollyhock is Campbell River; visitors first catch a ferry to Quadra Island, cross over, and catch a second ferry to Cortes Island. Water taxi passage to Hollyhock is available direct from Campbell River. It's not the sort of place you'd want to visit overnight—most travelers stay at least three nights, and many programs are weeklong events (with special pricing). Rates range from $129 up, meals included. For more information, visit www.hollyhock.ca, or call 250-935-6576 or 1-800-933-6339.

of warm Douglas fir and cedar trim, beams, and pillars. The Eagle Rock Lodge, a separate four-bedroom lodge house, is inexpressibly deluxe. Conceivably the most remote outpost in the exclusive Relais & Châteaux association, Sonora Resort is the sort of place for a honeymoon or 20th-anniversary trip—not for an ordinary family vacation, unless you have a most income-disposable family.

TSA-KWA-LUTEN LODGE
250-285-2042 or 1-800-665-7745
www.capemudgeresort.bc.ca
info@capemudgeresort.bc.ca
1 Lighthouse Rd., Quathiaski Cove,
BC V0P 1N0
On Quadra Island, 6⅛ miles (10 km) south of BC Ferries terminal

Price: Moderate
Credit cards: Yes
Handicapped Access: Full
Special Features: No pets, free WiFi

Owned and operated by the Cape Mudge band of the Kwakwaka'wakw First Nation, this striking, national park–style timber lodge occupies a bluff overlooking the channel, Discovery Passage, between Quadra and the Campbell River area. With huge cedar beams in the lobby and warm fir trim in all the rooms, the lodge reflects the woods that surround it. The lodge lobby is meant to evoke a traditional bighouse; accommodations range from spare, classic (and economical) lodge rooms to much more lavish suites and cottages. All the accommodations overlook the water and

Vancouver Island beyond; hiking trails lead through the forest down to the shoreline. The fabulous Nuyumbalees Cultural Centre is nearby.

DINING

CAFÉ AROMA
250-285-2404
www.aromacoffees.ca
685 Heriot Bay Rd., Quathiaski Cove (Quadra Island), BC V0P 1N0
Open: Daily 7 AM–5:30 PM
Price: Budget
Credit cards: Yes
Cuisine: Coffeehouse
Serving: B, L

Handicapped Access: Yes
Special Features: Yes, you should buy a sack of fresh-roasted beans to take home.

From this small facility near the ferry dock on Quadra Island come some of BC's best coffees, hand roasted here. Naturally it's a great place to get a small cup of coffee, but the baked goods and lunchtime soups and sandwiches are just as good—fresh bread baked daily, hearty soups, and chowders often made with local seafood. The café's billboard is a great place to eyeball the cultural rhythms of life on a small island on the BC coast—you might find a VW van for sale outfitted with a yoga studio, or perhaps a small mobile lumber mill, a Gibson guitar, or a used fishing net.

CULTURE

NUYUMBALEES CULTURAL CENTRE
250-285-3733
www.nuyumbalees.com
34 WeWay Rd., Quadra Island, BC V0P 1N0
Open: Daily 10 AM–5 PM, May–September
Admission: Adults $10, students and seniors $5

The cultural treasures here are not only superb examples of First Nations art—totems, boxes, masks, and ceremonial regalia—their story is a heartening one of loss and renewal. Most of the items were part of the potlatch-ban seizures in the early 20th century, when Canadian authorities prohibited this feasting ceremony integral to native life. The masks and other artworks confiscated then were sent around the world, sold to collectors or "donated" to museums, and the Cape Mudge Kwakwaka'wakw band has literally devoted generations to retrieving their stolen treasures. The two floors inside the museum hold totems, masks, capes, boxes, and other beautiful artworks; outside are petroglyph stones that were moved here for their protection. The museum is largely run today by the descendants of the families whose artwork was stolen and repatriated, and the artifacts on display remain the property of the families. Like U'mista, its sister museum at Alert Bay, Nuyumbalees is a truly special place.

Welcome figure, Nuyumbalees Cultural Centre
Nuyumbalees Society

Nuyumbalees Cultural Centre Leslie Forsberg

Nuyumbalees Cultural Centre Nuyumbalees Society

Alberni Inlet and Valley

Once just a decaying timber town halfway across the island from Nanaimo to Tofino, **Port Alberni** has enjoyed some surprising new prosperity in the new millennium as a . . . are you ready? . . . retirement center. Property values and living costs are low here. And, tucked into a narrow valley shielded on both sides by towering mountains whose flanks rise from the town suburbs, the climate is surprisingly benign. As the valley faces south-west, warmth gathers in the summer months sufficient that vineyards and cornfields have sprung up, supplying wine and fresh vegetables to residents and visitors. Retirees enjoy the two local golf courses eight months of the year. The town also fashions itself "Salmon Capital of the World," a title for which it competes with Campbell River and Ketchikan, Alaska, among others; the area's tourism slogan is "Bear Tracks and Lumberjacks," an inarguable description. Visitor infrastructure consists of mainstream restaurants and motels; for information, visit www.albernivalleytourism.com.

This is the departure port for the **MV *Frances Barkley*,** the famous mail/low-key-cruise boat that plies the Alberni Channel out into Barkley Sound, stopping in Bamfield, Ucluelet, and other remote hamlets. A sturdy boat that began life as a Norwegian ferry, the *Frances Barkley* hauls tourists and wilderness kayakers as well as supplies and mail; for information, visit www.ladyrosemarine.com.

Bamfield, at the end of a 37¼-mile (60 km) gravel road (two hours' driving time) from Alberni, is a remote West Coast outpost famed for its shoreline boardwalk and the fact the west side of the village has no road reaching it. This is the northern end of the West Coast Trail, so there is a longstanding community of outfitters serving trail trekkers, and a few hostel-style accommodations in town where backpackers enjoy their first hot showers and indoor beds in a week; visit www.bamfieldchamber.com. The **Bamfield Marine Sciences Centre** is one of the premier marine biology teaching and investigation facilities in North America (www.msc.bc.ca) but it has limited visitor facilities. It's on the road to Bamfield years ago that I saw my first wolves, a family of three wild canids poking along the side of the road.

LODGING

Few are the distinctive inns or lodges in the Alberni region, which is largely a waypoint between the West Coast and Nanaimo/Parksville. If you find yourself spending an unplanned night in Port Alberni, there are several decent motels in town; visit www.albernivalleytourism.com.

IMPERIAL EAGLE LODGE
250-728-3430
www.imperialeaglelodge.com
vacations@imperialeaglelodge.com
Bamfield, BC V0R 1B0
On the boardwalk, west side of Bamfield Inlet

Price: Expensive (Most packages include breakfast and dinner; two-night minimum weekends.)
Credit cards: Yes
Handicapped Access: Partial

Poised along the channel by the westside boardwalk in Bamfield, this is the best accommodation for many miles. The cottages and suites are decorated in modern country-inn style, the setting is splendid, and the cuisine quite naturally focuses on local seafood. Guests get a ride to the inn on its own water taxi, and the lodge offers fishing or sightseeing charters on its own salmon boat.

CULTURE

Its timber-industry history is the focus of attractions in the Alberni Valley, which has long been and still is a wood-products center.

MARTIN MARS WATER BOMBERS
250-724-7600
www.martinmars.com
On Sproat Lake, west of Port Alberni on Hwy. 4
Open: Daily 11 AM–3 PM, July and August
Admission: Free

Operated by a private company, these huge water-based planes are part of the West's forest fire–fighting arsenal. They are the largest water-based planes ever really flown (Howard Hughes's "Spruce Goose," though larger, made only one flight). When in service the highly maneuverable craft scoop water from lakes and rivers to dump on fires; yes, despite its temperate maritime climate, forest fires are a major hazard on the island and, especially, inland in BC. The company, based on Sproat Lake west of Port Alberni, has a visitor center where you can learn about the planes and firefighting, and tour a grounded aircraft (guided tour, $10). Lucky visitors may get to see the planes making practice runs, though not on any regular schedule.

McLean Mill National Historic Site
250-723-1376
www.alberniheritage.com
5633 Smith Rd., Port Alberni, BC V9Y 3B1
Open: Daily 9 AM–dusk
Admission: Adults $10, students $6, children under 12 free

Log trucks still rumble by every day in Alberni Valley, which is one of the most active remaining forest products centers in BC. This mill, though, harks back to the early heyday of the industry, when all the newly developed industrial equipment for the industry was steam powered. The historic site's namesake steam mill operated from 1926 to 1965, the province of pioneer logger R. B. McLean and his sons. Back then, it was a remote camp whose fallers plied the old-growth woods in the mountains abutting the valley. Today, visitors tour the old sawmill and lumber yards, gawk at huge pieces of machinery, and watch (summer only) a follies-type stage performance, *Saw Bites,* presented by a local theater troupe. Visitors can also ride a steam train, the Alberni Pacific Railway (now actually diesel, Thursday through Sunday, late June to early September) from downtown Port Alberni to the mill and back ($30). The whole experience is either a nostalgic look at the glories of the past or a vivid depiction of the destruction of the old-growth forest, depending on your point of view. The Alberni Valley heritage society also operates two small museums in the town, one devoted to community history, the other to maritime history, the latter housed in a handsome retired lighthouse.

RECREATION

The Alberni inlet is the gateway to Barkley Sound, and funnels salmon runs into the valley's rivers and streams. Thus it has been a center for decades for **salmon fishing**, chiefly for coho (silver salmon) runs in late summer and fall. The runs collapsed in the late '90s and the province suspended fishing for a few years; it has since resumed, but could be suspended again any time the runs plunge perilously low. Halibut, rockfish, and other types of salmon also draw anglers. Numerous skippers offer fishing charters out of Port Alberni; visit www.albernivalleytourism.com for a full list.

   Sproat Lake Provincial Park, west of Port Alberni along Highway 4, the Tofino road, has several excellent swimming beaches, and is a popular canoeing and fishing destination (www.env.gov.bc.ca/bcparks).

The Land of Giants

It's a long, long way to **Carmanah-Walbran Provincial Park**—three hours by gravel road from Duncan or Port Alberni—and that's probably fine with the visionaries whose protests led preservation of this world-class forest peering down at the Pacific Ocean. Slated for strip-logging in the late 1980s, environmental activists lobbied hard for park status for the valleys of Carmanah Creek and the Walbran River. Their efforts earned international attention when the world's largest Sitka spruce tree, the Carmanah Giant, was discovered in the area; the provincial park surrounding it was created in 1990 and expanded in 1995.

Visiting the park is a pilgrimage worth the effort for all who value the world's precious few remaining old-growth forests. Here are towering, thick-boled trees, Sitka spruces, Western red cedars, and Western hemlocks, standing tall beside tumbling streams whose amber waters splash reflected sunlight through the groves. A lovely path leads from the park entrance down into the valley, winding up at a particularly nice grove dedicated to the memory of Randy Stoltmann, the activist who led the campaign to save the forest. There is no trail to the 314-foot (96 m) Carmanah Giant, and access to and exact location of the tree are both stringently guarded. Anyone who has seen the damage done the famous, easily accessible giant redwoods in Northern California will understand why. But there are more than 225 other spruces in the valley taller than 225 feet (75 m), and the hills above hold many giant Western red cedars.

Here, too, you will see inescapable evidence of the fate that loomed over these trees—the last 3 miles (5 km) or so leading up to the park pass by barren clear-cuts (called cutblocks by the Canadian timber products industry) shorn of trees and looking much like strip mines do in the Appalachian Mountains of the United States. Serene and wonderful as the park is, even with the crystal waters of Carmanah Creek tumbling nearby, visitors will often hear the nearby sounds of chainsaws and industrial logging equipment.

There are limited camping and picnicking facilities at the park—a dozen walk-in sites near the parking area, and wilderness backpacking sites up the valley from there. Getting to the park involves a convoluted journey over gravel roads that I'll not attempt to describe here. Travelers must have a sturdy vehicle and a good spare tire, keep their headlights on, and remain alert to logging-truck traffic at all times. It is best to obtain maps from the visitor bureaus in your starting point; for more information, visit www.env.gov.bc.ca/bcparks.

NITINAT LAKE

250-745-3375
www.nitinaht.ca
About 37¼ miles (60 km) south of Port Alberni or west of Cowichan Lake

This long, narrow, drink-of-water tucked between two ridges along the coast southeast of Bamfield is one of the premier windsurfing locales in Western Canada. As thermals rise from the ridges each afternoon and air is sucked in off the ocean, reliable gales blow along the lake, which sports a lovely sand-and-gravel beach at the east end for launching. A short 1⅞-mile (93 km) channel connects the scenic 14¼-mile (23 km) lake to the ocean; averaging a little over ⅔ mile (1 km) wide, the lake's a natural wind funnel that draws windsurfers, kite surfers, and paragliders from around the world. Swimming, kayaking, and fishing are other options—best to paddle or fish in the morning, and reserve the afternoon for wind sports. Rentals and supplies are available at a local First Nations facility, the Nitinaht Visitors Centre.

Reaching Nitinat or nearby Carmanah-Walbran (see sidebar, p. 154) requires a three-hour journey over gravel roads that are active logging routes. Travelers must have a sturdy vehicle and a good spare tire, keep their headlights on, and remain alert to logging-truck traffic at all times.

West Coast

Nothing intervenes between the long, graceful strands of sand on Vancouver Island's West Coast and the North Pacific's tempestuous, breathtaking nature. So visitors watch towering spires of foam as breakers crash on rocky headlands. Surfers haul longboards out to the wave breaks 30 yards offshore. Elegant hotels beckon travelers in winter to dine behind floor-to-ceiling glass and watch storms lash the shore. Ancient spruce forests guard quiet coves, and in the back bays and seemingly infinite inlets of this convoluted coast, whales thump the waters, eagles ply the skies, oysters fatten in rich currents, and Vietnam-era draft dodgers grow old in remote hideaway homesteads.

Pacific Rim National Park, which preserves a large portion of this coast, is one of Canada's most-visited, drawing more than a million travelers a year. Tofino, the quaint/ funky town of 2,000 that hugs the northernmost ground reached by road, is a tourist mecca with a distinctive character formed by its logging and fishing past and its visitor-dependent present, spiced by a 1990s decade of cultural conflict over the rainforest environment that surrounds it. "Tough City," the town's nickname, draws on its real name, its "mild" but tempestuous climate, and its rugged industrial past.

Here, upscale international visitors mingle with tie-dye-clad holdover activists sipping coffee. Fishermen still chug the streets in net-laden old pickups; urban visitors arrive direct from downtown Seattle and Vancouver on floatplanes; and vacationers crowd into tour boats to look for whales, fish for halibut and salmon, or spend the day at a nearby waterfront hot spring unique on North America's west coast. The town's picturesque harbor offers bracing views of sapphire waters, thick-forested islands, and snow-draped peaks in the distance.

Ucluelet, the blue-collar town of 1,200 at the south end of the same peninsula, long defied the gentrification overtaking its northern neighbor. But the 21st-century plunge in resource extraction industries has led it to begin transforming its own logging and fishing past into a visitor economy as well. This is the embarkation point for wilderness kayakers trekking into the Broken Islands, a legendary group of small cays and skerries in Barkley Sound where paddlers can camp along deserted crescents of sand. Here, too, are ultra-budget backpacker lodgings and fusty eateries where chain-smoking locals gather on the porch (you'd never see that in Tofino), counterpoised against a sleek new upscale resort and a wonderfully quirky aquarium that returns all its denizens to the sea every fall.

LEFT: *On the continent's edge at Ucluelet's Wild Pacific Trail*   Leslie Forsberg

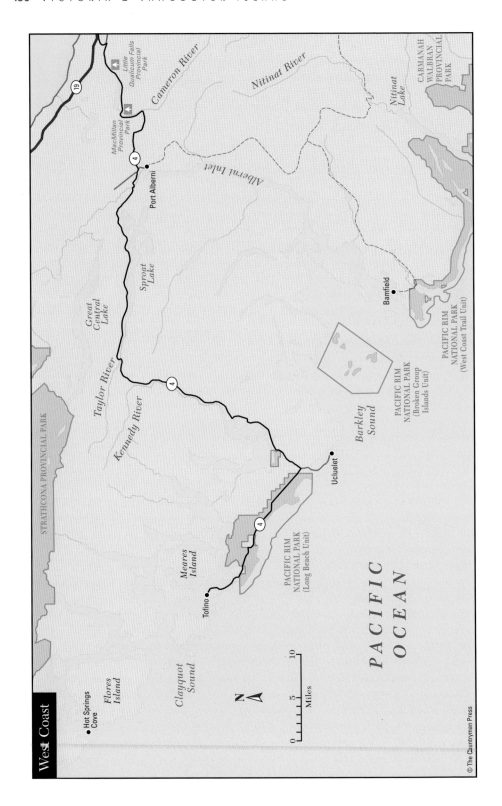

West Coast

MV Uchuck, *West Coast*   Boomer Jerritt/Tourism Vancouver Island

The peninsula that holds all this juts out from the main island like a swollen toe; and its backdrop is the virtually unbroken chain of mountains that form the spine of Vancouver Island proper. Between Ucluelet and Tofino is a largely undeveloped 31-mile (50 km) coastline of rocky headlands, wide sand beaches, thick spruce forest, and thundering surf—mostly wilderness, but just a few minutes' walk from the highway in many spots. Nowhere else is such a contrasting mix of wild and luxurious, funky and finessed, melded into one spectacular landscape.

The first thing visitors reach at the end of the long drive along Highway 4 from Port Alberni is the Pacific Rim Visitor Centre, a collaborative venture of the peninsula's twin towns, Tofino and Ucluelet, and Pacific Rim National Park. It's just before the intersection of Highway 4 and the Tofino-Ucluelet Road (250-726-4600, www.pacificrimvisitor.ca). Here you can find lodging, gather pamphlets for local restaurants, tour operators, and such, and obtain permits for national park activities ranging from camping to wilderness kayaking in Barkley Sound. Summer hours are daily from 9 AM to 7 PM starting July 1; hours are more limited from September through early March, with a Sunday/Monday closure.

Tourism Tofino's visitor center is at 455 Campbell Street (250-725-3414, 1-888-720-3414, www.tourismtofino.com). The Ucluelet visitor center is at 100 Main Street, in the Whisky Dock Landing, with limited hours (250-726-4641).

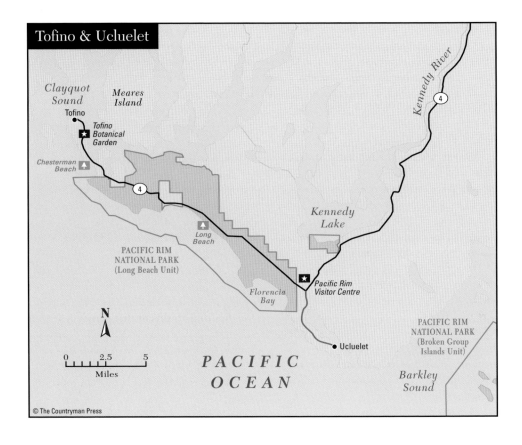

Tofino & Ucluelet

Clayquot Sound

Meares Island

Tofino

Tofino Botanical Garden

Chesterman Beach

Kennedy River

④

Kennedy Lake

④

Long Beach

PACIFIC RIM NATIONAL PARK (Long Beach Unit)

Florencia Bay

Pacific Rim Visitor Centre

N

Ucluelet

PACIFIC RIM NATIONAL PARK (Broken Group Islands Unit)

Barkley Sound

0   2.5   5
Miles

PACIFIC OCEAN

© The Countryman Press

HISTORY

Tofino and Ucluelet share a distinction few other locales in North America do—the arrival of road access came within living memory. Rough logging tracks threading the mountains between the coast and Port Alberni were not turned into a through road until the 1950s; before then, this area was a remote producer of seafood and timber, both shipped by boat to markets on the mainland. Prior to that, the coast had long been inhabited by Nuu-chah-nulth peoples who relied on cedar and salmon for a relatively prosperous lifestyle. European explorers came by over the centuries—most famously James Cook in 1778, who explored Nootka Sound, up the coast from Tofino, in March that year. Spanish explorers Galiano and Valdez made a more thorough survey of Vancouver Island in 1792, leaving behind numerous Hispanic place names that include Tofino, the surname of a hydrographer on the expedition.

Scattered homesteads coalesced into settlements in the early part of the 20th century, but the two towns at either end of the peninsula remained remote logging and fishing outposts until midcentury. Although the road was pushed through almost 60 years ago, visitors and residents were not allowed to use it weekdays when it was the province of logging trucks. Creation of Pacific Rim National Park in 1970 spurred paving of the road, and the area's great natural beauty and recreation opportunities began drawing ever more visitors.

That led, in 1993, to one of the most famous environmental battles of the recent past.

Government plans to issue timber-cutting licenses on Meares Island, home of vast old-growth forests and source of Tofino's water supply, drew conservation activists from around the world. Protests closed the highway and 1,000 activists were seized by police, but the largest mass arrest in Canadian history backfired on the government. An international campaign, including European boycotts, brought blistering pressure to bear on BC officials, and the logging plans were put on hold. A "peace" agreement several years later severely curtailed logging in Clayoquot Sound, and the area was declared a UNESCO Biosphere Reserve in 2000.

Today tourism is the mainstay of the economy from one end of the peninsula to the other, and home-grown visionary Charles McDiarmid's opening of the Wickaninnish Inn for storm watching has expanded the visitor industry into a year-round enterprise. The coastal climate means the weather is rarely very cold or very warm—though I have been to Tofino eight times, I have never seen a storm and in fact have ridden bikes along the beach in shorts in February. Summer months tend to bring morning fog; November through January is the rainiest period.

The area's colorful past persists in reminders that range from fine First Nations art galleries, to bayside wharves piled high with fishing nets, to floatplanes thrumming off the harbor waters, to the community billboard at Common Loaf in Tofino. When I first visited here in the late '90s, conservation groups were still fending off this or that planned clear-cut in nearby backwaters and protest announcements were pinned several layers deep on the corkboard. Now, protest campaigns are as likely to focus on a gold mine proposal in northern Canada or offshore drilling schemes along the BC central coast. But the whole wheat muffins are the same as ever, and the call of eagles rings through the streets of the towns and the paths in the forests as they always have.

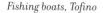

Fishing boats, Tofino

TRANSPORTATION

There are just two ways, by land or air, for visitors to reach the peninsula on which **Tofino** hugs the northernmost point and **Ucluelet** the southernmost. Highway 4 winds its way westward across the island's mountainous central spine from Parksville through Port Alberni to Tofino, a 103-mile (166 km) journey that takes three hours or more from the BC Ferries docks in Nanaimo, or more than five hours from Victoria. Although paved throughout, Highway 4 is a famously winding, narrow road that evinces its past as a logging track. Please, there is no need to compete with the occasional nitwits who believe they are Formula One drivers gunning their Porsches around the Riviera. **Greyhound Canada** buses travel between Nanaimo and Tofino twice a day. Beware—their Web site is extremely difficult to use (1-800-661-8747, www.greyhound.ca). **Tofino Bus** offers daily service to and from Victoria (250-725-2871, 1-866-986-3466, www.tofinobus.com).

Travelers with more expansive budgets can save time—and enjoy a memorable plane flight—by patronizing the regional carriers that offer charter service into Tofino. Passage is pricey, though—up to $900 US. **Kenmore Air** in Seattle (www.kenmoreair.com) and **Harbour Air** in Vancouver (www.harbour-air.com) are the two key carriers serving this market. Both operate sturdy floatplanes on routes that pass through spectacular scenery; Kenmore also offers wheeled-plane charters to the Tofino airport. If you can afford the cost, there's no more sensational way to reach the West Coast than on a DeHavilland Beaver banking in over Meares Island to set **down in Tofino Harbour.**

Budget Car Rentals has an outlet in Tofino (1-888-368-7368, www.bcbudget.com). **Tofino Taxi** (250-725-3333; tofinotaxi.com) provides service throughout the Long Beach Peninsula. Visitors staying at major hotels can reasonably plan to enjoy a week or so in Tofino without a car by advance planning to utilize shuttles and taxis.

Many Tofino area attractions, such as Meares Island, are reached by boat; **Tofino Water Taxi** is exactly what its name implies (1-877-726-6485, www.tofinowatertaxi.com) and

Chesterman Beach, Tofino

offers the sustainability benefit of operating a low-emission electric boat within its fleet. Reservations are advisable and essential during the summer peak travel season.

Visitors staying in Tofino proper can easily walk to many venues such as restaurants, and floatplane and water taxi docks. A paved off-street bike trail follows Highway 4 out of town several miles, providing access to the numerous hotels at Chesterman Beach and Cox Bay south of Tofino; a similar trail serves the Ucluelet area, so bicycle fans in either locale should consider renting bikes (**TOF Cycles**, 250-725-2453) if their hotels don't offer them.

LODGING

The inception of the storm-watching season in Tofino radically altered the lodging picture along the West Coast—resulting in the rare phenomenon of two distinct peak seasons. High prices thus pertain in July and August; and again in December through February. Bargain hunters are best advised to seek packages during the shoulder seasons of spring and fall. Late April and May can bring fine weather to the coast; storm-seekers may well get to watch waves crash in November or March. The price disparity can be significant, a $300 room in December going for $150 in April or October. Peak season lodging rates range $580 for a loft suite at the Wickaninnish Inn in January to $32 for a bed at Whalers Guesthouse hostel in summer.

Aside from the major resorts and hostels listed below, numerous small B&Bs and private campgrounds of varying quality welcome guests in both Tofino and, especially, Ucluelet. Consult the tourism Web sites for these. Over all, the two towns between them offer one of the best and most diverse selections of lodging in North America.

Pacific Rim National Park's one campground, **Green Point**, is open mid-March to mid-October. The 94 drive-in and 14 walk-in sites are near the shore (but also the highway), and are in huge demand from June 15 to September 15, so *reservations are absolutely essential* (1-877-737-3783, www.pccamping.ca). Book many months ahead if you are planning a summertime visit. Sites are $23.50 a night, plus a $10 reservation fee. There's also camping at the **Long Beach Golf Course**'s 76-site campground. Sites are $30 a night, and reservations are highly advised (250-725-3314, www.longbeachgolfcourse.com).

BLACK ROCK RESORT
250-726-4800 or 1-877-762-5011
www.blackrockresort.com
reservations@blackrockresort.com
596 Marine Dr., Ucluelet, BC V0R 3A0
⅔ mile (1 km) southwest of Ucluelet proper
Price: Expensive
Credit cards: Yes
Handicapped Access: Full
Special Features: Pets welcome, free WiFi, lavish spa

Ucluelet's brand-new big-deal destination resort has a lot to recommend it—not least a modern, stone-metal-and-glass design that dramatically sets it apart from the other West Coast hotels. Set just back from the edge of a headland outside Ukie, shaped like a flying wing so every room looks out over forest and the water, the hotel's uninspiring entrance is more than made up for by the sleek facility past the entry doors. Lots of rock (only some of it black) combines with conspicuous wood accents such as huge fir-block tables and vast walls of glass to meld inside and out. Rooms feature spare décor in beige, white, and sage, with black trim, that embraces the outside views, with the shower surrounds all black rock. All the art is by Vancouver Island artists. The resort's restaurant, Fetch, overlooks the ocean, and features an impressive rendition of West Coast cuisine, focusing on island seafood and BC meats and produce.

CABLE COVE INN

250-725-4236 or 1-800-663-6449
www.cablecoveinn.com
info@cablecoveinn.com
201 Main St., Tofino, BC V0R 2Z0
In Tofino proper
Price: Moderate to Expensive
Credit cards: Yes
Handicapped Access: Some units
Special Features: Pets welcome, free WiFi

Poised on a bluff above its tiny namesake cove in Tofino, this dandy small inn offers upscale luxury at more affordable prices, without the big-resort atmosphere of Tofino's high-profile beachfront lodges. (Although there is actually a brief ribbon of sand below the inn, between two headlands.) Dressed in neutral colors such as sage and sand, all rooms have either an in-room soaking tub or outdoor hot tub; and unlike the big resorts, the best storm-watching time is the low-rate season at Cable Cove. Tofino restaurants, shops, and attractions are within easy walking distance, five minutes in most cases.

CLAYOQUOT FIELD STATION

250-725-1220
www.tbgf.org/cfs
info@tbgf.org
1084 Pacific Rim Highway, Tofino, BC V0R 2Z0
At Tofino Botanical Gardens
Price: Budget
Credit cards: Yes
Handicapped Access: Full

Established to house researchers visiting Tofino, this spiffy newish facility is a great option for budget travelers, with all the advantages of a hostel (communal kitchen, laundry, etc.) and a more sophisticated cultural ethos. Rooms are more spacious than at the usual hostel, and the location at Tofino Botanical Gardens affords easy access to several of the area's best attractions—aside from the garden, Chesterman Beach is a short walk or bike ride away. There are private rooms; and even a private suite, with bath, which is a relative bargain at $138.

CLAYOQUOT WILDERNESS RESORT

250-726-8235 or 1-888-333-5405
www.wildretreat.com
info@wildretreat.com
Bedwell River, Clayoquot Sound; guests depart from south terminal, Vancouver International Airport, or from Tofino harbor
Price: Expensive—breathtakingly so
Credit cards: Yes
Handicapped Access: Call for arrangements

Once upon a time this wilderness resort consisted of an upscale log lodge housed on a floating barge in a backwater of its namesake sound. Then the resort hit upon the idea of installing a few safari-style tent cabins on land at a remote river mouth deep in the sound, and a new travel industry was born—"glamping." The resort's 20 tents at its Bedwell River Outpost are deluxe to the max, with Adirondack beds and furniture, gas-fired heating stoves, overstuffed armchairs, and plush Oriental rugs; and gourmet feasts served either in the tents or in the log-lodge-style pavilion. Guests spend their days fishing, wildlife watching, horseback riding, paddling, and hiking. It's very expensive (close to $10,000 per person per week, all-inclusive) and very memorable. Open mid-May through September only.

EAGLE NOOK WILDERNESS RESORT

604-760-2777 or 1-800-760-2777
www.eaglenook.com

info@eaglenook.com
Barkley Sound; guests depart by boat from
Ucluelet, or by floatplane charter
Price: Expensive
Credit cards: Yes
Handicapped Access: Some units
Special Features: Free WiFi, kayaks and
canoes

It'd be easy to call this the commoner's version of Clayoquot Lodge's wilderness
splendor, but that's giving short shrift to
this fine facility set on a very quiet back bay
in Barkley Sound. True, the faux-Bavarian
lodge building looks a bit odd in its setting
on a small spit between two coves, but the
rooms are comfy and spacious, and the
location affords easy access to all the wonders of the sound. It's a short hike to a vast
stretch of sun-warmed golden sand; the
paddling in nearby coves and bays is well
protected; and eagles, seals, otters, and
other wild creatures are regular sightings.
Although it's in our Expensive category, the
package price of $500 per person per night
includes transportation from Ucluelet, all
meals, recreation, and such.

LONG BEACH LODGE

250-725-2442 or 1-877-844-7873
www.longbeachlodgeresort.com
info@longbeachlodgeresort.com
1441 Pacific Rim Hwy., Tofino, BC V0R 2Z0
On Cox Bay, 2¼ miles (4 km) south of
Tofino proper
Price: Moderate to Expensive
Credit cards: Yes
Handicapped Access: Full
Special Features: Pets welcome, free WiFi

If Tofino can support one first-class lodge,
why not two? This exquisitely built post-
and-beam facility opened in 2000, just
back from the shore on Cox Bay, and offers
a slightly more economical, less elite alter-
native to the Wick. The massive great room,
perched just high enough to see out to the
ocean, is a wonderful place to linger in

front of the fire beneath huge fir beams.
The broad beach is literally just steps away
out the door; and the lodge specializes in
on-site surf lessons for guests. Rooms are
spacious, outfitted in somewhat brighter
colors than Northwest lodge standard—
autumn floral pattern fabrics, for instance.
But the usual warm-tone woods, mostly fir,
are omnipresent as well, perfectly comple-
menting the soothing, relaxed atmosphere
here.

PACIFIC SANDS

250-725-3322 or 1-800-565-2322
www.pacificsands.com
info@pacificsands.com
1421 Pacific Rim Hwy., Tofino, BC V0R 2Z0
On Cox Bay, 2¼ miles (4 km) south of
Tofino proper
Price: Moderate to Expensive
Credit cards: Yes
Handicapped Access: Some units
Special Features: Pets welcome, free WiFi,
bicycles available for guest use, babysitting
and child care

What was once a classic family-style beachfront resort—volleyball, picnic shelters,
compact kitchenette rooms with fold-
away beds—has been transformed with the
addition of 23 ultra-deluxe villas for
upscale travelers. Make no mistake, the
classic Sands resort is going strong: families packed into vans arrive for five-day
beachfront vacations in the original lodge
buildings, all of which have been renovated
and upgraded. The Sands has its own
peninsula headland with hiking trails, barbecue, picnic shelter, bike rentals, huge
lawn for rolling and tumbling, boogie
boards for mini-surfers, and more. All the
suites are airy and decorated in light colors
such as sand and sage, and have ocean
views. The villas are sensational, spacious,
superbly crafted loft units set in the spruce
fringe with gourmet kitchens, fireplace-
warmed sitting rooms, deluxe baths, and

skylight-lit master bedrooms. They're pricey (up to $730 for a three-bedroom unit in the summer) but are among the spiffiest lodging suites in Western Canada, and can comfortably house large families.

RED CROW GUESTHOUSE

250-725-2275
www.tofinoredcrow.com
relax@tofinoredcrow.com
1064 Pacific Rim Hwy., Tofino, BC V0R 2Z0
Price: Moderate
Credit cards: Yes
Handicapped Access: Full
Special Features: Free WiFi, hot tub, bicycles and canoes available for guest use

Two spacious guest suites and a lovely cottage comprise the lodgings at this peaceful retreat just outside Tofino. Set on 5 acres facing a back bay of Clayoquot Sound, the surroundings are notably peaceful and uncrowded. The suites and cottage all feature fine wood trim, light décor colors such as ivory, and luscious warm wood floors. The grounds invite contemplative strolling and bird-watching, and the lodge canoes offer a delightful way to enjoy the inland waters at high tide.

TERRACE BEACH RESORT

250-726-2901 or 1-866-726-2901
www.terracebeachresort.ca
manager@terracebeachresort.ca
1002 Peninsula Rd., Ucluelet, BC V0R 3A0
On Terrace Beach Bay, ⅔ mile (1 km) south of central Ucluelet
Price: Moderate to Expensive, children under 12 free
Credit cards: Yes
Handicapped Access: Some units
Special Features: Pets welcome

The various cottages and cottage suites that comprise this waterfront complex south of Ucluelet proper are tucked into old-growth spruce forest and linked by wood walkways in a fashion that brings to mind a movie set. While somewhat dark (hard to avoid within the depths of an ancient forest), they are cozy, warm, and comfortable, and much more spacious than the average hotel room. Although the kitchens lack ovens, most units have a barbecue, and many have soaking tubs or outside hot tubs. A few more compact "bachelor suites" offer economical lodging below $100. The cottages and suites at the southwesternmost edge of the complex afford what is probably the most genuine rainforest experience in West Coast lodging. A short boardwalk leads from the complex to a Wild Pacific Trail entry.

WHALERS ON-THE-POINT GUESTHOUSE HOSTEL

250-725-3443
www.tofinohostel.com
info@tofinohostel.com
81 West St., Tofino, BC V0R 2Z0
In Tofino proper
Price: Budget
Credit cards: Yes
Handicapped Access: Full

Yes, this fine hostel is indeed right on the point in Tofino proper. Guests can watch the harbor for floatplanes coming in or departing, and it's only a short walk to everything in town, including the grocery store just a couple blocks away. The green-roof wood-sided building is well kept and tidy, and the Caribbean colors in the lounge fend off the West Coast gloom. This is a definite cut above the usual backpacker hostel, and includes all the usual features such as a communal kitchen, games room, Internet access, laundry, and TV room. Not so usual are the free evening sauna; the storage for bikes, surfboards, and wet suits, and the scenic views. Private rooms are available (with small bath), up to $135 in high season.

WICKANINNISH INN

250-725-3100 or 1-800-333-4604
www.wickinn.com

info@wickinn.com
500 Osprey Lane, Tofino, BC V0R 2Z0
On Chesterman Bay, 1⅞ miles (3 km) south
of Tofino proper
Price: Expensive
Credit cards: Yes
Handicapped Access: Full
Special Features: Pets welcome, free WiFi,
bicycles available for guest use

Charles McDiarmid, son of the former
Tofino town doctor, is one of those who
remembers when the road to the "outside"
first opened in the '50s. After a career in
the hotel industry around the world, he
conceived the idea of opening a five-star
lodge on a headland south of town—his
family's old summer getaway—and attract-
ing visitors in winter to watch storms
thrash the shore, as the traditional two-
month summer tourist season was insuffi-
cient to support a world-class hotel. People
thought he was a lunatic, and for the first
few months, it looked like he was. Then the
bookings started to roll in (that was autumn
1996), and McDiarmid's vision not only
became prescient, it spread up and down
the Pacific Coast.

Today, "The Wick" has been accepted
into the ultra-fussy Relais & Châteaux lodging consortium, the original lodge building
has been boosted with the addition of a
newer wing sequestered in the spruce
fringe, and guests can not only watch
storms from the glass-enclosed comfort of
the Pointe dining room, they can enjoy an
island-seaweed body scrub in the little
shingle-sided cottage perched at the edge
of the cliff just above the water.

Although it is a large resort complex
(145 rooms and suites), the Wick rests
rather artfully in its surroundings—the
gray-toned finish on its main lodge, for
instance, blends into the headland rock.

Wickaninnish Inn, Tofino

Massive hand-carved yellow cedar doors greet guests; huge timber posts and beams bring the forest inside. Rooms are finished in tones of forest green and sage, with recycled clear (knot-free) fir trim and furnishings throughout, the wood salvaged from an old school in Victoria. All the rooms have beach or ocean views. Activities range from surfing in Chesterman Bay to simply strolling or riding bikes on the mile-long beach. The Pointe restaurant (see Dining) faces the ever-dynamic ocean. Although many first-time guests want to be in the original building out on the point, my favorite rooms are in the newer Wick-on-the-beach wing, where the balconies peek out on the broad expanse of sand through the spruce fringe. Open a window to bring in the susurration of the surf, draw a hot bath in the soaking tub, watch the last light of the sun play on the distant woods, and you could hardly be more relaxed.

DINING

The introduction of West Coast cuisine came a bit later to the area nicknamed "West Coast" than at its origins in Vancouver and Victoria—though cuisine in Tofino and Ucluelet, such as it was, has always incorporated local seafood. Crab, salmon, halibut: these were the mainstays of food in the region for decades, if not millennia. The opening of the Wickaninnish Inn's Pointe Restaurant brought high-style cooking to the area, and the customary ingredients from the sea have been vastly expanded to include shellfish, seaweed, ferns, mushrooms, and more from the island, as well as BC-grown produce and meat. Still, the quintessential Tofino supper remains grilled salmon; in Ucluelet, it's fish-and-chips. All worthy dishes to enjoy, whether in their simplest form at local pubs, or fancied-up at glittering lodge dining rooms.

One can have supper for as little as $10, or spend as much as $100 a person for a splurge dinner at The Pointe or Shelter. I'd say, enjoy both approaches.

CAFÉ VINCENTE
250-725-2599
441 Campbell St., Tofino, BC V0R 2Z0
Open: Daily 6 AM–3:30 PM
Price: Moderate
Credit cards: Yes
Cuisine: West Coast
Serving: B, L
Handicapped Access: Yes

Tofino's best coffeehouse is right along the main drag in town. The muffins, pastries, and other foodstuffs are all quite good, and the coffee preparations are the best in town. There's Internet access, of course, and even a couple on-site computers, a rarity these days.

COMMON LOAF BAKE SHOP
250-725-3915
180 First St., Tofino, BC V0R 2Z0
Open: Daily 7 AM–5:30 PM
Price: Budget
Credit cards: Yes
Cuisine: West Coast
Serving: B, L
Handicapped Access: Yes

Although the local slump in social activism has imposed a bit of decline on this once-stellar counterculture hangout, it's still a great place to, well, buy a loaf and, um, loaf. The fresh-baked muffins and morning pastries are good, the bulletin board is always entertaining (need a '67 Volkswagen bus for $200, throw in a surfboard for another $50?) and the sandwiches and soups at lunch are good. Possibly the best item on the menu is handmade pizza. Friendly customer service is not exactly a counterculture standard, but grin and bear it for the anthropological experience, if nothing else.

CYNAMOKA COFFEE HOUSE
250-726-3407
www.cynamoka.ca
1536 Peninsula Rd., Ucluelet, BC V0R 3A0
Open: Daily 6 AM–3:30 PM
Price: Budget
Credit cards: Yes
Cuisine: Bakery
Serving: B, L
Handicapped Access: Yes

The draws here are coffee fresh-roasted on-site (the best in Ucluelet) and fresh-baked breakfast goods including the ubiquitous cinnamon rolls, which are good enough if not memorable. Internet access and a cozy sitting area by the gas fire complete the atmosphere, though the cramped quarters can get a bit crowded at peak times.

DOCKSIDE PUB
250-725-3277
www.weighwest.com
634 Campbell St., Tofino, BC V0R 2Z0
Open: Daily 11 AM–11 PM
Price: Moderate
Credit cards: Yes
Cuisine: West Coast
Serving: L, D
Handicapped Access: Yes

Ask locals the best place for fish-and-chips and this answer will come up a lot—it's a classic Canadian tavern restaurant, and in Canada that's often the best place for supper. Part of the Weigh West complex on Tofino Harbour, the pub overlooks the water, but is notable more for its economical family meals. Best are the halibut burger at $15, or halibut fish-and-chips at $13; the $9 bowl of chili with corn bread is pretty good by Canadian standards, too.

JIGGERS
250-726-5400
Bay St. & Peninsula Rd. (1801 Bay St.), Ucluelet, BC V0R 3A0
Open: Daily 11 AM–5:30 PM
Price: Budget
Credit cards: No
Cuisine: Fast food
Serving: L, D
Handicapped Access: Yes

Widely considered the best fish-and-chips stand in the area, Jiggers is definitely nothing fancy—a truck, in fact, parked in the lot at an intersection on the main drag in Ukie. The burgers are also pretty good, but the standard fish-and-chips (cod or halibut) come in large portions, and both fries and fish are far less greasy than the usual. Advocates call this best in the world, which isn't quite so; but it's certainly best in Ucluelet.

MATTERSON HOUSE
250-726-2200
1682 Peninsula Rd., Ucluelet, BC V0R 3A0
Open: Daily 11:30 AM–9 PM
Price: Moderate
Credit cards: Yes
Cuisine: West Coast
Serving: L, D
Handicapped Access: Yes

Tucked into a refurbished heritage home along the main drag, this local favorite's menu is heavy on '80s-style burgers and pastas (cheese and mushrooms) but offers easy access, consistency, economy (their monster burger is $12, pasta plates all below $20), and a pleasant atmosphere.

NORWOODS
250-726-7001
www.norwoods.ca
1714 Peninsula Rd., Ucluelet, BC V0R 3A0
Open: Daily 6 PM–11 PM
Price: Expensive
Credit cards: Yes
Cuisine: West Coast
Serving: D
Handicapped Access: Yes

Until Black Rock Resort opened, fine dining in Ucluelet was represented by this gourmet outpost whose food is seriously better than its unprepossessing streetfront appearance. The intimate dining room (just a few tables and exhibition seating at the bar) faces the open kitchen, and the menu focuses on local fish in high-style, Asian-influenced preparations, such as salmon sashimi or lightly seared local scallops with a touch of cilantro. BTW, the name derives from chef-owner Richard Norwood, and has nothing to do with "north woods."

THE POINTE

250-725-3100 or 1-800-333-4604
www.wickinn.com
500 Osprey Lane, Tofino, BC V0R 2Z0
Open: Daily 7 AM–10:30 PM
Price: Moderate
Credit cards: Yes
Cuisine: West Coast
Serving: B, L, D
Handicapped Access: Yes
Special Features: Storm watching is at its best here—there are even microphones that bring the sound of the crashing waves inside.

The dining room at the Wickaninnish Inn is a shrine to both West Coast cuisine and the phenomenon that built the inn, storm watching. Vast glass window-walls look out directly on the water, and during massive winter storms the wave-wash occasionally reaches the roof. The menu changes often, but mainstays include octopus salad, smoked sablefish (black cod), seared wild salmon, and a dessert chocolate menu that offers milk, dark, and ultra-dark preparations.

THE SCHOONER

250-725-3444
www.schoonerrestaurant.ca
331 Campbell St., Tofino, BC V0R 2Z0
Open: Daily 5 PM–11 PM
Price: Expensive
Credit cards: Yes
Cuisine: West Coast
Serving: D
Handicapped Access: Yes

Long one of the benchmarks in Tofino dining, The Schooner has updated its half-century tradition with a West Coast approach that features organic Angus beef, free-range Fraser Valley poultry, and a separate vegetarian menu. However, the centerpiece of the menu remains seafood platters that range from halibut stuffed with crab to shrimp and cheese (Brie, in keeping with the New Age approach) to massive plates of salmon, halibut, crabs, shrimp, clams, and mussels. No one leaves unsated here.

SHELTER

250-725-3353
www.shelterrestaurant.com
601 Campbell St., Tofino, BC V0R 2Z0
Open: Daily 5 PM–11 PM
Price: Expensive
Credit cards: Yes
Cuisine: West Coast
Serving: D
Handicapped Access: Yes

Vancouver-type high style arrived in Tofino with the opening of this sleek bistro in 2003. The downstairs bar is a great place for drinks and tapas (calamari, thin-crust pizza, fried yams, and an especially good lingcod burger), and the concise dinner menu embraces salmon, curry, steak, crab, and chicken. The décor features lots of high-gloss wood and low lighting, and the convivial atmosphere typifies BC business casual. Wear your jeans, yes—freshly pressed.

SOBO

250-725-2341
www.sobo.ca

311 Neill St., Tofino, BC V0R 2Z0
Open: Daily 11 AM–9:30 PM
Price: Moderate
Credit cards: Yes
Cuisine: West Coast
Serving: L, D
Handicapped Access: Yes

"Sophisticated Bohemian" is what this restaurant's name stands for. Famously begun as a food cart in the parking lot at Tofino Botanical Gardens, SoBo moved to these expansive, spiffy new digs in 2008 as demand mushroomed for chef/co-owner Lisa Ahler's food. Although the daily menu is based on "the whims of nature," standout standards include fish tacos—the mainstay of the old food cart—the nightly island shellfish bowl, and wood-fired pizzas based on island cheeses. A wide array of ingredients, including of course seafood, is from island producers. The atmosphere is decidedly low-key and family friendly; feel free to arrive in sandals and shorts, and be sure to finish off with the chocolate-almond brownie.

TOUGH CITY SUSHI

250-725-2021
www.toughcity.com
350 Main St., Tofino, BC V0R 2Z0
Open: Daily 11 AM–9 PM
Price: Moderate
Credit cards: Yes
Cuisine: Sushi

Serving: L, D
Handicapped Access: Yes

The massive menu at this Tofino mainstay focuses on Pacific coast fish (salmon, halibut, tuna) but also expands to meet the local counterculture undercurrent. Witness the Smiling Buddha roll, a concoction of tuna, avocado, and spinach topped with tropical fruit. It's worth splurging (an extra $5) for real Dungeness crab in the California roll.

UKEE DOGS

250-726-2103
1576 Imperial Lane, Ucluelet, BC V0R 3A0
Open: Daily 11 AM–6 PM
Price: Budget
Credit cards: Yes
Cuisine: Fast food
Serving: L, D
Handicapped Access: Yes

A hot dog stand? Yep, a quintessential Ucluelet kind of place. Aside from gourmet hot dogs, handmade using sustainably raised BC meats, this fast-food stand also features meat pies (salmon Wellington—take that, gourmet chefs at stuffy restaurants), fresh-baked cookies, and cinnamon buns. There's little or no sitting room, depending on the weather, customer numbers, and such. Plan to enjoy the fresh air and perch on a curb, if necessary.

CULTURE

As the natural attractions on the West Coast are all-encompassing and all around you, the discrete tourist facilities are relatively few. This is a destination for beachcombing, bike riding, kayaking, surfing, nature hikes, and just plain relaxing by the fire. The attractions that are here naturally focus on the cultural and natural heritage of the area. The centerpiece is Pacific Rim National Park (see Recreation, p. 178) but innumerable other locales offer outdoor enjoyment—sometimes as low-key as simply riding a bike for an hour along the broad sands of Chesterman Beach.

CLAYOQUOT SOUND
www.clayoquotbiosphere.org

This vast inland sea is a maze of thick-forested islands, emerald bays and inlets, and long passages beneath mountains that climb skyward. Tides surge back and forth in constant flux; green anemones and orange sunstars glow beneath the water; eagles and gulls cry ceaselessly as they watch the waters below for herring and salmon. Numerous quiet back-water coves hold ramshackle homesteads, some of them housing Vietnam-era refugees from the States. Bears prowl the lowlands at river mouths, and humpback whales scout the deep channels for food while the occasional gray whale pores over shallow bays for krill. This is one of the world's richest ecosystems—though massive clear-cuts and old mining scars betray the ever-present threat posed by human activity. Declared a UNESCO Biosphere Reserve in 2000, after years of conflict over its preservation, the sound seems limitless to visitors who usually experience only a day—or just an afternoon—within it. Numerous tour operators in Tofino operate various kinds of journeys into the sound; my favorite is Michael White at Browning Pass Charters (250-725-3435, www.browning pass.com), who not only knows the area intimately, he treats it with the love and respect such intimacy demands.

HOT SPRING COVE/MAQUINNA MARINE PROVINCIAL PARK
250-474-1336
www.env.gov.bc.ca/bcparks
North Clayoquot Sound
Open: Daily dawn–dusk
Admission: $3 day use fee

Freedom Cove, Clayoquot Sound

Quiet cove, Clayoquot Sound   Leslie Forsberg

Reachable only by boat or, for those with bigger budgets, by floatplane, Hot Spring Cove is an attraction unique in BC, and certainly not common anywhere on earth. Here, geothermally heated water arises just 330 feet (100 m) or so above the shoreline, and tumbles down to the sea through rocky clefts, forming hot soaking pools along the way. Water emerges at about 122°F (50°C), and cools slightly as it cascades downward toward the sea. The lowermost pools are especially prized, as incoming waves wash over the hot water, then recede, providing a unique soaking experience.

So what's not to like? The park can become very, very crowded during nice days from May through September, and colorful jockeying takes place as visitors line up for a few minutes in the pools. As well, it's a long, long boat ride (more than an hour if ocean conditions demand an "inside" approach), and unless you are lucky enough to see whales during the journey, it's a bit of a slog. Millionaires are well advised to charter a floatplane, arrive early, and enjoy a flightseeing excursion there and back.

And, ahem, unlike most other "natural" hot springs in the West, clothing is not optional at Hot Springs Cove. Bring your suit, buckaroo.

MEARES ISLAND/BIG TREE TRAIL

Two decades ago this was an unofficial path through the woods on this deep-forested island east of Tofino; activists used it to illustrate the beauty and majesty of the cedar, fir, and hemlock old-growth forest that has been growing here for centuries. Now it's a board-walked stroll into old growth forest. Best way to get there is by Tofino Water Taxi (1-877-726-5485, www.tofinowtertaxi.com), whose operators will take you there and arrange to pick you up and bring you back for $25. The 15-minute crossing is invariably scenic and refreshing, too. The highlight of the trail is the legendary Hanging Garden cedar, a many-centuries-old grandfather tree whose numerous nooks and crannies are home to dozens of

Big Trees Trail, Meares Island

secondary trees, shrubs and plants. Poster tree for the early '90s Clayoquot Sound preservation campaign, it is truly an astounding sight, and bears witness to the steadfast durability of rainforest eco-systems—when they are not sawed to the ground.

TOFINO BOTANICAL GARDENS
250-725-1220
www.tbgf.org
info@tbgf.org
1084 Pacific Rim Highway, Tofino, BC V0R 2Z0
Open: Daily 9 AM—dusk
Admission: Adults $10, students $6, children under 12 free

Begun as a volunteer garden devoted to demonstrating the horticultural possibilities of the maritime climate, this has grown into an exquisite facility fostering

Tofino Botanical Gardens

appreciation of marine-climate ecosystems around the world. Here are plants native to the West Coast, as well as towering ferns from Chile, lilies from the Himalayas, kitchen gardens, and more. There are a total of 12 acres running down to the shore of Clayoquot Sound, with quiet paths throughout, a coffee shop and lunch counter, whimsical art installations, and innumerable educational offerings designed to elicit understanding and preservation of temperate rainforests around the world.

UCLUELET AQUARIUM
250-522-2782
www.uclueletaquarium.org
info@uclueletaquarium.org
Main & Cedar Sts. Ucluelet, BC V0R 3A0
Open: Daily 10 AM–6 PM May–October; 11 AM–5 PM spring and fall; closed Oct. 15–Mar. 15
Admission: Adults $5.50, children and seniors $3.50

Teaching respect for the marine environment is one of the key goals of this delightful small facility—and the most significant way it does so is by returning all its specimens to the sea each autumn (as part of a marvelous community festival). Visitors here see the colorful denizens of the underwater surroundings, such as chartreuse anemones and ivory nudibranchs; volunteers stand ready to answer questions about all they see in the various holding tanks. The aquarium is building a much larger new facility nearby, but plans to hew to its unique strategy of collecting specimens each spring and returning them to the wild every fall.

Temporary residents, Ucluelet Aquarium Leslie Forsberg

WILD PACIFIC TRAIL
www.wildpacifictrail.com
Reached by numerous trailheads throughout Ucluelet

Largely the result of unswerving dedication on the part of Oyster Jim, local shellfish entre-
preneur and community booster, this broad gravel path winds through spruce fringe and
along wave-tossed headlands in Ucluelet. Although it's ostensibly a recreation facility, it's
best suited just for walking, and it has become one of the peninsula's finest visitor attractions. Dipping into and out of the spruce fringe, curving up to rocky headlands that afford
sensational views of sea stacks, islets, incoming swells and all the marine life that inhabits
the landscape, the trail offers even casual strollers a marvelous window into the landscape.
The southernmost, 1¼-mile (2 km) loop circles a rugged peninsula tipped with photogenic
Amphitrite Lighthouse; a parking lot along Coast Guard Road affords easy access.

RECREATION

The centerpiece of nature along the West Coast is Pacific Rim National Park, but visitors
can experience all the wonders of the coast without ever setting foot in the park. Long
sandy beaches, moss-draped spruce forest, sparkling sapphire and emerald backwaters—
all these are the venues for the various recreational activities found here.

Several local naturalists offer explanatory tours in the area; consult tourism advisers or
hotel concierges for booking. One of my favorites, **Long Beach Nature Tours** (250-726-
7099, www.longbeachnaturetours.com) features the expertise and good humor of longtime Pacific Rim National Park naturalist Bill McIntyre, who knows just about everything
about everything here on this wild shoreline. Bill's the sort who can spy a hummingbird
nest hidden in a high branch of an evergreen huckleberry in a spruce forest—and tell you
when the hummingbirds arrived from California, when their chicks first fly, when they all
head back south.

Kayaking is popular not only in the Broken Islands of the national park but in Ucluelet
Inlet and Tofino Harbour. While almost anyone can sensibly undertake a paddling journey,
treacherous tidal currents and occasional winds can heighten the challenge; rank beginners are best advised to consider guided tours. Tofino Sea Kayaking is a long-established,
reliable operator in Tofino (250-725-4222, 1-800-663-4664, tofino-kayaking.com). In
Ucluelet, contact Majestic Ocean Kayaking (250-726-2868, 1-800-889-7644, www.ocean
kayaking.com).

Tofino is the Canadian capital for **surfing**, and Long Beach is the centerpiece of this
phenomenon. On mild-weather days when decent rollers are curling in just offshore, the
parking lot here looks like it might be Malibu—even down to the old "woody" station wagons, boards strapped on top, with young lads and lassies leaning against the fenders, eyes,
shaded, studying the waves. Dry suits are needed, but the surf is relatively mild and suited
for beginners (except in bad weather) and rentals, classes, and general guidance are available at **Tofino Surf Shop** (1184 Pacific Rim Highway, 250-725-4464) and **Long Beach
Surf Shop** (630 Campbell St., Tofino, 250-725-3800; 2060 Peninsula Rd., Ucluelet, 250-
726-2700; both at www.longbeachsurfshop.com). **Pacific Surf School** offers lessons for
all (www.pacificsurfschool.com), and **Surf Sister** specializes in classes for women (www
.surfsister.com).

Although there are better-known locales for ocean **fishing** in British Columbia, the

Surfer girl, Chesterman Beach Leslie Forsberg

West Coast holds its own on the basis of open-water halibut fishing, and the king and coho salmon runs that usually throng local waters in late summer and autumn on their way to spawning streams in the mountains. Any of the area's lodgings can arrange a day fishing with one of numerous local guides; the most conspicuous venue is **Canadian Princess Resort**, contained on a permanently moored historic coastal ship in Ucluelet Harbour. The key offering at the resort is daily fishing expeditions; accommodations onboard ship are basic (bunk-bed cabins), but there's also a landside hotel with more spacious rooms. A one-night stay with a day on the water fishing can be had for less than $200 (250-598-3366, 1-800-663-7090, www.canadianprincess.com). The area's visitor information site lists many other fishing charter operators at www.pacificrimvisitor.ca.

LONG BEACH GOLF COURSE

250-725-3332
www.longbeachgolfcourse.com
1850 Pacific Rim Highway, Tofino, BC

A legacy of World War II days, when a considerable military base occupied this peninsula, Tofino's golf course is a surprisingly challenging nine-hole championship layout (yes, there is such a thing) with a couple tough par-4s. But rates are just $24 for 9 holes, $36 for 18. Tucked into the pines on the northeast side of the highway, the course is shielded from the ocean winds, and offers a welcome respite from the otherwise water-focused recreation menu on the West Coast.

PACIFIC RIM NATIONAL PARK RESERVE

250-726-3500
www.pc.gc.ca
pacrim.info@pc.gc.ca

One of Canada's most famous and most visited national parks (more than 1 million visitors a year) is a sprawling preserve that embraces huge swaths of wilderness coast and sound, from Port Renfrew west of Victoria, north to the edge of Tofino. Virtually all the human activity in the park is confined to the relatively small 11-mile (18 km) -long section between Ucluelet and Tofino, known as the **Long Beach Unit** for the major feature within it, the 10-mile (16 km) shore of Wickaninnish Bay. All the unit's main features are well signed and reached by short roads or trails leading from Highway 4. Here, curving strands of broad sand beckon beachcombers, quiet trails lead through dank spruce forest to wave-tossed headlands, and surfers scan the horizon offshore for incoming swells. The park's **Wickaninnish Interpretive Centre** (open daily 10–6, closed mid-October to mid-March) introduces visitors to the rich and hardy ecology of the coast from its bracing locale atop a headland. The short drive to the top of **Radar Hill** affords panoramic views in every direction.

Visitors stopping anywhere in the Long Beach unit must obtain a **park pass**, available at the Pacific Rim Visitor Centre at the junction of Highway 4 and the Tofino–Ucluelet Road, or at vending machines at most parking areas. It's $7.80 per adult; other fees apply to beach hiking.

Elsewhere in the Long Beach unit, short hikes of ⅔ mile (1 km) or less lead through spruce fringe rainforest, or down to various coves and beaches within the park. My favorites are **Schooner Cove**; **Shorepine Bog**, featuring the coast's version of lodgepole pine; and **Halfmoon Bay**, a delightful little strand of sand. One longer trail, **Nuu-Chah-Nulth**, is a historic First Nations pathway that introduces visitors to indigenous culture.

The Long Beach Unit's one campground, **Green Point**, is open mid-March to mid-October. The 94 drive-in and 14 walk-in sites are near the shore (but also the highway), and are in huge demand from June 15 to September 15, so *reservations are absolutely essential* (1-877-737-3783, www.pccamping.ca). Book many months ahead if you are planning a summertime visit. Sites are $23.50 a night, plus a $10 reservation fee.

The **Broken Group Islands** section of the park lies within Barkley Sound south of Ucluelet, and is a sea kayak paradise for *experienced wilderness paddlers*. More than 100 islands dot the sound, ranging from 100-yard (90 m) -long atolls to ⅔-mile (1 km) -long forested humps. Here, curving strands of white sand beach front emerald water coves in which seals play and underwater anemones flash vivid hues in the sun. Tricky tidal currents and sudden winds and storms demand wilderness experience; check with local guiding companies if you are not an expert. Park permits are needed to camp within the islands, and camping is limited to designated sites on seven islands. No, I don't know why the islands' name is backward.

The legendary (and notorious) **West Coast Trail** is for experienced wilderness trekkers who like challenge—such as scaling steep headlands on rope ladders and dodging incoming high tides—seclusion . . . and mud. Originally carved out of the wilderness in 1907 as an escape route for shipwrecked mariners who washed up on this notoriously rough coast, the so-called Graveyard of the Pacific, the corridor became part of the national park in 1973. The 46⅔-mile (75 km) trail and the thin strip of shoreline around it comprises the south-

Whale Watching on the West Coast

Whales are gentle beings that inhabit the food-rich waters of the Pacific Coast. Humans are not-so-gentle beings that, when they desire something, sometimes thrust aside all manner of compassion and common sense. The result is the troubling phenomenon of natural systems being loved to death, and so it is with whales in many spots around the world. The whale-watching industry has ballooned into a massive global enterprise that, while it introduces travelers to the beauty and wonder of these creatures, also can make their lives miserable. Imagine if you spent your days, dusk to dawn, with the sound of hundreds of helicopters directly overhead: That's what life is like for inland orcas and other whales along some parts of the Pacific Coast, where hundreds of Zodiacs chase and hound marine mammals every summer day. The situation is not so out of hand in Clayoquot Sound, but visitors should take responsibility for ensuring that they patronize whale-watching operators who observe decent distances (more than 60 yards [100 m]) from their "quarry", do not chase after the whales, and put safety and environmental respect ahead of guaranteeing sightings. There are no guarantees in nature, and that's as it should be. The coast's best-known and longest-established tour operator is Jamie's Whaling Station (250-725-3919, 1-800-667-9913, www.jamies.com).

I much prefer the marine tour services of Michael White at Browning Pass Charters (250-725-3435, www.browningpass.com), who uses a 36-foot (11 m) yacht whose quiet, inboard engine is far less damaging to sea life. White's careful seafaring and thoughtful appreciation of the spectacular environment he traverses makes the experience richer and better, and he knows his territory exceptionally well. He'll not only take you through the splendid waters of Clayoquot Sound, he'll help you understand its unique natural and cultural environment, from the plankton that feeds the great whales, to the back bays that hold quiet homesteads of those escaping the haste of modern life.

ernmost unit of the park; trailheads are in Bamfield and Port Renfrew (see p. 70), along with Parks Canada entry stations. *Permits and reservations are required* before venturing onto the trail, and hikers seeking positions during the best-weather (if there is such a thing) months are advised to apply far in advance. About 6,000 hikers manage the journey each year. It's closed in winter, when the weather is even worse.

Throughout the park, and on all ocean beaches, please be alert for rogue waves, which can arise at any time. These rare but powerful swells carry a few incautious beachgoers out to sea each year along the Pacific Coast.

SHOPPING

A couple fine galleries in Tofino offer artwork representing First Nations styles. **Eagle Aerie Gallery** (35 Campbell St., 250-725-3235) is the home studio of Roy Henry Vickers, an unusual artist whose heritage is Tsimshian, Haida, Heiltsuk, and Canadian-British. His carvings, prints, paintings, and jewelry offer a modernist take on traditional motifs such as raven, bear, eagle, and whale. Other artists' works are on offer, too. **Himwitsa Native Art Gallery** (300 Main St., 250-725-2017) has a less sophisticated inventory of baubles, carvings, lithographs, and such; lower prices, but for the most part lesser quality.

5

NORTH ISLAND

Once you get north of Campbell River, Vancouver Island changes dramatically. A tempestuous climate of storms driven south from the Gulf of Alaska, only one main road, and a complicated topography of mountains, fjords, forests, and rivers makes the region—a third of the entire island geographically—lightly populated, much more forested, less developed, and not nearly as tourist oriented as the lower island. Most travelers here are on their way to Port Hardy to ship aboard the BC Ferries two quasi-cruise routes departing there . . . or perhaps to Telegraph Cove to seek orcas, or to Cape Scott Park for a no-holds-barred wilderness experience.

It's tempting to say that's a shame, but then the untrammeled nature of the region comprises a big part of its charm. Yes, there are clear-cuts; but there are also untouched forests (Cape Scott, for instance), gem lakes, stunningly beautiful beaches, quaint small harbors, and wild animals in great numbers. Here, once, a mountain lion came within 10 yards of me, its research collar making the sensor ping frantically in the hands of the wildlife biologist I was hiking with. But so thick was the forest that we never saw the cat, and it caught our scent and ghosted away. Here, I camped in a wonderful birch-fir forest with my family by a rushing river, and awoke to ravens cackling their secret jokes in the mists of dawn. Here, I hiked into San Josef Bay, in Cape Scott Park, and stood almost breathless at the sight of one of the world's most beautiful stretches of sand, without another soul around.

And here, at Alert Bay, is one of the world's greatest cultural treasures, the matchless potlatch mask collection that was retrieved from its "civilized" captors by the Kwakwaka'wakw people there, and put on public display for all to see. North Island is like a tidy, compact jewelry store on a back alley that's hard to find—you'll see natural and human gems of great value here, whether trees or whales or First Nations artwork, rarely seen by other travelers.

TRANSPORTATION

There are just two ways to reach north Vancouver Island for most travelers—drive north out of Campbell River on Highway 19, or arrive in Port hardy after sailing south on a BC ferry from Bella Coola or Prince Rupert. Either travel venue is far from major gateways of any sort—Port Hardy is, at best, an eight-hour drive from Victoria, or six hours from Nanaimo. Highway 19 becomes two lanes out of Campbell River, and so it remains, coursing north and

LEFT: *'Namgis Burial Grounds, Alert Bay*   Boomer Jerritt/Tourism Vancouver Island

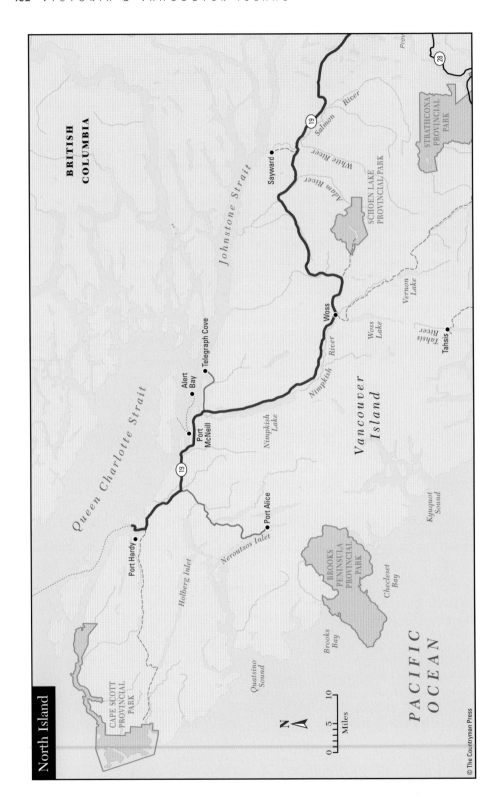

North Island

BRITISH
COLUMBIA

STRATHCONA
PROVINCIAL
PARK

28

19

Salmon River

White River

Adam River

Sayward

SCHOEN LAKE
PROVINCIAL PARK

Johnstone Strait

Vernon
Lake

Woss

Woss
Lake

Tahsis
River

Tahsis

Nimpkish River

Telegraph Cove

Alert
Bay

Queen Charlotte Strait

Nimpkish
Lake

Vancouver
Island

Port
McNeill

19

Port Alice

Kyuquot
Sound

Port Hardy

Neroutsos Inlet

BROOKS
PENINSULA
PROVINCIAL
PARK

Checleset
Bay

Holberg Inlet

Brooks
Bay

CAPE SCOTT
PROVINCIAL
PARK

Quatsino
Sound

PACIFIC
OCEAN

N

0   5   10
       Miles

© The Countryman Press

east, then west and north, along long stretches of blacktop that have only mile markers to indicate civilization. The two towns on the way, Sayward and Telegraph Cove, are off the highway. The end of the paved road, in Port Hardy, is about four hours from Campbell River.

BC Ferries' two routes that sail into and out of Port Hardy, the Inside Passage and Discovery Coast, are hugely popular car-ferry "cruises" that ply the scenic channels and fjords of the BC central coast. The **Inside Passage** sailing, which operates year-round, docks 18 to 24 hours north in Prince Rupert, from which many travelers head on up to the Yukon on the remote Cassiar Highway, then on to Alaska, or back home along the Alaska Highway to Alberta. The **Discovery Coast** itinerary, which sails only May through October, docks after 12 to 16 hours in Bella Coola, from which many travelers head east up the legendary "Freedom Highway" into the wild Chilcotin highlands. Both routes are superb ways to see spectacular fjords, sapphire passages past remote islands, whales, porpoises, sea lions, eagles, and waterfowl of every description. Both, though far more expensive than a ferry trip from, say, Horseshoe Bay to Nanaimo, are infinitely less expensive than an Inside Passage sailing on the major cruise ships that ply these same waters—about $300 for a couple with a regular vehicle between Port Hardy and Prince Rupert. Both require reservations, which must be made far, far ahead; for information, visit www.bcferries.com.

LODGING

No major lodges await travelers here; no big hotels, either. There is a smattering of small inns in Telegraph Cove and Port McNeill, largely serving travelers who come here for the popular whale-watching expeditions that sail into the rich waters here in which a large pod of resident orcas lives. The major venue is the **Telegraph Cove Resort**, a large compound in its namesake hamlet that offers cabins, camping, dining, marina services, and activity bookings (www.telegraphcoveresort.com). Port McNeill's **Black Bear Resort** is a spiffy new hotel with spacious rooms ranging from king-size-bed kitchenette suites to standard queen-size-bed hotel rooms. Rates are moderate to expensive (www.port-mcneill-accommodation.com).

Port Hardy has a modest collection of motels and inns, largely serving outbound travelers on the BC Ferries routes. There is an unexceptional but clean hostel, **C&N Backpackers**, which offers the usual bargain single beds ($25) and private rooms; it's closed in winter (www.cnnbackpackers .com/porthardy). **Glen Lyon Inn**, one of the largest in town, is on the waterfront and offers standard hotel accommodations in fairly spacious rooms at moderate rates up to $200 (www.glenlyoninn.com).

Alert Bay is the home of an excellent inn, the **Alert Bay Lodge**, small but well kept and perfect for families who wish to spend more than an afternoon admiring the island's superb First Nations treasures. Rates are budget to moderate, and the friendly atmosphere is priceless (www.alert baylodge.com).

CULTURE

Aside from U'mista, almost as famous, and culturally significant in its own right as an icon of modern life, is the **Shoe Tree**. Located along the Holberg/Cape Scott Road, about 12½ miles (20 km) west of Port Hardy, this hoary old cedar has become one of the best-known pieces of folk art in North America. It began as a lark in 1989 when an area resident nailed an old pair of boots to the tree. Other residents pitched in (or tacked on, to be accurate) and the tree soon was festooned with dozens, then hundreds, of pairs of old shoes, boots, high heels, duck boots, slippers—every imaginable kind of footwear, all attached to the tree like an elaborate layer cake. Many is the pair of hiker's boots tucked in here after being wrecked by a wilderness trek in Cape Scott Park (p. 186).

Much photographed, the tree has spawned dozens of other shoe trees around North America, including Nevada, Texas, Oregon, and the BC interior.

U'MISTA CULTURAL CENTRE

250-974-5403
www.umista.org
#1 Front St., Alert Bay, BC V0N 1A0
Open: Daily 9 AM–5 PM May–September, closed Sundays and Mondays rest of year
Admission: Adults $8, seniors and students $7, children under 12 $1

Words can hardly describe the remarkable treasure that rests here in a simple, purpose-built bighouse-style museum in this small town on a remote island at the north end of Vancouver Island. Here stands a large portion of the potlatch regalia that was stolen from the island's Kwakwaka'wakw people in the early 20th

Shoe Tree, Holberg Road Lana Kingston/Tourism Vancouver Island

century. Carefully and lovingly, the Alert Bay band has spent decades in the arduous task of finding and bringing home its artworks from around the world. The highlight here is the Hall of Masks, a stunning display of unimaginably beautiful and vivid carved examples of this art form. Resplendent in shape and color, feather and decoration, the masks vary from fierce to evocative, from simple to multifaceted. Most affectingly, they are behind no glass or barrier of any kind—simply mounted on stands so visitors may breathe the same air as these spirit works. Too long imprisoned, the museum explains, it was decided the masks should stand free of restraint. Other displays hold totems and various other artifacts of traditional First Nations life. I have been to no world-famous museum in New York, London, or Asia that offers a more memorable experience than U'mista. Please go and see for yourself.

Outside, the village has erected the world's tallest totem, a fairly ungainly spire that's held in place by guy wires. Along the town's waterfront, a small cemetery holds priceless small totems and mortuary poles—some of them slowly disintegrating, as longstanding First Nations cultural tradition says they should, to return to nature.

RECREATION

The second of Vancouver Island's two great wilderness parks lies here (Cape Scott, below). Aside from that, several smaller parks along or near Highway 19 are popular summer recreation sites, or decent camping spots for travelers. **Woss Lake** and **Marble River** parks are both wilderness parks with excellent hiking and camping opportunities; both are accessible by boat or foot only, but are relatively close to Highway 19.

The north island also holds another recreation secret whose advocates claim is overlooked, but perhaps better so—a ski area whose immense torrents of winter powder may even exceed those at Mount Washington. **Mount Cain** defies the Canadian penchant for circumspection by claiming "Vancouver Island's best powder," an assertion one could never prove either way. Uphill lift capacity is limited to two T-bars, it's generally open only weekends and holidays, and accommodations consist of a couple of hostels and a couple of rental cabins. But there is 38 feet (150 m) of snowfall a year and never a lift line. It's near Woss, three hours north of Nanaimo (www.mountcain.com).

Kayaking and **whale watching** are extremely popular activities in the Robson Bight area outside Telegraph Cove. I do not recommend thoughtful travelers take part in motorized whale-watching tours because of the severe impact on orcas, in particular (see p. 63); kayaking is another matter entirely. This low-key way to travel the waters and experience whales is not only environmentally respectful, it significantly enhances the wonder of the experience. Guided tours are not only best, they are safest in these wilderness waters;

Hall of Masks, U'mista Cultural Centre   Boomer Jerritt/Tourism Vancouver Island

numerous operators offer trips in the region. For information, consult BC Tourism at www.hellobc.com.

Great Bear Nature Lodge is a boat or plane-access-only facility about 50 miles (80 km) from Port Hardy that offers fishing, kayaking, wildlife watching, and general relaxing (www.greatbeartours.com).

CAPE SCOTT PROVINCIAL PARK
250-956-2260
www.env.gov.bc.ca/bcparks
39¾ miles (64 km) west of Port Hardy on the Holberg/Cape Scott road
$3 day-use fee

Northernmost of Vancouver Island's three great parks, Cape Scott is also the wildest and in some respects most remote. Anchoring the farthest corner of the island, it offers a palpable sense of being at the edge of the continent—nothing intervenes between here and Asia, and the area is often pummeled by fierce storms. Near here a Canadian government buoy once registered the largest non-tsunami wave ever recorded, at 130 feet or so. No road actually reaches the park, but a good gravel road from Port Hardy (two hours' drive) does end in a parking lot next to the park. From here, it is a pleasant and fairly easy half-hour (1½-mile, or 2.4 km) walk down to **San Josef Bay**, a truly stunning wilderness locale

San Josef Bay, Cape Scott Park   Lana Kingston/Tourism Vancouver Island

The Potlatch Ban

For centuries the indigenous Kwakwaka'wakw people lived on the north part of Vancouver Island and the subsidiary islands between it and the mainland, fishing for salmon, harvesting shellfish, berries, and wild game; building sturdy longhouses of cedar; and devoting the long hours of winter to art-carving, storytelling, and feasting. The biggest, most important, and rarest of the feasts was the pot-latch, a ceremonial gathering during which gifts were exchanged; chants, songs, and dances were performed to tell the people's stories; clan ties were renewed; and the people's many spirits were honored. Modern "history" says the potlatch was also a major wealth redistribution activity—chiefs and wealthy clan leaders demonstrated their status by giving away much of their wealth, supposedly—but some First Nations figures dispute this, calling it a story concocted by religious and government officials to justify their efforts to erase an allegedly communist practice. Whatever the case, "stamp it out" was the policy of Canadian and religious officials in the second half of the 19th and early part of the 20th centuries, regarding potlatch. The practice was declared illegal by government act in 1885, but the potlatch per-sisted, especially in the islands along the Inside Passage. Finally, between 1917 and 1927, in a series of raids, authorities arrested various Kwakwaka'wakw leaders and charged them with violating the law. Their families were offered a rude choice—surrender their potlatch regalia, such as masks, staffs, and other garb, or have their loved ones clapped in prison for extended periods. The potlatch artifacts seized were gen-erally given or sold to collectors around the world—a practice that had been common for decades with totems, bentwood boxes, and other First Nations artwork.

First Nations cemetery, Alert Bay Leslie Forsberg

The ban was repealed in 1951. Potlatch resumed among the indigenous peoples of the Northwest Coast—occasionally visitors are welcome—and the tribes and bands began to attempt to recover their stolen treasures. Many of them have been returned to the families that owned them; much of the best is on display in the museums at Alert Bay (p. 184) and Cape Mudge, and it is among the world's finest and most meaningful cultural art.

But not all has come home. I myself have seen a Haida funeral box on display in a museum in a major European capital—which is no more defensible than would be a Haida museum having on dis-play a coffin from a cemetery in Paris.

San Josef Bay Trail, Cape Scott Park
Lana Kingston/Tourism Vancouver Island

whose broad white sands are backed by ancient spruce forest. San Josef beach is one of the most spectacular spots on earth that I know of for a picnic lunch. The rest of the park is for serious and experienced wilderness travelers only; trails are rough, the weather is tempestuous; help is far away if anything happens. Wilderness fans believe this is a more challenging, more spectacular and more memorable trek than the much-better-known West Coast Trail in Pacific Rim National Park.

SCHOEN LAKE PROVINCIAL PARK
250-974-5556
www.env.gov.bc.ca/bcparks
87 miles (140 km) north of Campbell River, 7½ miles (12 km) off Highway 19
$3 day-use fee

This low-elevation mountain park clasps a shimmering lake in its peak-rich surroundings. The small campground has nine vehicle sites; swimming, fishing, boating, hiking, and wilderness trekking are the attractions, aside from scenery. Campsites are first-come, first-served.

A

Abigail`s Hotel, 37–38

Abkhazi Garden, 54

Acme, 122

Alberni Inlet and Valley: cultural activities, 152–153; lodging, 152; recreation, 153–155

Alcheringa Gallery, 63

Alert Bay Lodge, 183

Alpine Point Lodge, 144

Amethyst Inn, 38

Apple Festival, 85

aquariums, 77, 175

art galleries: Salt Spring Island, 93; Tofino, 179; Victoria, 54–55, 58–59, 63, 67

Art Gallery of Victoria, 54–55

ArtSpring Theatre, 90

Ashcroft House, 38–39

Asian art, 55

Atlas Café, 137

B

Bamfield, 152

Bamfield Marine Sciences Centre, 152

Barb's, 45–46

Barb's Bakery, 88

bastion (fort), 108

Bastion Square, 55

bathtub races, 118

Bay Centre, 62

BC Ferries, 32–33, 81–82, 108, 183

BC Forest Discovery Centre, 114–115

BC Liquor Guys, 44–45

Beacon Drive-In, 46

Beacon Hill Park, 61

Beacon Inn, 73–74

Beaconsfield Inn, 39

The Beagle Pub, 46–47

Bear Mountain Resort, 61

Belfry Theatre, 54

Bernard Callebaut Chocolatier, 64

Between the Covers B&B, 86

bicycling, 84

Bigleaf Maple Syrup Festival, 115

Big Tree Trail, 173–174

Birdie's Bistro, 95

Bistro la Pommeraie, 112

Black Bear Resort, 183

Blackburn Meadows Golf Course, 91

Blackfin Pub, 137

Black Rock Resort, 163–164

Blue Bridge Repertory Theatre, 54

Blue Fox, 47

Blue Grouse winery, 110

Blue Water Bistro, 145

The Bluffs Preserve, 99

Bon Rouge, 47

Botanical Beach, 70
Brentwood Bay Resort, 74
Broken Group Islands, 178
Browning Pass Charters, 179
Bubby Rose's, 45
Budget Car Rentals, 162
bus travel: Victoria, 35
Butchart Gardens, 76–77

C
Cable Cove Inn, 164
Cadboro Bay Village, 45
Café Aroma, 150
Café Brio, 47–48
Café Vincente, 168
Caffe Fantastico, 45
Camille's, 48
Campbell River: cultural activities,
    145–146; dining, 145; lodging,
    143–145; museums, 145–146;
    parks, 146–147; recreation,
    146–147; transportation, 108
camping, 71, 94, 95, 101, 163, 178
Canada Day lamb barbecue, 99
Canadian Princess Resort, 177
Cape Scott Park, 181
Cape Scott Provincial Park, 186–187
Capital Iron, 64
Carmanah-Walbran Provincial Park,
    154
Carr, Emily, 55
car rentals. see transportation
Carr House, Emily, 56–57
"Car Stops," 100
castles, 56, 57
Cathedral Grove/MacMillan
    Provincial Park, 128–129
Centre of the Universe, 78–79
Chemainus, 110

Cherry Point winery, 110
China Beach, 71
Chinatown, 55–56
Chronicles of Crime, 64–65
Clayoquot Field Station, 164
Clayoquot Sound, 172
Clayoquot Wilderness Resort, 164
climate, 17–18, 36–37
C&N Backpackers, 183
Common Loaf Bake Shop, 168
Comox Air Force Museum, 137–138
Comox Valley: cultural activities,
    137–138; dining, 137; ferries,
    133–134; golf, 139–140; lodging,
    135–137; museums, 137–138, 139;
    parks, 140, 142; recreation,
    139–142; transportation, 133–134
Comox Valley Airport, 108
Compass Rose Cabins & Marina, 74
Cook Street Village, 44
Cortes Island, 147
Courtenay. see Comox Valley
Courtenay & District Museum, 137
Cowichan Bay Kayaks, 118
Cowichan Bay Maritime Centre, 115
Cowichan Bay Village, 117–118
Cowichan Valley: cultural activities,
    114–118; dining, 112–114; festivals,
    115; lodging, 110–112; museums,
    115; parks, 114–115
Craigdarroch Castle, 56
Crow & Gate Pub, 122
Crown Isle Resort Golf and Country
    Club, 139–140
cultural activities: Alberni Inlet and
    Valley, 152–153; Campbell River,
    145–146; Comox Valley, 137–138;
    Cowichan Valley, 114–118;
    Discovery Islands, 150; Nanaimo,

124–125; North Island, 183–184; Parksville/Qualicum, 128–131; Saanich Peninsula, 76–78; Salt Spring Island, 90–91; Victoria, 53–60; West Coast, 171–176

cultural etiquette, 23–25

Cumberland, 139

Cumberland Museum, 139

Cusheon Lake Resort, 86

Cynamoka Coffee House, 169

D

Della Falls, 147

Denman Island, 133

Denman Island Chocolate, 134

Departure Bay, 108

Descanso Bay Regional Park, 100

Dick's Fish-and-chips, 145

Dinghy Dock Marine Pub, 122–123

dining: Campbell River, 145; Comox Valley, 137; Cowichan Valley, 112–114; Discovery Islands, 150; Gabriola Island, 103; Nanaimo, 122–124; Parksville/Qualicum, 128; Pender Island, 95; Saanich Peninsula, 75–76; Salt Spring Island, 88–90; Sooke and West Coast, 69–70; Tofino, 168, 169, 170–171; Ucluelet, 169, 171; Victoria, 44–53; West Coast, 168–171

Discovery Islands: cultural activities, 150; dining, 150; lodging, 148–150; visitor information, 147

Dockside Grill, 76

Dockside Pub, 169

Dodge City Cycles, 136, 139

Dolphins Resort, 143–144

Don Mee, 48

Drumbeg Provincial Park, 101

Duke Point, 108

Duncan, 109–110

E

Eagle Aerie Gallery, 179

Eagle Nook Wilderness Resort, 164–165

East Sooke Regional Park, 71

Elk/Beaver Lake Park, 79

Elk Falls Provincial Park, 146

Emily Carr House, 56–57

The Empress Hotel, 39

Englishman River Falls Provincial Park, 131

Entrance Island Lighthouse, 101

Estevan Village, 45

F

Fairburn Farm, 110–111

Fairholme Manor, 40

Fall Fair, 85

Fanny Bay, 133–134

Fanny Bay oysters, 134

Fan Tan Alley, 55, 62

fauna, 16–17

Feast of Fields, 29

ferries: Comox Valley, 133–134; Mid-Island, 108; Mill Bay, 73; Nanaimo, 118; North Island, 183; Victoria, 32–33, 35

Ferris' Oyster Bar, 49

festivals: Cowichan Valley, 115; Nanaimo, 119; Salt Spring Island, 85; Victoria, 29

fishing, 146, 153, 176–177

floatplanes, 35

flora, 14–16

Fol Epi Bakery, 49

Folk Dance Festival, 85
Foo Asian, 49
Fort Street, 62, 64–65
Foxglove Farm, 86
Free Spirit Spheres, 127

G
Gabriola Island: dining, 103; lodging, 101–103; parks, 100–101
Gabriola Sands Provincial Park, 100
Galiano Inn, 97
Galiano Island: dining, 98; kayaking, 96; lodging, 97; parks, 99; recreation, 98–99
Galiano Island Books, 96
Galiano Kayaks, 96
Galloping Goose Trail, 61–62
gardens. *see also* parks: Brentwood Bay, 76–77; Mayne Island, 100; Parksville/Qualicum, 130–131; Tofino, 174–175; Victoria, 54, 57, 76–77
Gate of Harmonious Interest, 56
Genoa Bay Café, 112
Georgina Point, 100
Glen Lyon Inn, 183
Glenterra winery, 110
Goldstream Provincial Park, 79
golf: Comox Valley, 139–140; Salt Spring Island, 91; Tofino, 177; Victoria, 61; West Coast, 163
Government House, 57
Government Street, 62
Gray Line, 35
Great Bear Nature Lodge, 186
Green Point, 163, 178
Greyhound Canada, 108, 162
Guld Islands: transportation, 81–84
Gulf Islands National Park, 94, 99

H
Haig-Brown House, Roderick, 144–145
Halfmoon Bay, 178
Harbour Air, 35, 82, 162
Haro's, 75
Hastings House, 86–87
Haterleigh Heritage Inn, 40–41
Hatley Castle, 57
Haven Resort and Institute, 101
Helijet, 34
Helliwell Provincial Park, 140
Helmcken House, 59
Heriot Bay Inn, 148
Hilary's Cheese and Deli, 117
Hill's Native Art, 65
Himwitsa Native Art Gallery, 179
historic sites, 153
HI Victoria Hostel, 41
Hollyhock, 149
Hope Bay Café, 95
Hornby Island, 134
Hornby Island Recycling Depot, 138
Horne Lake Caves Provincial Park, 129–130
horse-drawn carriages, 58
Hotel Grand Pacific, 41
Hotel Oswego, 41–42
Hotel Rialto, 42
Hot Spring Cove/Maquinna Marine Provincial Park, 172–173
House Piccolo, 88–89
Hummingbird Pub, 98

I
Imperial Eagle Lodge, 152
Indigenous art and culture: Alcheringa Gallery, 63; Hill's Native Art, 65; Himwitsa Native Art

Gallery, 179; Kwakwaka'wakw peoples, 59, 107, 181, 184, 187; North Pacific Coast Indigenous art and culture, 58; Nuu-Chah-Nulth, 178; Nuyumbalees Cultural Centre, 150; potlatches, 187; Quw'utsun' Cultural Centre, 116–117; U'Mista Cultural Centre, 184

Inn at Laurel Point, 42–43
The Inn on Pender Island, 94
Inn the Estuary, 120
Inside Passage sailing, 183
Irish Linen, 65

J
James Bay Inn, 43
Jamie's Whaling Station, 179
Japanese Garden, 100
JazzFest International, 29
Jazz Festival, 85
Jiggers, 169
John's Place, 50
Juan de Fuca Provincial Park, 71
Juan de Fuca Trail, 71
Jupiter Ranch, 102

K
kayaking: Cowichan Bay, 118; Galiano Island, 96; North Island, 185; Victoria, 61; West Coast, 176
Kenmore Air, 35, 162
Kingfisher Resort, 135
Kiss and Tell, 65
Kwakwaka'wakw peoples, 59, 107, 181, 184, 187

L
La Berengerie, 98
The Landing Grill, 128
La Pause B&B, 135

Latch Inn, 74–75
legal details, 23–25
Little Qualicum Falls Provincial Park, 131–132
Lochside Regional Trail, 62
lodging: Alberni Inlet and Valley, 152; Campbell River, 143–145; Comox Valley, 135–137; Cowichan Valley, 110–112; Discovery Islands, 148–150; Gabriola Island, 101–103; Galiano Island, 97; Nanaimo, 120–122; North Island, 183; Parksville/Qualicum, 127–128; Pender Island, 94–95; Saanich Peninsula, 73–75; Salt Spring Island, 86–88; Sooke and West Coast, 68–69; Victoria, 37–44; West Coast, 163–168
Long Beach Golf Course, 163, 177
Long Beach Lodge, 165
Long Beach Nature Tours, 176
Long Beach Surf Shop, 176
Long Beach Unit, 178
Lunds Auctioneers, 64

M
Magnolia Hotel, 43
Malaspina Galleries Community Park, 100
Maquinna Marine Provincial Park, 172–173
Marble River, 185
Maritime Museum of British Columbia, 55
Martin Mars Water Bombers, 152–153
Matterson House, 169
Max and Moritz Spicy Island Food, 98
Mayne Island, 100
Mayne Island Resort, 100
McLean Mill National Historic Site,

153
Meares Island/Big Tree Trail, 173–174
Merridale Cidery, 116
Mid-Island: transportation, 108–109
Mill Bay Ferry, 73
Milner Gardens, 130–131
Ming's, 50
miniature golf, 132
Monday Magazine, 54
Mon Petit Choux, 123
Montague Harbour Provincial Park, 99
Moonstruck Organic Cheese, 93
Morningside Café and Bakery, 89
Mount Cain, 185
Mount Galiano, 98
Mount Golden Hinde, 147
Mount Maxwell, 91
Mount Norman Park, 95
Mount Parke, 100
Mount Washington Alpine Resort, 141–142
Munro's Books, 66
Murchie's Tea & Coffee, 66
Museum at Campbell River, 145–146
museums: Campbell River, 145–146; Comox Valley, 137–138, 139; Cowichan Valley, 115; Nanaimo, 124; Sooke, 68; Victoria, 55, 58–60
MV *Coho*, 34
MV *Frances Barkley*, 152

N
Nanaimo: cultural activities, 124–125; dining, 122–124; festivals, 119; lodging, 120–122; museums, 124; recreation, 126; transportation, 119–120
Nanaimo Airport, 108
Nanaimo bars, 118

Nanaimo Museum, 124
Netherlands Centennial Carillon, 60
Newcastle Island, 124–125
Nitnat Lake, 154–155
Nordic winter sports, 147
North Island: cultural activities, 183–184; ferries, 183; kayaking, 185; lodging, 183; parks, 186–187, 188; recreation, 185–188; transportation, 181–183
North Pacific Coast Indigenous art and culture, 58
Norwoods, 169–170
Nuu-Chah-Nulth, 178
Nuyumbalees Cultural Centre, 150

O
Oak Bay Village, 45
Oceanside Inn, 94
Ocean Wilderness Inn, 68
Old Farm Inn, 111
Old House Village Hotel, 135–136
Outer Island R&R, 136
Out of Ireland, 66

P
Pacific Antiques, 64
Pacific Coach Lines, 35
Pacific Editions, 64
Pacific Mist Hydropath, 135
Pacific Opera Victoria, 54
Pacific Rim National Park, 157, 178–179
Pacific Rim Visitor Centre, 159
Pacific Sands, 165–166
Pacific Surf School, 176
Painted Turtle Guesthouse, 120
Painter's Lodge, 144
Paprike Bistro, 50
Paradise Fun Park, 132

parks. *see also* gardens: Alberni Inlet
and Valley, 153–154; Campbell
River, 146–147; Comox Valley, 140,
142; Cowichan Valley, 114–115;
Gabriola Island, 100–101; Galiano
Island, 99; North Island, 186–187,
188; Parksville/Qualicum, 128–130,
131–133; passes, 178, 179; Pender
Island, 94, 95; Saanich Peninsula,
79; Salt Spring Island, 91–92; West
Coast, 157, 172–173, 178–179
Parksville/Qualicum: cultural activi-
ties, 128–131; dining, 128; lodging,
127–128; parks, 128–130, 131–133;
recreation, 131–133
Parliment Buildings, 58
passes, park, 178, 179
passports, 24
Pegasus Gallery, 93
Pender Island: dining, 95; lodging,
94–95; recreation, 95
Pender Island Bakery, 95
Penfold Farm, 111–112
permits. *see* passes, park
Pizzeria Prima Strada, 44
Plenty Epicurean Pantry, 66–67
Poets Cove Resort, 94–95
The Pointe, 170
Point-To-Point Resort, 68–69
Port Renfrew, 68
Prime Steakhouse, 50–51
Prior Centennial Campground, 95

Q
Quadra Island, 147
Qualicum. *see* Parksville/Qualicum
Quw'utsun' Cultural Centre, 116–117

R
Radar Hill, 178

Raspberry's Jazz Restaurant, 103
Rathtrevor Beach Provincial Park,
132–133
recreation: Alberni Inlet and Valley,
153–155; Campbell River, 146–147;
Comox Valley, 139–142; Galiano
Island, 98–99; Nanaimo, 126;
North Island, 185–188;
Parksville/Qualicum, 131–133;
Pender Island, 95; Saanich
Peninsula, 78–79; Salt Spring
Island, 91–92; Sooke and West
Coast, 70–71; Victoria, 60–62; West
Coast, 176–179
Red Crow Guesthouse, 166
Red Fish Blue Fish, 51
Reid, Bill, 59
rental cars. *see* transportation
Riding Fool Hostel, 136
Ripple Rock, 147
Riptide Marine Pub, 145
Robert's Place, 103
Rock Cod Café, 112–113
Rock Salt Restaurant, 89
Roderick Haig-Brown House,
144–145
Roe Lake Park, 95
Roger's Chocolates, 67
Roger's Jukebox, 64
The Roost, 75
Royal BC Museum, 58–60
Ruckle Provincial Park, 91–92
Russell Books, 64

S
Saanich Peninsula: cultural activities,
76–78; dining, 75–76; lodging,
73–75; recreation, 78–79; transportation, 71–73
Saanich Wineries, 76

safety, 22–23

Salish Sea, 63

salmon fishing, 153, 176–177

salmon fishing/snorkeling, 146

salmon snorkeling, 146

Salt Spring Adventure Company, 91

Salt Spring Coffee, 89

Salt Spring Island: art galleries, 93; cultural activities, 90–91; dining, 88–90; festivals, 85; golf, 91; lodging, 86–88; parks, 91–92; recreation, 91–92; shopping, 92–93

Salt Spring Island Air, 82

Salt Spring Island Bread, 93

Salt Spring Island Cheese, 92–93

Salt Spring Spa Resort, 87

San Josef Bay, 186–187

Saturday Market, 85

Saturna Island, 99–100

Saturna Island Estate Winery, 99–100

Saturna Lodge, 100

Schoen Lake Provincial Park, 188

Schooner Cove, 178

The Schooner, 170

Seabreeze Lodge, 136–137

SeaGrille, 74

Second Beach, 71

Selkirk Guest House, 43

Serious Coffee, 45

Shaw Ocean Discovery Centre, 77

Shelter restaurant, 170

Ships Point Inn, 137

Shoe Tree, 183–184

shopping: Salt Spring Island, 92–93; Victoria, 62–68; West Coast, 179

Shorepine Bog, 178

Sidney Pier Hotel, 75

Sidney Spit, 94

Silk Road, 67

Silva Ray Inn, 101

skiing, 141–142

snorkeling, 146

SoBo, 170–171

Sombrio Beach, 71

Sonora Resort, 148–149

Sooke: dining, 69–70; lodging, 68–69; recreation, 70–71

Sooke Bed and Breakfast Association, 68

Sooke Harbour House, 69–70

Sooke Potholes Provincial Park, 71

Sooke Region Museum, 68

Spinnaker's Gastro Brewpub, 51–52

Spinnakers Guesthouse, 43–44

Sproat Lake Provincial Park, 153

Stage, 52

St. Ann's Academy, 60

Steeples, 113

St. Mary Lake Resort, 88

Stone Soup Inn, 113

Strathcona Park Lodge, 145

Strathcona Provincial Park, 146–147

Sturdies Bay Bakery, 98

surfing, 176

Surf Lodge, 101–102

Surf Sister, 176

Swan Lake Nature Sanctuary, 62

Symphony Splash, 29, 53

T

Tarbell's, 136

taxis, 162

Telegraph Cove Resort, 183

Terrace Beach Resort, 166

Thetis Island, 110

Third Street Café, 76

Three Gates Farm, 102–103

Thunderbird Park, 58–59

Tigh-Na-Mara, 127–128

TOF Cycles, 163

Tofino: art galleries, 179; dining, 168, 169, 170–171; gardens, 174–175; golf, 177; history, 160–161; transportation, 162

Tofino Botanical Gardens, 174–175

Tofino Bus, 35, 162

Tofino Surf Shop, 176

Tofino Taxi, 162

Tofino Water Taxi, 162–163

totem poles, 110

Tough City Sushi, 171

Tourism Tofino, 159

Tourism Victoria, 29

tourist information. *see* visitor information

transportation: Campbell River, 108; Comox Valley, 133–134; floatplanes, 35; Guld Islands, 81–84; Mid-Island, 108–109; Nanaimo, 119–120; North Island, 181–183; rental cars, 162; Saanich Peninsula, 71–73; taxis, 162; Victoria, 32–35; water taxis, 162–163; West Coast, 162–163

Tree House Café, 89–90, 91

Tribune Bay Provincial Park, 142

Trincomali Farms, 96

Troller's Fish and Chips, 123–124

Trounce Alley, 62

True Grain, 117

Tsa-Kwa-Luten Lodge, 149–150

U

Ucluelet: dining, 169, 171; history, 160–161; transportation, 162

Ucluelet Aquarium, 175

Udder Guys, 117

Ukee Dogs, 171

U'Mista Cultural Centre, 184

V

Venturi-Schulze winery, 110

Via Rail, 108

Victoria: art galleries, 54–55, 63, 67; cultural activities, 53–60; dining, 44–53; ferries, 32–33, 35; festivals, 29; gardens, 57, 76–77; inner harbour, 58; kayaking, 61; lodging, 37–44; museums, 58–60; recreation, 60–62; shopping, 62–68; tourist information, 29; transportation, 32–35

Victoria Bug Zoo, 60

Victoria Clipper, 34

Victoria Dragon Boat Festival, 29

Victoria Film Festival, 29

Victoria International Airport, 32

Victoria Regional Transit, 35

Victoria Symphony, 53

Victoria Tea Festival, 29

Vigneti Zanatta, 113–114

Villa Marco Polo, 44

vineyards, 110

visitor information: Discovery Islands, 147; park passes, 178; Victoria, 29; West Coast, 159

W

Wasabiya, 145

Washington State Ferries, 33–34

water taxis, 162–163

weather, 17–18, 36–37

West Coast: cultural activities, 171–176; dining, 168–171; golf, 163; history, 160–161; kayaking, 176; lodging, 163–168; parks, 157, 172–173, 178–179; recreation, 176–179; shopping, 179; transportation, 162–163; visitor information, 159

West Coast Air, 35

West Coast Trail, 70, 178

West End Gallery, 67

Whalers on-The-Point Guesthouse Hostel, 166

whale watching, 63, 179, 185

Wickaninnish Inn, 166–168

Wickaninnish Interpretive Centre, 178

Wild Fire Bakery, 52

wildlife watching, 60

Wild Pacific Trail, 176

WildPlay Element Park, 126

Willie's Bakery, 52–53

wineries, 110

Woodfire Pizza & Pasta, 103

World Parrot Refuge, 130

Woss Lake, 185

Y

Yellow Point Cranberries, 120

Yellow Point Lodge, 120–122

Z

Zanatta winery, 110

Zen Zero, 137

zoos, 60

JAN - - 2012